Table of Contents

MW00785638

Creativity: Mysteries Revealed

Creative Genius Lesson Plans

(See complete listing next two pages)

Reproducibles

Appendix

Creative Genius Lesson Plans

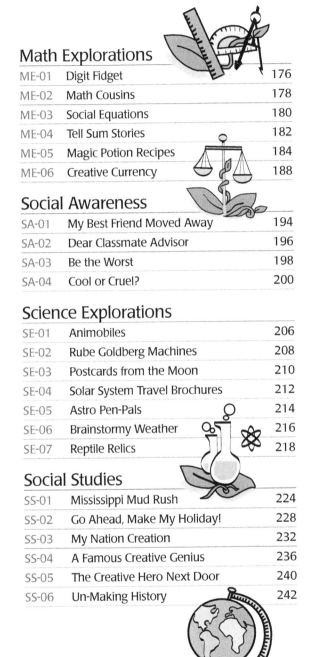

"All you've done is chisel all day! Do something useful,
like helping your brother drag those rocks up the hill."

When I was in fourth grade our teacher, Miss Malkin, gave us an unusual assignment. She wrote a word on the chalkboard and allowed us ten minutes to list as many words as we could think of using only the word's letters.

When the time was up, Miss Malkin asked the top student in our class how many words she had. Bonnie announced that she had 34 words. The teacher asked if anyone had more.

I was the only other student who raised a hand, and I reported that I had 116 words. As Miss Malkin approached my desk she declared loudly, "You must have done it incorrectly." But when she scrutinized my list, she saw that I had made no mistakes.

Miss Malkin was slack-jawed, and sat staring at me for the longest time. (I didn't think I had done anything special—to me, the assignment was a snap.) But Miss Malkin was clearly astonished, for I was a bright student, but rarely earned the highest grades in our class.

Miss Malkin didn't know anything about creativity. If she had, she would have known that creative thinking embodies the skills at work in a task such as this, and that high intelligence and high creativity operate independently. The most highly intelligent among us are not necessarily the most highly creative. The most highly creative are usually very intelligent, but not always top students. And they may not be the students you would expect. A mind-wandering student with a B-minus in science just might become the Thomas Edison of tomorrow!

Be on the lookout to identify potential creative geniuses in your classroom. Encourage them by acknowledging their talents and conveying to them that their creativity is a valuable gift.

The lesson plans in *Creative Genius: How to Grow the Seeds of Creativity Within Every Child* are designed to be fun, to spark the fire of creativity in every student, and to shine a bright light on the creatively gifted who might otherwise go unnoticed.

Within each and every student is the potential of creative genius. This book is a how-to guide for teaching creativity.

Creativity is priceless. It enables us to solve problems, both personally and professionally. Creativity has driven our highest achievers in every endeavor throughout history and across all cultures.

It is innovation that keeps our economy flowing, and new discoveries and inventions improve the quality of our lives. The most creative among us have power to make our world a better place.

On a personal level, imaginative minds can improvise Plans B, C, D, or Z to overcome obstacles. Creativity gives us hope for the future and uplifts us as we contend with the rocky roads of life. Creativity is an important life skill, and we all can cultivate it.

Creative geniuses are not always our most intellectually gifted people. Creative talent abounds among high-level, average-level, and even learning-challenged students. In fact, all children have remarkable creative potential. Our classrooms are filled with highly creative minds waiting for a chance to grow.

Think Outside the Tests

In recent years, educators have focused on standardized testing as the means of assessing a child's progress. In preparing for such tests, creative activities are often viewed as unnecessary diversions. What's more, educators often believe that creative thinking is something only for the gifted or the very artistic. With this "teaching to the tests" mentality, educating students in creative thinking is not viewed as part of the core curriculum.

Enter *Creative Genius,* which allows students to exercise creative thinking in dramatic arts, language arts, music, math, social studies, science and the visual arts. As a teacher, you'll find that these activities support your efforts to meet your requirements, but does so in a lively and challenging way—one in which all your students will benefit.

How the Book is Organized

The book is divided into four parts. In *Creativity: Mysteries Revealed* you'll enjoy a roundup of practical information about creativity, the creative process, and divergent and convergent thinking. This section introduces a valuable process called S.C.A.M.P.E.R., and includes useful brainstorming guidelines and techniques that you can immediately apply in your own classroom. We explain the characteristics of highly creative people so you and your students can learn to keep the creative juices going in daily life.

The next section of the book consists of the lesson plans. It starts with *Creative Calisthenics*, twenty warm ups for creative thinking that are complete and fun lessons in their own right. Next are over eighty lesson plans in the areas of Dramatic Arts, Language Arts, Music Awareness, Math Explorations, Social Awareness, Science Explorations, Social Studies and Visual Arts. Try using lesson plans that are outside of subject areas that you normally teach. A main theme of this book and, indeed, our work at *Jr Imagination,* is that with creative thinking individuals can strengthen their skills in one area by exploring other areas that might appear to be unrelated.

Creative Genius is organized so that you, as a teacher, can quickly see the gist of any given lesson plan by reading its Quick View. A special effort was made to make the lesson plans easy to follow, step-by-step. Yet they are designed to be flexible enough so that you can customize them to suit your needs. If need be, start with shorter or less complex lesson plans, then build to more challenging ones.

Reproducibles are found in the next section of the book. There are easy to copy pages of Object Cards, Creature Cards, and Personality Cards, all of which are used throughout various lesson plans. In addition, there is a reproducible Award for Creative Excellence, or "A.C.E. Award," for outstanding creative thinkers who deserve recognition for their accomplishments. Finally, resources for students and teachers are found in the Appendix.

Material Importance
Most of the lesson plans require everyday materials which would typically be found in your classroom, such as scissors, paper, glue, paper clips, markers, pencils and chalk, as well as many "found" or household items such as newspaper, flowers, and utensils. There are no expensive supplies to buy.

Creativity is as important to a student's future as any other educational goal. Here is a practical guide and an array of lesson plans for teaching creative thinking. When added to a foundation of knowledge, creative thinking leads to breakthrough problem solving. People who display this ability are often called creative geniuses, and any child has the potential to become one.

*

A Special Note To Teachers and Grammarians
In the interest of gender-neutrality, we've chosen to use the plural pronouns, "them," "their, " et. al., when referring to a non-gender specified singular noun such as "student" or "child." We believe that breaking this rule of traditional grammar in our case helps make our material reader friendly.

"I decided to think outside the box."

Creativity: Mysteries Revealed

Creativity: Mysteries Revealed

ACHIEVING GREATNESS
Nurturing Our Nature

What do Albert Einstein and Oprah Winfrey have in common? How about Martin Luther King and Jonas Salk? From Marie Curie to Mariah Carey, what is the key ingredient these great achievers share? It's creativity. These movers and shapers each acquired different kinds of knowledge, but all used high levels of creative thinking to bring new ideas to their fields and execute them. Each is a creative genius in their own special way.

Creative thinking skills are rarely addressed in school, yet they are a significant factor that often distinguishes our great achievers from the ordinary in every field. Combined with knowledge, hard work, and determination, creative thinking works wonders.

Creativity is natural to all of us. Within every child is a potential creative genius. By nurturing their creativity we help our children grow to become contributors to our world in brilliant and distinctive ways yet to unfold.

> "Knowledge is power, but dreamers shape the world."
> – Anonymous

WHAT IS CREATIVITY?
Out of the Box on Purpose

Creativity is about problem solving in a new way. It is using skills to generate ideas and bring about something unique and valuable. Although the creative process involves imagination and self expression, it also must be purposeful in reaching beyond the bounds (out of the box) to solve a problem, meet a need, or accomplish a goal.

The creative process is not a mystery. Some of us are innately more creatively inclined, but we all can learn creative thinking skills and get in the habit of using them for problem solving in life, work, and play. The results will amaze you.

DIVERGENT AND CONVERGENT THINKING
Outwardly Bound, and Bound to Be Great

There are two types of thinking that make up a dynamic balance in the creative process. This is the interplay between divergent and convergent thinking.[1] Understanding and learning how to harness these types of thinking leads to breakthrough problem solving.

1 J.P. Guilford, "The Nature of Human Intelligence" (New York: McGraw-Hill, 1967)

Divergent Thinking leads you to diversify and explore. Creative thinkers use divergent thinking to generate new ideas. In divergent thinking you start with an idea or information and move outward from it, looking at related ideas or things, and going wherever thoughts lead. This type of thinking resists closure and seeks to explore options and possibilities. This type of thinking is free and open to anything and everything.

Convergent Thinking helps you choose and refine. In convergent thinking, we select ideas or information and focus to eliminate the irrelevant by filtering various input. Convergent thinking leads to a specific point. This approach holds ideas up to scrutiny by determined criteria. Convergent thinking seeks closure and definitive answers, and screens out that which does not lead toward the goal. It uses constructive judgment to help refine and improve ideas, even those that don't make sense to begin with.

If an idea is not fully practical, use *divergent thinking* once more to think of ways to make the idea work. Now go back to *convergent thinking* to refine those ways. Creative thinkers move back and forth, either deliberately or intuitively, between these two thought types many times until a valuable new idea is formulated.

This interplay of the two thinking types produces ideas that are unique and have value. The two thinking types do not take place simultaneously; they must alternate:
- Use *divergent thinking* to explore possibilities
- Use *convergent thinking* to choose the best idea

One approach without the other is ineffective; both are integral to the creative process. Divergent and convergent thinking are essential for generating successful problem solving and will lead to achievements in school, career, and personal life.

Our children often get opportunities to practice the convergent type of thinking in school, but they need more opportunities to exercise divergent thinking along with it.

22 Questions: Evaluating An Idea

Here is a checklist for evaluating the usefulness of an idea. Some of these questions may be more relevant than others to the solution being sought.

1 What do I like about this idea?
2 What problem does it solve?
3 What need does it meet?
4 Is my idea really new?
5 What else exists that solves the same problem?
6 How is my idea better?
7 How does it work?
8 How can my idea be made?
9 What materials is it made from?
10 How expensive is it to make?
11 How long would it take to implement?
12 Will it break easily?
13 Can it be simplified?
14 How does it excite me or will excite others?
15 Does it appeal to the senses?
16 Is it safe?
17 Is it legal?
18 Does it create any new problems?
19 Who would use my idea?
20 Who would find my idea appealing?
21 Who might object to my idea, and why?
22 How can my idea be put into action?

If the answer to any of these questions shows that the idea is not so great, don't give up. See how the idea can be refined, then evaluate it again.

Creativity: Mysteries Revealed

Use Creative Thinking to Plan a Vacation

1 Fluency: *Think About Different Destinations* such as Myrtle Beach, Antarctica, Patagonia, Disneyland, Europe, Washington D.C.

2 Flexibility: *What Kind of Vacation?* Historical, beach, humanitarian, resort/spa, backpacking, cruise, RV trip, adventure, guided tour package

3 Originality: *Unique or Uncommon for You or Your Family*, such as seeing an active volcano, scuba diving, space camp, mountain climbing, culinary school, painting workshop; or even an 'impossible' trip to space, or a V.I.P. trip behind the scenes to the U.S. capital

4 Elaboration: *Details About What to Do*, for example, an historical trip to Washington D.C. might include visiting the Library of Congress, Supreme Court, and the Vietnam and Lincoln Memorials. It could include seeing Congress in session, touring the Smithsonian museums, and attending a Kids State Dinner at the White House

THE CREATIVE PROCESS
Spinning Thoughts into Gold

During creative development, divergent and convergent thinking weave in and out in a dynamic balance. Here is a model of the stages of the creative process:[2]

- **Clarify a Problem** – What is it you want to accomplish? Have you found the *right* problem to solve? Gather ideas and information. The more knowledge you have about your subject, the more food for creative thought you will have.
- **Generate Ideas** – Explore ideas and twist them around. Make connections. Play with possibilities. Stretch your imagination in unexpected ways. Generate a multitude of concepts, from practical to unusual to wild.
- **Develop Solutions** – You recognize one (or more) good idea that has bubbled to the top. Think about how to build it, write it, or bring it into being. Examine its pluses and minuses. (See sidebar, "22 Questions: Evaluating an Idea," pg. 3.)
- **Implement** – Make it real. Test it. Present it. Try it out. Does your idea work well? Is it valid? If not, make adjustments and try again.

THE MAGIC FOUR
May the "Fours" Be With You

There are four main components to creative thinking[3]:
1 **Fluency** – the ability to generate quantities of ideas
2 **Flexibility** – the ability to create different categories of ideas, and to perceive an idea from different points of view
3 **Originality** – the ability to generate uncommon or unique ideas
4 **Elaboration** – the ability to expand on an idea by embellishing it with details or the ability to create an intricate plan

When we are thinking creatively, all four components usually interact together. At other times only one, two, or three of the components need be in play. Brainstorming techniques, explained later in this guide, suggest ways to use the four creative thinking components. With practice, creative thinking becomes an easy habit, great fun, and applies to all areas of your life. (See sidebar, "Use Creative Thinking to Plan a Vacation.")

2 For more information, visit www.foursightonline.com. See Gerard J. Puccio, "FourSight Technical Manual," 2002, FourSight, www.foursightonline.com <http://bit.ly/SiBKpF>

3 E. Paul Torrance, "Guiding Creative Talent," (Prentice-Hall, 1962) pgs. 46 – 47

Four Components of Creative Thinking

Fluency
the ability to generate
quantities of ideas

Flexibility
the ability to create different categories
of ideas, and to perceive an idea
from different points of view

Originality
the ability to generate new, different,
and unique ideas that others are
not likely to generate

Elaboration
the ability to expand on an idea by
embellishing it with details, or the
ability to create an intricate plan

Connecting the Dots

Dot Dot Dot Dash

Samuel Morse, who invented the telegraph in 1844, was having trouble creating a signal strong enough to be sustained over great distances. One day, during a journey, he observed some exhausted horses being exchanged for fresh horses at a travel relay station. This gave Morse the idea for boosting the signals' energy along the way, so messages could travel long distances and be received clearly. Morse had made a mental connection between horse travel and electronically sent signals, two seemingly unrelated ideas.[3]

Painted Dots And Dashes

Another example of a famous connection was made by the French painter Georges Seurat in the late 1800's.

As Seurat gazed at a green field dotted with yellow wildflowers, he observed that the field looked solid yellow-green. Yellow-green was the exact color that would result by mixing the dark green color of the field plants with the yellow color of the wildflowers.

Seurat speculated that if the eye can mix the separate colors of nature in a large field, why couldn't the eye mix separate colors of paint on a canvas? Seurat experimented with dots and dashes of paint, and introduced pointillism to the world. Seurat had made a mental connection between a field of flowers and dots of paint on a canvas.

3 Michael Michalko, *Cracking Creativity* (Berkeley: Ten Speed Press, 2001) pg. 141

CREATIVE CONNECTIONS
Getting from There to Here

A major characteristic of creative thinking is the ability to make connections between seemingly unrelated things. This includes a facility for forming metaphors, seeing analogies, and applying a system for one activity to another. It involves imagining associations between dissimilar things.

Marshall Vandruff, a well known illustrator and art instructor in Southern California, tells his students an important secret about creativity: "Creative people play with metaphors. They look at one thing as if it were another thing," says Vandruff. "For example, look at every person and ask, 'What kind of animal is this person? What kind of food or car or weather?'"

Vandruff continues, "When you explore an idea, ask 'What other thing in nature is this idea like?'" For example, *my idea for a painting of a dragon is like the image of a spiraling tornado.* Or, *my innovative new sport shoe idea is like a grasshopper.*

Creating new connections between the unconnected occurs by interactions of the four components of creative thinking—*flexibility, fluency, originality, and elaboration.* The flexible mind finds new angles for thinking about something and new points of importance, while the fluent mind looks for a parallel with other things. The flexible mind juxtaposes one object or idea with another, searching for a common denominator or a connection between them.

Once a connection is found, the stage is set for *originality*. Here originality is the ability to identify and formulate something previously unknown, which has emerged out of the new connections. Now it takes *elaboration* for further development.

BRAINSTORMING
A Climate for Creativity

Brainstorming is a divergent thinking technique for generating the free-flow of ideas for the solution to a problem within a short time period. Brainstorming can be practiced by individuals or groups.[4]

Groups sometimes use a facilitator, whose role is to present a problem that needs a solution, to encourage participation, to record ideas, to keep order, and to remind participants to defer judgment of ideas, however wild they may seem. Group sessions offer valuable benefits beyond generating ideas. They boost confidence, warm up creative muscles, improve classroom spirit, and create a trusting social climate. Creative thought flourishes in positive psychological environments.

An effective system for generating ideas is to start with a short group brainstorming session as a warm up, then have participants continue brainstorming individually.

"It is easier to tone down a wild idea than to think up a new one."
– Alex Osborne

4 Alex F. Osborn, "Applied Imagination: Principles and Procedures of Creative Thinking," (New York: Charles Scribner's Sons, 1953) pgs. 151-153

Creativity: Mysteries Revealed

Hitchhiking

Ride the Storm Together
Hitchhiking[5] is a technique used by two or more people in a brainstorming session. A participant may use the ideas of another person to spark more ideas (fluency). One may also build on another's idea by adding details (elaboration) or by offering a variation (See "The S.C.A.M.P.E.R. Techniques," next page).

Letting your mind catch a ride on another's idea can take you to wonderful places you might not have thought to go.

Three Teacher Tips

1 **Set a time limit** – 10 or 15 minute sessions work well
2 **Record all ideas** – Use the chalkboard, a voice recorder, appoint a note taker, or have each participant write down their own ideas as they emerge
3 **No lengthy discussions** – This allows time for all to contribute and to cover the most ground

BRAINSTORMING GUIDELINES
Taking Ideas by Storm

The purpose of brainstorming is to produce a "checklist of ideas" for problem solving that can be evaluated later through convergent thinking. Brainstorming can be done by any size group. Groups of three to eight work best, although it can be done effectively in pairs or by an individual, as well. These guidelines should be followed:[6]

- **No value judgments of anyone's ideas** – All ideas have value, and should not be screened during the creative process (but moral and ethical boundaries must be set). Something seemingly stupid, misunderstood or silly may be the seed of an idea for a great invention or a wonderful work of art.
- **Welcome wacky ideas** – The more ridiculous the idea, the better! Ideas that are way out of the box have a life of their own. They lead us into territory we normally would not explore—territory that might contain gold.
- **Go for quantity, not quality** – Resist the temptation to evaluate the ideas being tossed about. Instead, keep the ideas flowing.
- **Combine and improve** – Encourage participants to offer ways to build upon ideas of others (see sidebar, "Hitchhiking").

CLASSROOM CONDUCT FOR BRAINSTORMING
Break Any Rules Except These

Brainstorming teams work most harmoniously when they embrace each others' contributions:
- **No interrupting** – When participants are speaking their thoughts, they deserve respectful consideration and should be heard.
- **No right or wrong answers** – All ideas are possibilities at this stage. Evaluate ideas later, but not during brainstorming.
- **No laughing at anyone's ideas** – This includes your own, unless the idea is meant to be humorous. Laugh *with* others, not *at* others.
- **Lighten up and have fun** – Humor itself grows out of the creative process, because humor can involve exaggeration or odd combinations, techniques used in creative thinking. This is to be expected, and helps us relax and get our creative juices flowing.

5 6 Alex F. Osborn, "Applied Imagination: Principles and Procedures of Creative Problem-Solving," (New York: Charles Scribner's Sons, 1953) pgs. 154-156

THE S.C.A.M.P.E.R. TECHNIQUES
Brainstorming Idea Generators

S.C.A.M.P.E.R.[7] is an acronym made from the initials of seven words that suggest how a topic can be transformed. It is based on the premise that one can create something new through a transformation of something that already exists. Using S.C.A.M.P.E.R. as a brainstorming tool helps generate the maximum array of new ideas out of a topic.

These are divergent, idea-getting techniques that help overcome creative blocks and stimulate productive thought. Authors, artists, inventors, and other creative leaders use the techniques, either consciously or intuitively. They can be used effectively by groups as well as by individuals during the *Generate Ideas* phase of the creative process (see "The Creative Process," pg. 4). Try these techniques next time you need to generate new ideas. Not all techniques are applicable to every situation, but some of these will be fruitful. (For a full page reproducible of a S.C.A.M.P.E.R. mini-poster, turn to pg. 342.)

> "Do not follow where a path might lead. Go instead where there is no path and leave a trail."
> – Ralph Waldo Emerson

S **substitute** a part for something else

C **combine** things or add something new

A **adapt** by changing the kind of materials or procedure

M **modify** by enlarging, reducing, or changing proportions

P **put** to a new use

E **eliminate** something or simplify

R **reverse** or rearrange

7 Bob Eberle, "SCAMPER," (Waco: Prufrock Press, 1996) pg 6;
and Michael Michalko, "Cracking Creativity," (Berkeley: Ten Speed Press, 2001)

Using the S.C.A.M.P.E.R. Techniques
Two examples putting S.C.A.M.P.E.R. into action

Example 1:
Porcelain tea cup and saucer set (a product)
You have been asked by the manufacturer to brainstorm to make it more interesting.

S Substitute an ice cream dish for the tea cup, but keep the saucer, which is a practical idea for an ice cream dish.

C Combine the saucer and the cup so they are attached. Add a lid to the cup to keep the tea warm. Add designs around the cup.

A Adapt the tea cup and saucer by making the cup out of plastic. Or by making the saucer out of sponge. (This set would be great for kids.) Or by smashing the set and using the pieces in a mosaic design.

M Modify by making the tea cup tall and narrow, or by making it a tiny tea set for a doll, or by changing the color.

P Put to a new use by filling the tea cup with candle wax and a wick. Or by turning the set upside down and using it as a base for a small sculpture.

E Eliminate the handle and have a juice cup.

R Reverse or rearrange by having a tea cup that is wider at the bottom and narrow toward the top to prevent spills.

Example 2:
Game of catch (a procedure)
You and your friend are playing a boring game of catch with a ball. It's time to brainstorm something new.

S Substitute by throwing a cupcake or a banana instead of a ball. Or substitute throwing the ball with carrying the ball on two fingers to the other player.

C Combine the ball with a spring and see how it bounces. Add another ball to the opposite end of the spring. Add more players and more balls. Add a paddle. Write rules for new games that use these items.

A Adapt the ball by making it of clear plastic filled with water and colored gel. Or by adapting the game by having to give a math fact every time you throw the ball, with the catcher needing to answer.

M Modify by making the ball five feet in diameter. Or by making the players stand several yards apart. Or side by side.

P Put to a new use by inking the ball and bouncing it on a large canvas for stamping designs. Or by writing on the ball and sending messages back and forth.

E Eliminate one of the players and bounce the ball against a wall. Eliminate half the ball, so it will be flat on one side. Eliminate the ball and play a game of pantomime catch.

R Reverse or rearrange by playing a game of "don't catch the ball." Can you resist catching a soft sponge ball coming toward you? Stand backwards when you throw the ball, trying to hit your target.

TAKING IT LATERALLY
Somewhere Out There

Lateral Thinking[8] refers to thought processes for solving problems by non-logical methods. It includes techniques for changing concepts and perceptions.

Lateral thinking is in contrast to "vertical thinking" (critical thinking), which is concerned with validity, focus, and seeking errors. Lateral thinking is concerned with breaking routine patterns of thought, widening the search for ideas, and examining ideas from unexpected points of view.

Some lateral thinking techniques include:
- **Random Inclusion** – Choose an object or word at random and associate it with the area you are thinking about. Terrific outside-the-box ideas can emerge. For example, imagine you are thinking about a way to increase your closet space. You randomly select the word, "mouse." Perhaps you can create little "mouse holes" in a wall to hold small items.
- **Outlandish Provocation** – Choose and apply a provocative statement, using wishful thinking, exaggeration, reversal, controversial statements, and more. This technique challenges the limits of our perceptions, and forces us to re-think possibilities. For example, imagine you are thinking about a better way to get butter to melt on your toast. "I wish I could press my toast with a steam iron" could inspire you to invent something new.
- **Challenge-it** – Take the position that the accepted way of doing things, or the accepted beliefs about things, is not the best. This method is not meant to generate harsh criticism, but rather, is intended for questioning and exploring why we do things as we do. This technique often leads to improvements and useful alternatives.
  For centuries, luggage was carried by hand. Perhaps someone thought, "I'd rather drag this heavy thing!" That thought may have led to the innovation of wheels on luggage. And why does luggage need to be carried or wheeled? Imagine luggage that you can ride on or that you can program to follow along by your side.
- **Fanning-out** – Expand the range and number of ideas you will consider in order to end up with a broadened range of concepts from which to develop solutions. For example,

"Innovation distinguishes between a leader and a follower."
– Steve Jobs

---

8 The term, "Lateral Thinking," was coined by author Edward De Bono to denote a creative problem-solving style. See "Lateral Thinking: Creativity Step by Step," (New York: Harper & Row Publishers, 1970)

imagine you want to write a musical play based on an existing story. You could broaden your search for storylines to nursery rhymes, foreign stories, operas, country song lyrics, picture books, sitcom episodes, messages written on the backs of old postcards, blogs, and so forth.

- **Contrary Proving** – Take the opposite point of view about something and try to convincingly validate your position. You may inadvertently generate new ideas that are appropriate and useful. For example, most teachers and parents believe that students should do homework every day. Suppose you took the position that homework interferes with a student's mental growth. To support that point of view, consider what a student would do with their time at home instead. They might engage in: social interaction, creative activities, charitable work, or physical exercise. These activities are also beneficial, and may lead to assigning a new kind of "homework."

AWESOME ATTRIBUTES
Analyze This

Attribute Listing[9] is a specific idea-finding technique by which you identify and list every characteristic of an item or procedure. The goal of this "deconstructing" analysis is to let you observe the subject clearly and objectively, which leads to increased ideas for modifications.

For example, a tennis shoe has these attributes: size, shape, color, materials, removable parts (laces and inner soles), decorative elements, weight, flexibility, texture, and more. Think how each of these could be modified to create a better or new kind of shoe, or how the components could be used for other purposes.

An example of a procedure is an elementary school's morning drop-off system. The attributes are: the time frame, the drop off street, traffic patterns, the number of drop-off cars, safety issues, city laws, volunteer helpers, and so forth. By examining each characteristic, one can more clearly design an excellent drop-off system.

The strength of attribute listing is that it encourages the problem solver to thoroughly examine a situation from several points of view.

9 Alane Jordan Starko, "Creativity In The Classroom: Schools of Curious Delight," (Mahwah, N.J.: Lawrence Erlbaum Associates, 2001), second edition, pgs. 180 – 184.

Idea Catcher

Your Journal for Capturing Ideas

An important habit characterizing creative geniuses is that they regularly record and keep ideas for future reference. A simple notebook can be a storehouse of fuel for your creative explorations.

Creative achievers jot down ideas, thoughts, insights, observations, clippings, and inspirations, and keep them close at hand wherever they go. One never knows when an amusing daydream or powerful insight will surface.

Ideas are precious because they are the raw material of inspiration and achievement. A random idea today could be the seed of greatness to come. But ideas are fleeting; capture them before they drift away.

Your Personal Journal

Find, buy, or make some sort of journal that fits into your backpack, bag, or pocket along with a pen.

Consider making a pouch with a shoulder strap or using a fanny pack to hold your journal and pen. It is important that your journal be on hand the moment you need it.

Useful Journals:

- A small sketchbook with a cover that you can decorate
- A small spiral bound notebook with a cover that you can decorate
- Index cards held together with a clip
- Pieces of any paper with holes punched and bound with brads or ribbon
- Sketchbooks or notebooks in any suitable size
- Digital systems that are quickly accessible
- A new style of journal that you invent

Always keep a pen with your journal. You can clip a ballpoint pen to a spiral edge or use a pouch to keep journal and pen together. Perhaps you can invent a great way to keep your pen with your journal.

Tips

Decide whether you prefer lined paper, blank paper, or some of each. If you use marker pens, make sure your paper is heavy enough to prevent bleeding through. If you like pencils, use an automatic one so you don't have to sharpen it. A glue stick and colored pencils can be useful, but they're not essential.

Collecting Ideas

Go scouting for ideas everywhere and anywhere. Observe nature. Listen to words. Discover things in stores, books, museums, the movies, your backyard, and your aunt's living room. Try to come away from every excursion with at least one new idea for your journal.

Sometimes ideas will just pop into your head out of nowhere. They could be wacky or wonderful, but know that they are all worth recording.

Look through your journal entries often and reflect on the ideas you've recorded. Play with your unfinished ideas, adding notes, sketches, and more ideas. List problems that need solutions. Add inspiring quotes, jokes, and positive thoughts.

Discover and develop your own special talents with your journal. Use it as your creative companion, letting it become the launch pad for your inspiration and achievement.

> "Creativity is the ability to see relationships where none exists."
> – Thomas Disch

Problems Creative People Tackle

- How to write a thrilling novel
- How to improve the function of an appliance
- How to help the homeless
- How to tag an animal for scientific study
- How to tie a shoe without using a shoelace
- How to melt butter on toast
- How to make a delicious meal from available ingredients
- How to express emotion in a painting
- How to find the cure for cancer

MORPH CHARTS
Having Morph Fun

Morphological Synthesis[10] is a variation of attribute listing by which the attributes are placed onto a chart in rows and columns (see "Sunglasses Morph Chart"). Doing this may help spark new ideas through combining, eliminating, and other modifications. Apply any subject to a morph chart. It will display surprising combinations.

In addition to listing word attributes, images can be used. For example, in attempting to invent a fantasy creature, list heads on the vertical axis and bodies on the horizontal axis. Each space on the chart represents a different head/body combination (see "Creature Combo Morph Chart"). See which combo sparks your imagination.

THE PROBLEM-FINDERS BANK
Make Frequent Deposits

Problem Finding[11] means identifying a problem that needs solving. Problems are the foundation of most creative accomplishments. Highly creative people don't wait for problems to present themselves; they actively search for them. Creative thinkers manipulate materials, wonder why things are as they are, challenge ideas, question established beliefs, investigate behaviors, are curious about all sorts of things, and notice everyday annoyances. If "necessity is the mother of invention," problems generate the necessity. (For only a few examples, see sidebar, "Problems Creative People Tackle.")

Ask students in your classroom to look for problems, large and small, and jot them down on separate slips of paper. Invite them to collect concerns and complaints from friends and family, as well. Decorate a shoebox, use a large coin bank, or improvise something to hold all your students' slips of paper. Encourage students to "deposit" problems into the bank on a regular basis. Withdraw a few from time to time to use as classroom idea sparkers. These also will be valuable later for brainstorming and problem-solving activities.

10 11 Alane Jordan Starko, "Creativity In The Classroom: Schools of Curious Delight," (Mahwah, N.J.: Lawrence Erlbaum Associates, 2001), second edition, pgs. 184 – 186, and pgs. 104 – 114

Sunglasses Morph Chart – Word Attributes

LENS	FRAME STYLE	COLOR	MATERIAL	OTHER FEATURE
DARK	CAT'S EYE	SILVER	METAL	GLOW IN THE DARK
RAINBOW	WRAP-AROUND	HOT PINK	PLASTIC	FOLDS UP
MIRROR	BIG ROUND	BLACK	RUBBER	TV RECEPTOR
DARK TO LIGHT	SQUARE	CLEAR	CARDBOARD	PLAYS MUSIC

Creature Combo Morph Chart – Image Attributes

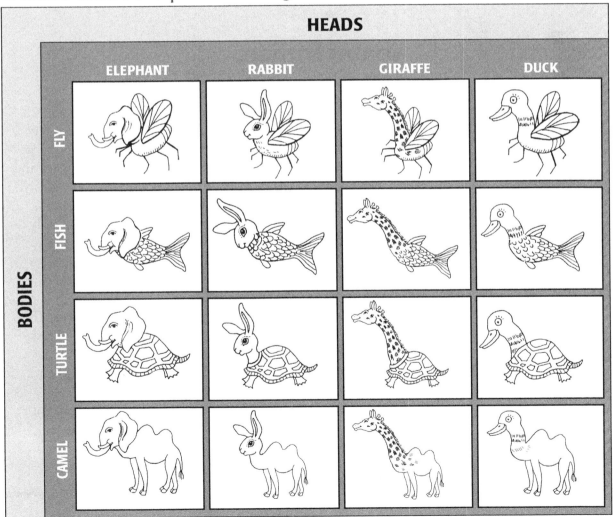

HEADS: ELEPHANT, RABBIT, GIRAFFE, DUCK

BODIES: FLY, FISH, TURTLE, CAMEL

Creativity: Mysteries Revealed

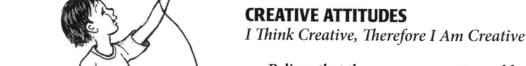

CREATIVE ATTITUDES
I Think Creative, Therefore I Am Creative

- **Believe that there are answers to problems** – Do not ask if there is only one answer. Instead, know there are many answers and search for them.
- **Be self-expressive** – Get in touch with your own tastes and beliefs, know who you are, and show your own special self.
- **Value all ideas, both yours and others'** – It makes for a richer world. All ideas are worth something, even if only to show you what you do not believe.
- **Value creative efforts** – A failed attempt with a new idea will strengthen your creative thinking skills more than copying something already done.
- **Don't give up** – Be tenacious. Accept failure as part of the creative process and continue on until you attain success.
- **Be self-motivated** – Keep your enthusiasm and determination. Passion is a fuel that propels you forward. This is called creative energy.
- **Have courage** – Don't worry about others scoffing at your ideas, your failures, or your interests. You're too busy making the world a better place.
- **Dare to dream** – Believe in yourself and the power of your imagination.

THE 9 HABITS OF HIGHLY CREATIVE PEOPLE
Being on Your Best (Creative) Behavior

1 **Keep a notepad and pen with you** – You never know when a terrific idea will float through your head. You must capture it before it disappears. (See sidebar, "Idea Catcher," pg. 13.)

2 **Ask "what if?" a lot** – Start a list of "what ifs" and add a few to your journal every day. What if you asked others to add to your list?

3 **Ask "why?" and "why not?"** – Creative people are curious, and regularly question everything. Find your own answers to "why? and "why not?"

4 **Learn about creative people** – They're not always famous. You may know a struggling artist, a successful engineer, or a great school teacher. Ask them about their lives, their work habits, their ideas.

5 **Practice thinking of ideas** – As with anything else, the more you practice the better you will be at it. Exploring possibilities will become a habit.

6 **Take risks** – Test your ideas. It's okay to do an ugly painting, to bake a yucky cake, or to mastermind a failed experiment. When you let a failure stop you, it remains a failure. When you learn from a failure and try again, it becomes a stepping stone on your path toward achievement.

7 **Associate with other creative people** – You can inspire each other, share ideas, and support each other's creative activities. Is there a project you can work on together, combining your talents?

8 **Take a flight of fancy every day** – Exercise your creative wings and fly as far as your imagination takes you. Allow yourself to go to wonderful and strange places. (See sidebar, "Let Your Imagination Soar.")

9 **Have fun** – Having fun makes you feel optimistic and opens your mind to creative thoughts and fresh ideas. Make it a habit to enjoy yourself.

Let Your Imagination Soar

Taking a "flight of fancy" is a creative workout and strengthens your skills. In your mind you can visit hidden worlds never seen before. Using your imagination, you can fly back and forward in time, or shrink yourself so small that the center of a flower becomes a wide open space. You can morph into any creature to experience the world from its special point of view. The possibilities are endless.

You'll allow yourself to go great distances if you believe you'll return with feet firmly on the ground and that you are in control of your "flights." You're empowered and your creativity grows upon your return, carrying wonderful "souvenirs" from your journeys in your mind.

"Creative achievement comes with creativity and hard work. Creativity is not always easy.... There needs to be determination and motivation. We need to teach our students with small tasks and then build to more challenging problems."
– Cyndi Burnette

THE CREATIVE ADVANTAGE
Every Child Can Have It

Creativity is the passion to explore, invent, and express with a purpose in mind. Having such a purpose, one can generate something new that has value. This is how we define creativity.

We often call our greatest achievers creative geniuses. Exactly how they do what they do is not a mystery. They build upon acquired knowledge and apply the creative thinking techniques described in the previous pages, either deliberately or intuitively. Both formal and informal studies have shown that by teaching and encouraging creative thinking skills, students make enhanced gains in their creative performance.[12]

Every child deserves to experience the joy of being creative. Children who are offered the chance to express their creativity:
- *stay motivated in school* because learning is more gratifying
- *increase their self esteem* by getting results in their endeavors
- *are better prepared to cope with life's challenges* because they know how to problem-solve
- *have open attitudes and are optimistic* because challenges are interesting

> "The real voyage of discovery consists not in seeking new landscapes, but in having new eyes."
> – Marcel Proust

WHEN LESS IS NOT MORE
Giving Children a Significant Advantage in Life

Schools often eliminate creative activities from their curriculums in an attempt to balance budgets. This deprives children of strengthening an important set of thinking skills. Creativity helps children learn to think for themselves and to be self motivated achievers throughout their lives. Creative children are more:
- confident and courageous
- flexible in working with others
- fun to be around
- open to new ideas
- self reliant
- willing to take on challenges

The lesson plans in *Creative Genius* offer fun-filled practice of creative thinking skills and an opportunity for your students to astonish you.

12 Karlyn Adams, "The Sources of Innovation and Creativity," 2005, pg. 48, National Center on Education and the Economy, www.ncee.org < http://bit.ly/SHQ2kA>

Creative Genius Lesson Plans

GROWING A GENIUS IS CHALLENGING AND FUN

All of the *Creative Genius* lesson plans practice divergent thinking and other skills associated with creativity. The Creative Calisthenics are for warming up and getting the creative juices flowing. The rest of the lessons complement traditional curriculum standards. You don't need to take precious time away from curriculum requirements to foster creativity.

The lesson plans were designed with a teacher's realities in mind:
- **Age Appropriate** – The subjects fit interests and abilities of the intended ages and grades.
- **Class Size** – There are lesson plans for individual students, small teams, and large groups. Many lessons can be adapted to work for individuals or any size groups of students.
- **Quick** – Most lessons require small amounts of time.
- **Easy** – Minimum preparation is needed by the teacher for the lessons.
- **Inexpensive** – The lessons use basic materials teachers have on hand, such as pencils, scrap paper, and crayons.
- **Productive** – The lessons result in take-home items, stories, invention ideas, or other satisfying accomplishments.

TEACHER'S ROLE

Brainstorming phase: The teacher leads classroom discussions, and writes lists on the board. They may add to the lists to keep ideas flowing, but should encourage class participation, showing enthusiasm for all contributed ideas, especially unusual ones.

Reassure the class that outrageous (but not offensive) ideas are welcome. It is important to keep an atmosphere of acceptance and non-ridicule, so every student feels safe enough to freely voice all their ideas. Keeps ideas flowing by encouraging students to go where their imaginations lead them. They may ask helpful questions such as, "And then what happened? or "What does that look like?"

Offer reference materials, such as picture books and posters to the students to help spark ideas and fill out details.

Development phase: The teacher should keep the lesson moving by offering helpful suggestions to students if they are stuck. They also need to make sure teams are working together harmoniously, and that students have the materials they need. The teacher may remind students how much time they have left, and may also suggest they employ particular creative thinking techniques as needed.

EXTENSIONS

At the end of many lesson plans extensions are listed. There are numerous ways a lesson plan can inspire more ideas. These lesson plans were designed to be flexible and adapted easily to specific subject, grade level, and classroom size needs. Use the creative thinking techniques, such as "substitution" for customizing lesson plans to meet your classroom's particular needs. Keep notes on ways you have used lesson plans as jumping off points for new lesson plans.

HOW TO EVALUATE

Evaluations of lesson plans should be based on how effectively students have demonstrated creative thinking skills to solve problems. Of course, there is much subjectivity in the evaluation process, and every lesson requires different considerations. Some of the criteria below may not apply to each lesson plan, while some criteria may matter more than others for a particular lesson plan.

Here are some things to think about when assessing a creative task:

- **Fluency** – How many ideas were generated before settling on a final choice?
- **Quality of Idea** – How appropriate or useful is the idea for solving a problem? How well does the creative solution meet the task?
- **Flexibility** – Did the student reconfigure or rethink an existing idea, turning something known into something new?
- **Originality** – How unusual, intriguing, or novel is the idea? If many others thought of similar ideas (without copying) it may be a predictable solution and not unique.
- **Elaboration** – Is the idea highly developed with much detail and depth of thought?
- **Following Directions** – Did the student solve the problem asked to be solved? Although they might have come up with something wonderful, addressing the right problem at the right time is important in school and in life.
- **Completion** – Did the student complete the task in the time allotted? Follow-through matters in school and in life. A fabulous invention that is only half worked out is not useful (except as inspiration for continuing development).

Consider devising your own point system using the above list as a guideline for evaluating students' creative works.

Keep in mind that evaluations should be based on the merits of the ideas, not the sophistication of artwork, writing skills, or knowledge. Try to separate out the creative factors in a solution to a problem. For example, a roughly drawn picture of a robot that cooks breakfast may show more creativity than a beautifully illustrated but typical stove. Both are answers to "a way to fry eggs," but one shows creative thinking skills, while the other shows expert drawing skills.

AWARD OF CREATIVE EXCELLENCE

It's fun to have the class vote for its favorite creative accomplishment. Hand out an *Award of Creative Excellence (A.C.E. Award* certificate) for the winner(s). (See *Reproducibles,* pg. 341.) Also, consider expanding the awards to include "Funniest," "Most Original," "Most Beautiful," and so forth.

Notes

Creative Calisthenics

Grade Level: 2 through 8
Participants: Teams of two to four
Objectives: Exercise flexibility, originality, elaboration, brainstorming and identifying relationships as well as storytelling, writing, and sketching skills
Time: ½ hour to 1 hour

Quick View

In this exercise in making connections, students work in small teams to forge relationships among randomly-selected objects. Through brainstorming and collaboration, students create unique inventions or original narratives featuring the items on their object cards.

Examples

Invention – A glove, a bell, and a drinking straw are combined to become a wagon. The glove is used as a seat, cross sections of the straw form the wheels, and the bell heralds the wagon's arrival.

Story – A toy robot, a flower, and a roller-skate inspire a story in which the robot and the flower fall in love, get married, and ride away on the stylish roller-skate.

Take Home
A highly original invention or story to share with friends and family

Materials
- Object Cards (see *Reproducibles,* pg. 320) or equivalent
- Pencils
- Paper
- Index cards (optional)
- Scissors (optional)
- Glue stick (optional)
- Magazines for clip-art (optional)

Getting Ready
- Make copies of Object Cards and cut them out; or
- Have students make their own object cards by drawing a few objects on cards or cutting pictures from magazines to glue onto cards.

Activities and Procedures

1 Divide students into teams of two to four.

2 Have a student from each team pick four cards at random. Tell students that they can imagine the objects to be any size, from tiny to giant.

3 Explain that the task is to find a relationship among the objects on the cards.

4 Discuss the examples above to inspire brainstorming.

5 Tell students that they may eliminate one of the cards and focus on the remaining three.

6 Teams brainstorm to either:
   - "Invent" something new from the objects shown; or
   - Make up a story featuring their objects.

7 Encourage students to write or sketch their ideas, adding as much detail as possible.

8 When the final product is complete, ask students to give their story or invention a creative title.

9 Allow teams to present their inventions and stories to the class. Inventions should be described and demonstrated, if possible, and stories may be either recited or performed.

Extensions
- *Ultra-challenge:* Have students complete the activity with the goal of finding relationships among six objects.
- *Uncommonly Common:* Explain the term "common denominator," and have individuals or teams list as many "common denominators" among their objects as they can. For example, "They all have metal parts or they all have circular shapes in them" (see lesson plan, "Connect The Ducks and Boots" on pg. 42). Hold a contest to determine which team can find the most common denominators within a ten-minute timeframe.

Invent-a-Toy

Grade Level: 2 through 5
Participants: Individual or group
Objectives: Exercise fluency, flexibility, originality, elaboration, brainstorming
Time: 1 to 2 hours

Quick View

In this exercise in entertainment ingenuity, students invent new toys by brainstorming ways to improve existing toys. Technical realities are of no concern for this activity; rather, being imaginative and having fun are what's important! Students work independently to conceptualize their invention, sketch and label the parts, and give their toys brand names.

Examples

Students create a new and improved version of an ordinary teddy bear. The upgraded toy changes color by touch, sings and dances, has secret compartments and a fully-functioning built-in clock, has the capability of transforming into a giant sleeping bag or a bicycle seat, is part of a set of charms for a bracelet, or holds a paintbrush and can paint real pictures.

Take Home
Students take home a detailed, labeled drawing for their new toy with its own brand name.

Materials
- Three "nothing-special" toys (e.g. A plain teddy bear, doll, toy car, board game, box of crayons, group of blocks, etc.)
- Pencils
- Paper
- Chalkboard and chalk or equivalent

Getting Ready
- Display three simple toys. Show the creative S.C.A.M.P.E.R brainstorming techniques for the students to see as you lead classroom discussions. (See *Reproducibles,* pg. 342.)

| Basic Teddy Bear | Storytelling Night Light | Bracelet | Tricycle Basket |

Activities and Procedures

1   Begin the classroom discussion by selecting a toy and asking your students to suggest ways to make it more interesting. Students may build on each other's ideas or offer their own. Write the students' ideas on the board. As they offer ideas, encourage them to use S.C.A.M.P.E.R to develop them further. For example, a student may mentally combine magnets with the teddy bear by putting magnets in its paws; when it wraps its arms around something, it will give a "real" bear hug when the magnetic paws connect.

2   Next, encourage students to select one of the three plain toys for re-inventing as a fun, "never-seen-before-on-this-planet" toy.

3   Give students 5 to 10 minutes to brainstorm as many ideas as possible for their toy re-invention. While they are thinking of ideas, invite them to let their imaginations run wild and not to concern themselves with exactly how their toys would be made. At this stage of the brainstorming process, every idea should be listed; there should be absolutely no screening as even perceived weird, silly, and/or stupid ideas could contain seeds of brilliance! (Refer to "Brainstorming," pgs. 7–8 in *Creativity: Mysteries Revealed*.)

4   Once time is up and students have completed their lists, ask them to return to each concept and evaluate it in order to decide on the best of their great ideas. (Refer to "22 Questions: Evaluating an Idea," pg. 3.) At this point, students may wish to alter or elaborate on the ideas listed. Explain that with changes, a mediocre idea could become something great. For example, suppose a student brainstormed "a ball with legs that run toward you." Silly? Yes, but what if the ball had a magnet inside it, and you had an attracting magnet in your glove? This could be the start of a really fun game! What if the magnet in your glove repelled, so it was hard to catch?

5   Next, have students sketch their toys, adding notes and details to explain working parts or special features. Instruct them to construct additional sketches and diagrams to show close-ups of details, alternate views, or other explanatory material.

6   Once students have developed their new toy concept, encourage them to think of an original brand name for their toy. You might suggest combining feature words, such as "magnets" and "teddy bear" to create "Maggie Bear", "Nettie Bear", or "Ted-Net." Allow students to use a dictionary, rhyming dictionary, or thesaurus to help spark name ideas as well.

7   Finally, ask student inventors to write short descriptions of their toys concepts and explain them to the class in a brief presentation.

Extensions
To enhance this lesson, have teams:
- Write scripts for TV commercials promoting their toys
- Shoot their own "infomercials" or other promotional videos
- Enact a skit featuring a child playing with their new toy
- Take on the role of the toy itself and interact with other students in the classroom.

For a more comprhensive lesson plan on naming, see lesson plan, "Name Us Famous," pg. 96.

The Perfect Pet

Grade Level: 2 through 5
Participants: Individual or group
Objectives: Exercise fluency, flexibility, originality, elaboration, brainstorming
Time: Approximately 1 to 2 hours

Quick View

In this exercise in preferences, students list their likes and dislikes about all kinds of animals. They then design perfect pets by combining their likes and eliminating their dislikes. By drawing and naming their pets, writing descriptions about them, and staging a Perfect Pet Show, students demonstrate their ingenuity and conceptualization skills.

Examples

Turtles that have fuzzy shells; a family dog large enough to ride to school; cats with monkey hands that can open their own cans of food; tiny giraffes that can be kept in a bird cage; a fish that talks like a parrot

Take Home
Enhanced visualization and conceptualization skills and a drawing of a unique pet

Materials
- Pencils
- Paper
- Markers or crayons
- Pictures of mammals, reptiles, birds, sea creatures, and more
- Tape
- Dictionary, thesaurus, rhyming dictionary (optional)

Getting Ready
- Gather and display pictures of all kinds of animal life.

Activities and Procedures

1 Ask students to share their favorite pets and animals with the class. Then, ask them to describe the things they like and dislike about these various animals. Make a list on the board. A student may say, "I love elephants, but I wish they were small enough to sleep in my bedroom," or "I love soft, furry bunnies, if only they could catch a Frisbee." Discuss the characteristics that make great pets. Ask the kids, "What things would you like your pet to be or be able to do?"

2 Have students working individually to create a new kind of pet—their own perfect pet—by combining their likes and eliminating their dislikes.

3 Invite students to create large color drawings of their pets, adding as many details as possible.

4 Instruct students to name their new species, and suggest ways that they might do so. For instance, a combination dog and cat could be a "Docat" or a "Climbing Canine." Allow students to use the dictionary, thesaurus, or rhyming dictionary to spark ideas.

5 Encourage students to write about their pets, answering the following questions as they create their descriptions: What are the physical characteristics of your pet? How do you play with your pet? How do you take care of your pet? What does your pet eat? Can your pet do any tricks? What mischief does your pet get into?

6 Invite students to stage a "Perfect Pet Show" by standing around the room holding their drawings. Each student has a turn to explain their pet to the class. The pet owner may demonstrate the way their pet walks or acts. If the pet makes a sound, the pet owner may vocalize it.

7 Have classmates vote for The Best of Show, Cutest Pet, Most Fun Pet, Most Helpful Pet, Most Mischievous Pet, Cuddliest Pet, Funniest Pet, Most Unusual Pet, etc. There could be something for everyone!

Extensions
- Instruct students to create the Scariest Animal using the steps in this lesson plan.
- Invite students to make stuffed animals from their Perfect Pet concepts, following these steps:
  1 Make a large drawing of a Perfect Pet and cut it out.
  2 Trace the outline onto a second piece of paper and cut it out.
  3 Staple or glue the edges of the cut-out drawing to the edges of the second paper shape. Leave an opening to stuff with newspaper, then seal.
  4 Insert a ruler into the bottom of the stuffed animal to hold it upright, or attach a string handle at the top for holding or hanging.

For a more comprhensive lesson plan on naming, see lesson plan, "Name Us Famous," pg. 96.

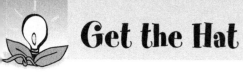

Grade Level: 3 through 8
Participants: Two teams of any size
Objectives: Exercise fluency, flexibility, originality, brainstorming, problem solving, and writing skills
Time: Approximately 30 minutes

Quick View

In this fun problem-solving activity, teams compete to find the best solution to a specific problem—getting a hat down from a high shelf without the use of a ladder or step stool. After receiving their randomly-dealt Object Cards, teams brainstorm to discover the best method of retrieving the hat using the items on their cards.

Examples

A team receives 3 Object Cards: a paper bag, a stapler, and a pen

- Tear the bag into strips and staple them together to form one very long strip. Tie one end of the stapled strip to the pen. Toss it onto the shelf until the pen pushes the hat off the shelf; or

- Use the stapler to gouge holes in the wall. Climb up the wall and retrieve the hat. Ignore the bag and the pen.

Take Home
Enhanced problem-solving skills and a written account of both good and bad plans

Materials
- Object Cards (see *Reproducibles,* pg. 320)
- Paper
- Pencils
- Timer
- Magazines for clip-art (optional)

- A hat or sketch of a hat
- Index cards or similar (optional)
- Glue stick (optional)
- Scissors (optional)

Getting Ready
- Make copies of Object Cards and cut them out; or
- Have students make their own object cards by drawing a few objects on cards or cutting pictures from magazines to glue onto cards.

Activities and Procedures

1 Explain to the class that they will participate in a contest called "Get the Hat."

2 Display a visual representation of a hat. To do this, you might place a real hat up high where students can see it, sketch a hat high on the chalkboard, or tape a sketch of a hat high on a wall.

3 Ask students to brainstorm aloud to identify various ways to get the hat down without a ladder or stepstool. Encourage them to be creative and assure them that no idea is too wild or imaginative as long as it is feasible given the proper resources.

4 Make a list of their ideas on the board. Use some of the examples below to inspire ideas:
- Use something long to swipe it down
- Knock the hat shelf off the wall by throwing something at it
- Gouge holes in the wall to use for climbing up to get it
- Blow it down
- Train a homing pigeon to get it

5 Explain and display the following contest rules. (See sidebar, "Rules for Get the Hat.")

6 Divide the class into teams, and appoint a scorekeeper for each team.

7 Randomly deal each team three Object Cards (except the card showing a ladder).

8 Start the timer, and invite teams to begin brainstorming ways to use the items shown on their cards to retrieve the hat. Teams may continue to draw one more card at a time until they devise a plan, but remind them that they are penalized for each additional card that they draw.

9 Encourage the brainstorming process by asking students to ponder the following questions:
- In what other ways can the item be used besides its obvious, intended use? For example, think of other things you could do with a football besides throwing it. If you puncture it, will a stream of air blow out? What if you fill it with water?
- Think of the item as its individual parts rather than the whole. For example, if you cut the football, what could you do with the skin and the thread?
  These questions will enable students to think about their objects in new ways.

10 Ask teams to jot down all of their plans and ideas, even those they rejected, to share with the class.

11 Instruct students to announce "I Got the Hat!" as soon as they have devised a successful plan.

12 When time is up, tally up the points, and announce a winner!

Extensions
Have students use their Object Cards to:
- Design a chair.
- Escape from a small enclosure.
- Get a message to someone across the street without delivering it in person.
- Get the penny from the bottom of a tall, narrow jar.

Rules for Get the Hat

Object of the Contest
To be the first team to devise a successful plan to get the hat down by drawing the fewest number of Object Cards.

Play
- Teams start with 20 points and three object cards each
- Teams do not need to use all their cards.
- Teams may add additional cards, as needed, until they form a plan
- Teams have five minutes or less to create a plan to get the hat

Scoring
- The team who announces "I got the hat!" first earns 5 extra points
- Teams are penalized 1 point for each card drawn over their original three cards
- Teams that use only two cards get 3 extra points
- Teams that use only one card get 6 extra points
- The team who earns the most points wins

Combo Contraptions

CC-05

Grade Level: 2 through 8
Participants: Individuals or small teams
Objectives: Exercise fluency, flexibility, originality, elaboration, brainstorming, sketching and writing skills
Time: Approximately 1 to 2 hours

Quick View

In this imaginative, trial-and-error activity, students become inventors by listing existing tools and combining them at random until some creative and useful ideas emerge. After determining the utility of their new inventions, students create sketches of their contraptions and present them to the class.

Example

Combine a tricycle with a vacuum cleaner to make "Ridervac," a vacuum cleaner you ride.

Take Home
Increased brainstorming skills and sketches for an original invention

Materials
- Pencils
- Plain paper
- Chalk and chalkboard or equivalent

Getting Ready
- Gather pictures of all kinds of inventions, both old and new.
- Discuss the concept of "utility" and how inventions meet needs.
- Discuss power sources and movement processes such as electricity, water power, wind, mechanics, springs, batteries, magnets, pulleys, gears, levers, gravity, and human muscle. List several of these on the board and ask students to add their own ideas to the list.
- Discuss how the items on the list contribute both old and new inventions.
- Invite students to brainstorm as many inventions as possible such as the water faucet, clock, electric toothbrush, television, bicycle, computer, cell phone, pencil sharpener, three-ring binder, electric light, helicopter, piano, roller-coaster, skates, remote control car, and windmill.
- Make a list on the board, and ask students to contribute their own ideas to the list.
- Choose several of these inventions and discuss how they are useful and what life would be without them.

Activities and Procedures

1 Ask students to take an imaginary walk through their homes, school, and town and name the inventions they see.

2 Then, ask students to combine two existing inventions to create a new invention. They may use the inventions on the list or come up with their own.

3 Encourage the students to try random combinations, jotting down all of their thoughts until an idea for something useful emerges.

NOTE: Tell them not to be concerned with technical realities at this point.

4 Now, ask students to evaluate each of their combo-invention ideas by assessing its usefulness. Instruct them to ask themselves what kind of person might use the new invention and for what purpose. For example, a combination lawnmower/flashlight might be used by someone who prefers to mow the lawn at night and needs light cast onto the lawn.

5 Invite students to ponder the following questions to determine the overall utility of their combo-inventions:
- What does your invention do?
- Why is it used?
- Who would use it?
- When and where is it used?
- How is it used?
- What is the benefit of using it?

6 Next, have students name their inventions using creative and descriptive titles. (See lesson plan, "Name Us Famous," pg. 96.)

7 Once the inventions have been named, tell students to sketch their inventions, label the important parts, and write titles above their sketches.

8 Then, instruct students to write a description of how someone might use the invention and why it would benefit that person to use it.

9 Finally, invite students to present their new inventions to the class.

Extensions
- For a super challenge, combine three existing inventions to create a new invention.
- Connect this lesson plan to a social studies unit about famous inventors.
- Integrate this activity into a science unit on mechanics and physics.
- Have students write a sales pitch touting their new invention and deliver it to the class.

The Next Great Invention

CC-06

Grade Level: 2 through 6
Participants: Individuals or small teams
Objectives: Exercise fluency, flexibility, originality, elaboration, brainstorming, identifying and solving problems, writing and sketching skills.
Time: 1 to 2 hours

Quick View

In this exercise in creative problem solving, students brainstorm a list of everyday problems, big or small, and devise unique inventions to solve those problems. Inspired by images of working parts such as gears or electrical parts, students refine their ideas by keeping a journal of their notes and sketches.

Examples

Problem: The dog eats my homework.

Creative Solution:

- A spray coating for homework papers that tastes horrible to dogs.
- A pulley system that attaches to your homework and is activated by warm breath. When a dog gets close, the papers are pulled high out of reach.

Problem: I have too many things to carry to school.

Creative Solution:

- A remote control system with sensors and wheels that attach to your books and projects. By using the remote, you can make your belongings follow you to school.
- A molecule compactor that compresses things to pocket size. Pull a string to re-expand the molecules once you arrive at school.

The Amazing "Follow-Me" Remote

Take Home
Enhanced problem-solving skills and an inventor's notebook featuring the development of "The Next Great Invention"

Materials
- Pencils
- Plain paper
- Chalk and chalkboard or equivalent

Getting Ready
- Gather pictures of various contraptions and working parts such as gears, pulleys, wings, etc.

Activities and Procedures

1 Invite the class to brainstorm a list of little problems and annoyances in daily life. Share the following examples to spark ideas, or select a problem from a Problem Finders Bank. (See *Creativity: Mysteries Revealed*, pg. 14.)
   - It's too cold to get out of bed in the morning.
   - I usually miss the bus.
   - When tall people sit in front of me at the movie theater, I can't see the screen.

2 Have students brainstorm ways these problems could be solved by inventing something. Mention several kinds of working parts to help get ideas flowing, and tell students not to be concerned with technical realities; ideas are the important factors.

3 Ask students to jot down a few of their ideas and select one to develop.

4 Invite students to make sketches, changing and refining their concepts until they are satisfied with their designs. The sketches do not need to be perfect, but they should be clear.

5 Tell students to make notes to clarify the concepts, and title their inventions. (See lesson plan, "Name Us Famous," pg. 96.)

6 Finally, have students collect their sketches and bind them together to show the development of their concept. Students can decorate paper covers and bind the notebooks with staples or holes and string, or they may paste the papers into spiral notebooks.

Extensions
- Make 3-D "prototypes" of "The Next Great Invention" with materials such as construction paper, wire, found objects, discarded toys, clay, and paper mache.
- Integrate this activity into a social studies unit on inventions and how they have changed our lives.

Concoct a Recipe

Grade Level: 2 through 6
Participants: Individual or group
Objectives: Exercise fluency, flexibility, originality, elaboration, brainstorming
Time: Approximately 1 hour

Quick View

This quasi-culinary activity is sure to end in groans and laughter. Each student picks food words at random like "tomato," "broccoli," "or "hot fudge." Working individually or in teams of three or four, students combine their foods to concoct an original recipe, featuring the list of ingredients and cooking instructions. The recipes can be delicious or disgusting—it's all part of the fun!

Example

See "Jelly Bean Soup" and "Froggy's Feast."

Take Home

Unique recipe cards

Materials

- Pencils
- Plain paper
- 1 Paper bag
- 3″ x 5″ index cards
- Chalk and chalkboard or equivalent

Getting Ready

- Gather some examples of recipes. Children's cookbooks and online web sites are great resources.
- Cut some of the plain paper into dozens of small scraps, approximately 2″ square.
- Optional: Display measuring cups and a conversion chart for the class to see.

Froggy's Feast

Ingredients*
7 flies
4 beetles
1 can of peas
1 cup milk
1 cup corn flakes
1 tbsp ketchup
2 large sunflowers

Directions
Mash the peas and corn flakes together. Add milk and ketchup and mix thoroughly in bowl. Sauté the flies and beetles until crispy. Add the ingredients from the bowl and cook on medium heat for 8 minutes. Let stand 2 minutes. Pour over large sunflowers.
Serves two hungry frogs.

Jelly Bean Soup

Ingredients*
12 red jelly beans
12 yellow jelly beans
1 tsp cinnamon
½ cup chopped cherry pie
2 cups orange soda
2 cups small marshmallows

Directions
In a large pot, combine all ingredients except marshmallows. Stir together. Heat on low until jelly beans start to melt. Remove from heat. Let stand for 5 minutes. Serve in cups with marshmallows on top.
Serves four.

*Measurement abbreviations:
tbsp = tablespoon, tsp = teaspoon

Activities and Procedures

1 Through classroom participation:
   - Brainstorm a list of foods such as peas, potato chips, banana pudding, broccoli, hot fudge, etc. Hint: food doesn't have to be for human consumption – it could be a pet or animal food, etc.
   - Brainstorm a list of spices and condiments such as hot sauce, honey, garlic, ketchup, etc.
   - Brainstorm a list of cooking processes such as stir, mash, chop, blend, whip, heat, bake, fry, boil, etc.

2 Show the class some examples of recipes. Point out the distinct parts of a recipe including title, ingredients, measurements, directions, and serving suggestions.

3 Discuss measurements such as cups, ounces, tablespoons, teaspoons, etc.

4 Hand out several of the 2″ paper scraps to each student. Ask students to write one food or spice on each paper and then drop these "ingredients" into the bag.

5 Instruct each student to randomly pick one ingredient out of the bag.

6 Divide the class into teams, approximately three students to a team. Have the teams combine their foods and spices to concoct an original recipe. Teams may eliminate one ingredient and are allowed to add one or two more ingredients of their choice. Multiplying foods is allowed as well. For example, "potato" can be interpreted as several potatoes.

7 Instruct teams to brainstorm some recipe ideas and decide on the best one.

8 Tell teams to first write their recipes on plain paper and once their idea is approved, transfer the recipe onto an index card, adding decorations, special lettering, and borders as desired.

9 Allow each team to share their recipe with the class.

George Washington Carver

January 1864 – January 5, 1943

George Washington Carver was a great innovator in concocting recipes using peanuts! He was an American scientist, botanist, educator and inventor whose studies and teaching revolutionized agriculture in the Southern United States.

Carver once published a popular "practical bulletin for farmers" that contained 105 food recipes, all using peanuts. He also created or identified approximately 100 products that could be made from peanuts that were useful for the house and farm, including cosmetics, dyes, paints, plastics, gasoline, and nitroglycerin. Carver's work on peanuts was intended to provide an alternative crop to cotton which, through repeated farming, depleted the soil.

He wanted poor farmers to grow alternative crops both as a source of their own food and as a source of other products to improve their quality of life.

Extensions

- Have students make a "Creative Concoctions Cookbook." In doing so, students learn about the parts of a book, refine their writing skills, learn editing skills, and practice illustrating. A cookbook is a great class project to display at Open House or Back to School Night!
- Use this lesson for a more in-depth study of standard measurements and conversions.

What <u>Can</u> You Do with a Paper Clip?   CC-08

Grade Level: 2 through 8
Participants: Individuals and teams
Objectives: Exercise fluency, flexibility, originality, and brainstorming skills
Time: 15 to 30 minutes

Quick View

In this exercise in creative brainstorming, students work individually to think of as many uses for paperclips as possible. Students then combine their lists with their teammates and compete for both fluency and originality.

Examples

There are many possible uses for paperclips: Bracelet, key chain, earrings, pendulum, photo holder, sculpting tool, braces for teeth, jump rope, hamster cage. See sidebar, "The Many Uses of Paper Clips!"

Take Home

Enhanced brainstorming skills and a collection of new ideas for paperclips

Materials

- Pencils
- Paper
- Dozens of regular size paperclips
- 1 box of large paperclips
- Chalk and chalkboard or equivalent
- Timer

Getting Ready

- Review "Brainstorming Guidelines" and "Classroom Conduct for Brainstorming" on pg. 8. in *Creativity: Mysteries Revealed*. These rules are important and shouldn't be overlooked.
- Provide a small pile of paperclips for each student to use as a brainstorming aid.
- Ask the class to think of as many uses for paperclips as possible within a three-minute timeframe, and list each idea on the board.

Activities and Procedures

1 Inform students that they will be participating in a contest called "What *Can* You Do With a Paper Clip?"

2 Ask students to review the list on the board and begin thinking of additional uses for paper clips.

3 Encourage students to observe, touch, and manipulate their paperclips to facilitate the brainstorming process.

4 Divide the class into two teams, and instruct each student to create an individual list to contribute to the team's "master" list at the end of the contest.

5 Set the timer for three to five minutes, and encourage students to strive for quantity, not quality.

6 When time is up, have students combine their individual lists and select students from each team to take turns reading their master lists out loud. For example, Team A reads one entry, then Team B reads one, and so on.

7   Award Teams 2 points for each item on their list (fluency), and 5 points for each use that was not duplicated by the other team (originality).

For example, Team A reads "necklace." If Team B has "necklace" on their list also, they call out "We have it." Both teams are "awarded" 2 points for "necklace."

If Team B did not have "necklace, "however, then Team A is awarded 5 points.

NOTE: For extra fun, award large paperclips instead of points.

8   Have students continue reading until both lists are completed.

9   Tally up the points, and announce the winner!

Extensions

Complete the activity above, but instead of asking students to think of uses for paper clips, invite them to think of uses for:

- Ball of string
- Bars of soap
- Bricks
- Buttons
- Cans of soup
- Crayons
- Drinking straws
- Erasers
- Pocket combs
- Rolls of tape
- Tennis shoes
- Toothbrushes

The Many Uses of Paper Clips!

- Attaching things to ring binders
- Bell swinger
- Belt
- Book mark
- Braces for teeth
- Button hook
- Chain
- Chain used as a jump rope
- Chains to support a swing
- Compass
- Craft tool
- Dog leash
- Door knocker with hard item attached
- Ear cleaners (don't try this!)
- Electric light component
- Electrical current conductor
- Fill a bag and use as an anchor
- Fish hook
- For supporting hanging vines
- Fork
- Game part
- Gardening tool
- Garland support for flowers
- Glue to floor mat
- Hair clip
- Hold papers together
- Inside a rainstick
- Inside box to make noisemaker
- Jewelry – necklace, bracelet
- Key chain
- Keyboard cleaner
- Magnetize it to make magnets
- Magnetized to create sculpture
- Magnetized chain for retrieving things from narrow spaces
- Make a covering for something by attaching pieces of paper
- Make a cage for a small pet
- Manicure tool
- Melt them to cast into candle holder or other household items
- Mobile
- Net for fishing
- Pants/blouse fastener
- Paper weight – fill a container with them
- Pendulum by making a chain and attaching a weight
- Percussion musical instrument
- Pick a lock
- Plumbline by making a chain and attaching a weight
- Printing tool by attaching pieces of sponge, clip is handle
- Puncture holes in pie crust
- Radio component
- Sculpting tools
- Shoe fastener
- Spring – form it into this
- Staple puller
- Stirrer
- Stopper for model airplane glue
- Strainer
- Stylus for etching
- Support for baking
- Texturizer on canvas for painting
- Texturizer tool for marbling paint
- Thumb tack
- Tiny fence for a doll house
- Tooth cleaner (don't do this!)
- Tree ornaments
- Weapon (slingshot part)
- Weight for helium balloon
- Zipper pull

SAFETY WARNING: The ideas listed are just that, ideas only. Don't allow children to do anything that could cause harm to themselves or others.

What Can't You Do with a Paper Clip? CC-09

Grade Level: 2 through 8
Participants: Individuals and teams
Objectives: Exercise fluency, flexibility, originality, elaboration, critical thinking, and brainstorming skills
Time: 15 to 30 minutes

Quick View

In this companion lesson to "What Can You Do With a Paper Clip?" students go head-to-head to prove that virtually anything is possible with an ordinary paper clip. As students brainstorm seemingly impossible feats, or CANNOTS, their opponents counterattack with YES, YOU CANS, proving the tasks feasible after all.

Take Home

Enhanced brainstorming and critical thinking skills as well as a collection of ideas for transforming ordinary things into original creations.

Examples

CANNOTS:

- Spaceship
- Megaphone
- Window
- Compass
- Children's Book
- Road Sign
- Writing Tool
- Food Bowl

YES YOU CANS: A student might suggest creating a Food Bowl by forming the wires into a bowl shape and adding a wax paper lining. Or, one could use a paper clip as a Writing Tool by scratching messages onto any painted surface.

Materials

- Pencils
- Paper
- Dozens of paper clips
- Chalk and chalkboard or equivalent
- Timer

Getting Ready

- Refer to "The Classroom Conduct for Brainstorming" so that students feel comfortable to participate and do their best (see *Creativity: Mysteries Revealed*, pg. 8). These rules are important and should not be overlooked before you begin.
- Place a small pile of paper clips on each student's desk as a brainstorming aid.

Activities and Procedures

1 Inform students that they will be participating in a contest called "What *Can't* You Do With a Paper Clip?"

2 Tell students that they will be listing as many things as possible that they believe absolutely, positively CANNOT be done with one or more paper clips.

3 Divide the class into two teams, and instruct each student to create an individual list of CANNOTS to contribute to the team's "master" list at the end of the contest.

4 Set the timer for three to five minutes, and encourage students to strive for quantity, not quality.

5 When time is up, a student from each team will begin reading their list of CANNOTS as follows:

A member of Team A reads a CANNOT from the master list.

Team B then has 10 seconds to respond with "YES, YOU CAN!" and state how the task in question could be accomplished.

For example, if Team A says "You CANNOT use paper clips as a warm blanket," Team B could say, "YES, YOU CAN!" and explain that one could use paper clips to attach small scraps of fabric or tissue paper to each other, creating a warm blanket."

Now, Team B reads a CANNOT from their master list, and Team A has ten seconds to respond with a "YES, YOU CAN!" For example, Team B might say, "You CANNOT use paper clips for food," and Team A could respond with "YES, YOU CAN!" Paper clips make a great breakfast cereal for robots."

NOTE: The "YES, YOU CANS" can be wildly imaginative as long as they are logical within their own context.

If the other team remains silent for ten seconds without countering with a "YES, YOU CAN," the CANNOT is considered unchallenged. For instance, if Team A says, "You CANNOT use paper clips to hold water," and Team B does not have a "YES, YOU CAN" response within ten seconds, the CANNOT remains unchallenged and Team A reads the next CANNOT on their list.

Teams alternate CANNOTS and YES, YOU CANs until both lists are completed.

6 Award points and announce a winner according to the following guidelines:

2 points for each CANNOT that goes unchallenged.

4 points for each acceptable YES, YOU CAN

The Team with the highest number of points wins the contest!

Extensions
Complete the activity above, but instead of asking students to think of CANNOTS for paper clips, invite them to think things that cannot be done with:

- Ball of string
- Bars of soap
- Bricks
- Buttons
- Cans of soup
- Crayons
- Drinking straws
- Erasers
- Pocket combs
- Rolls of tape
- Tennis shoes
- Toothbrushes

Connect the Ducks and Boots

Grade Level: 2 through 8
Participants: Individuals or small teams
Objectives: Exercise fluency, flexibility, originality, finding relationships, and analytical skills
Time: Approximately 30 minutes

Quick View

This mind-bending activity will test students' analytical skills as they brainstorm to discover commonalities between two seemingly unrelated items. Working independently or as a team, students race to connect randomly-chosen items in surprising new ways.

Example

"Duck" and "Boot"

- Both are often wet. (usage and materials)
- Both can make similar sounds (sound)
- Both are relatively small. (size)
- Both have an outer skin. (structure)
- Both were made on Earth. (location)
- Both can be made of animal materials. (material)

- Both can be yellow. (color)
- Both have flat feet. (shape)
- Both have one syllable. (word)
- Both have four letters. (word)
- Both are spelled with a consonant at the beginning and a consonant at the end. (word)

Take Home

An interesting list of items which proves that with a little creativity and analysis, anything can be related!

Materials

- Pencils
- Paper
- Paper bag
- Chalk and chalkboard or equivalent

Getting Ready

- On the board, list some qualities such as shape, materials, and usage for students to refer to as they complete the activity.
- Gather several scraps of paper for students to write on.
- Discuss the meaning of "relationships" with your class.

- Tell them to consider the qualities listed on the board when looking for relationships between two unrelated things.
- Point to two dissimilar items such as a stapler and a chair, for instance, and ask the following thought-provoking questions: Even though they are different things, what do they have in common? How do they look similar to each other? What can they do that is similar? Some responses might include: both have hard surfaces, both are used at school, both have metal parts, etc.

Activities and Procedures

1 Have students write down object words on individual scraps of paper. Encourage students to think of unusual items or look around the classroom for ideas. They may also wish to mentally picture items in each of their rooms at home.

2 Place all the papers in a bag, and have each student pick two papers at random.

3 Have individuals or teams brainstorm and list as many commonalities as they can think of for their chosen items within a ten-minute timeframe.

4 Share the results with the class. Discuss interesting or debatable responses.

5 Repeat the activity as time permits.

Of Pumpkins and Backpacks

Discovering relationships between things that are not obviously similar is a task that demands creativity. Therefore, students may wish to analyze the items from various points of view. Below are some category suggestions to facilitate brainstorming.

Comparing a Pumpkin and a Backpack

Category	Relationship
Color	Both can be orange
Construction	Both are hollow
How they work	Neither has electrical parts
Location	Both can be found at home
Materials	Neither is wood
Perspective	Both are found on Earth
Physical property	Both are solids
Shape	Both are kind of round
Size	Both are bigger than a bar of soap
Sound of the word	Both have two syllables
Sounds it makes	Both make a thud when dropped
Spelling	Both have two vowels
Weight	Both weigh more than an ounce
Temperature	Both are medium temperature
Time	Both exist in modern times
Usage	Both can hold things

Extensions

- *Object Cards:*
  Use copies of Object Cards in place of written words on slips of paper. (See *Reproducibles,* pg. 320.)
- *Contest:*
  Each student or team is given the same two items and has ten minutes to list as many similarities as possible. The student/team with the longest list wins the contest.
- *Super Challenge:*
  Students are encouraged to find relationships among three or four items.
- *Language Arts Connection:*
  Students compose poems featuring similes and metaphors based on their comparisons.

Brainstorm Boot Camp

Grade Level: 3 through 8
Participants: Individuals
Objectives: Exercise fluency, flexibility, originality, elaboration, and brainstorming skills
Time: Approximately 1 hour

Quick View

In this exercise in transformation, students learn the power of brainstorming and creative thinking by applying the S.C.A.M.P.E.R. techniques to enhance ordinary objects or even transform them into spectacular inventions.

Examples

See the sidebar, "S.C.A.M.P.E.R. Examples," for an example of how the techniques can apply to both a "Chair" and a "Ball." The possibilities are endless!

Take Home

Enhanced brainstorming skills and a S.C.A.M.P.E.R. Worksheet featuring ideas for new inventions

Materials

- Pencils
- Plain paper
- Scrap paper
- S.C.A.M.P.E.R Worksheet Form (optional) (For a free downloadable Worksheet Form, go to www.jrimagination.com/printables)
- S.C.A.M.P.E.R. brainstorming poster (see *Reproducibles*, pg. 342)
- Tape
- Chalk and chalkboard or equivalent
- Timer
- Common objects for brainstorming such as a chair, pen, book, backpack, or anything else you have on hand

Getting Ready

- Crumple seven pieces of paper into separate balls. Write the S.C.A.M.P.E.R. words on strips of paper and tape each to a crumpled paper ball, then put the balls aside. These will be used for "The Game of Brain Toss."
- Display copies of the S.C.A.M.P.E.R. Brainstorming Chart.
- Share the "S.C.A.M.P.E.R Examples" in the sidebar and in *Creativity: Mysteries Revealed*, pgs. 9–10.

S.C.A.M.P.E.R. Examples

CHAIR
Substitute the legs for skis, so a wheelchair bound person can ski.
Combine a heater with a chair to create a chair that warms you.
Adapt a fuzzy teddy bear into a chair to make a comfy, cozy chair.
Magnify a chair big enough for four friends. **M**inimize a chair to hold an iPod.
Put to new use as an exercise apparatus.
Eliminate the seat so that the arms and back provide support while standing.
Reverse or rearrange the parts to make a comfortable lounge chair.

BALL
Substitute the smooth surface for little springs to make it bounce higher.
Combine a ball with glue to create a ball that sticks to the surface it hits.
Adapt a bouncy ball to a remote for a TV, so you can bounce it to another person.
Magnify a ball to a size that fills your yard. Minimize it so it fits on top of a pencil.
Put to new use as a bathtub plug.
Eliminate half of it to create a rubber hat.
Reverse or rearrange it by curving it into the shape of a boomerang.

- Discuss with your class the various ways of improving an item such as making it more useful, changing its use, making it more fun, more beautiful, or more unusual. Then ask students to consider how S.C.A.M.P.E.R. might be applied to accomplish these goals.
- Distribute paper and pencils to each student.

Activities and Procedures

Individual Practice

1 Hand out the S.C.A.M.P.E.R. Worksheet Form, but if it is not available, ask students to create their own by writing out each of the words along the left margin, leaving room to write examples beside each technique, and leaving a little space at the top.

2 Display the common objects, then instruct students to select one and write the name of the object at the top of the page.

3 Have the students apply S.C.A.M.P.E.R. to reinvent the item, writing an example next to each word. NOTE: Decide if all ideas must be feasible, or if non-feasible ideas are allowed.

4 Continue practicing as time permits.

Game Play

5 Inform students that they will be participating in a game called "The Game of Brain Toss."

6 Begin the game, and proceed according to the following guidelines:
- The object of the game is to generate ideas for improving an item by using S.C.A.M.P.E.R.
- Students sit facing a single object on display.
- The teacher stands near it, and tosses a paper ball to a student to catch.
- The student who catches the ball has ten seconds to say an idea by using the technique written on the ball.
- If the student cannot come up with an idea, they hand the ball to another student who has ten seconds to generate an idea.
- The student who successfully produces an idea tosses the ball back to the teacher.

For example, a chair is on display. A student catches the ball labeled "Adapt." The student says, "Adapt by making the chair icy cold" and tosses the ball back. The teacher tosses another ball with a different label, and play continues until all the balls have been played. Over the duration of the game, the simple chair will take new forms many times over, demonstrating the limitless power of effective brainstorming.

Extensions

Use S.C.A.M.P.E.R. to transform or reinvent the following items:
- Clothes hanger
- Fork
- Shopping bag
- Book
- Band-aid
- Tire/wheel
- Toy car
- Fishing rod
- Flashlight

S.C.A.M.P.E.R.

S substitute a part for something else

C combine things or add something new

A adapt by changing the kind of materials or procedure

M modify by enlarging, reducing, or changing proportions

P put to a new use

E eliminate something or simplify

R reverse or rearrange

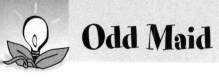

Odd Maid

Grade Level: 2 through 6
Participants: Individuals or small teams
Objectives: Exercise fluency, originality, elaboration, sketching, categorizing, and social skills
Time: Approximately 1 to 2 hours

Quick View

In this creative spin-off of a popular card game, students brainstorm lists of common noun pairs such as cup and saucer or ball and bat, and sketch their pairs on small cards to create an original card game. By designing their own cards, students demonstrate their artistic talent while exercising categorization and concept development skills as well.

Example

For an example visit www.jrimagination.com/printables.

Take Home

Enhanced concept development skills and an original version of a classic card game to share with friends and family

Materials

- Index cards or equivalent (26 to 42 per student or team)
- Pencils
- Rulers
- Crayons or markers
- Medium-size rubber bands
- Chalkboard and chalk or equivalent

Getting Ready

- List some common noun pairs on the board to inspire student brainstorming (see sidebar, "Common Pairs," for ideas).

Activities and Procedures

1 Explain or review the meaning of the word "noun."

2 Have the class brainstorm pairs of nouns that are commonly found together, such as salt and pepper, and add them to the list on the board.

3 Instruct each student to make a list of 12 to 25 pairs to use for their cards. They may combine pairs listed on the board with their own pairs if they wish.

4 Have students draw rectangular cards, approximately 2½" x 3½" each, or use small, blank index cards.

5 Invite students to sketch and color their pairs on separate cards, one item per card.

Common Pairs

- Ball and bat
- Bread and butter
- Bride and groom
- Comb and brush
- Cream and sugar
- Cup and saucer
- Ham and eggs
- Hammer and nails
- Hat and coat
- Horse and saddle
- Milk and cookies
- Needle and thread
- Pail and shovel
- Paint and brush
- Pancakes and syrup
- Peanut butter and jelly
- Pen and ink
- Pencil and paper
- Salt and pepper
- Shoes and socks
- Soap and water
- Song and dance
- Sticks and stones

6 Direct students to write the pair name on each card. For example, the pair Peanut Butter and Jelly would feature a drawing of a jar of peanut butter on one card and a drawing of a jar of jelly on the other, but both cards would say "Peanut Butter & Jelly".

7 Encourage each student to draw only one "Odd Maid" card. This card can be silly, weird, wacky, or simply creative, but it must not be paired with any other card.

8 Have students cut out their cards if necessary.

9 To finish, invite students to create a title card featuring the name of the card game and the student's name, put it on top of the deck, and put a rubber band around the deck.

10 Allow students to share their games with the class and have fun playing a few rounds of "Odd Maid" with one another.

Rules For "Odd Maid" Card Game

Players
- 2 to 4 players

Deck
- 25 cards (12 pairs plus one) to 41 cards (20 pairs plus one)

Goal
- To avoid being the player who ends up holding the Odd Maid card, which has no matching pair.

Setup
- Select a dealer who shuffles the cards and distributes them evenly to all the players. It's ok if some players have one card more than the others.

Play
- Players sort their cards, looking for pairs. They lay down any pairs they have.
- The dealer then offers their hand, face down, to the player on their left. That player randomly selects one card from the dealer.
- If that card matches a card they have in their hand, the player lays the pair down. If it doesn't complete a pair, the player keeps it in their hand.
- Continue playing clockwise until there are no more pairs, and only the card that has no pair is left. The player holding that card (the Odd Maid) loses the game.

Extensions

Have students play the game featuring different kinds of pairs such as:
- Opposites – big and small, in and out, hot and cold, open and close, young and old, etc.
- Famous couples – Romeo and Juliet, Jack and Jill, Lewis and Clark, etc.
- Math equations – two different math problems that result in the same sum are pairs

Have students use two identical items for both cards:
- Animals
- Bugs
- Christmas things
- Countries – draw shape of each country
- Geometric shapes
- Leaves
- Monsters
- Sea creatures
- United States – draw shape of each state
- Vehicles

Use this game as part of any lesson or unit by adapting the cards to fit the theme or subject that your students are currently exploring.

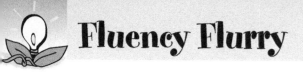

Grade Level: 2 through 8
Participants: Individuals or small groups
Objectives: Exercise fluency, originality, imagination, brainstorming, and classifying skills
Time: Approximately ½ hour

Quick View

In this fun, fast-paced contest, students exercise classifying and fluent thinking skills. Time is of the essence as students race to think up as many items in a given category as possible. Points are awarded for quantity and creativity.

Example

Things in the Sea

1 Bubbles	12 Mermaids	15 Rusty anchors	18 Sea shells
2 Clams	13 Octopus	16 Sand	19 Seaweed
3 Coral	14 Oysters	17 Sea horses	20 Sharks
4 Crabs			21 Shellfish
5 Dolphins			22 Sting rays
6 Eels			23 Sunken ships
7 Fish			24 Tuna
8 Flounder			25 Turtles
9 Jellyfish			26 Volcanic rock
10 Krill			27 Water
11 Lobsters			28 Whales

Take Home

An impressive list of items which demonstrates the student's fluency and ability to classify. This list may spark future brainstorming or even inspire a family game.

Materials

- Pencils
- Lined paper
- Timer
- Awards or prizes for incentives

Getting Ready

- Write one or two categories on the board for the class to see. Invite the class to suggest items for each category, and list a few relevant items as examples. Use student responses as an opportunity to model classifying strategies.
- Choose a category for the activity. You can make up your own or choose from the list in the sidebar, "Category Suggestions."

Activities and Procedures

1 The teacher announces a category, and allows students to work independently or in small groups to list as many category-specific items as they can think of within a five-minute time period.

2 When time is up, the teacher asks the student or team with the most items to read their list aloud. Other students raise their hands when they hear an item that matches one on their list.

3 The teacher then asks if anyone has an item listed that was not mentioned, and students are invited to share these responses.

4 After all items are discussed, points are assigned. One point is awarded for each item listed and three points are awarded for each unique item (one that no other student has listed). Points are tallied, and the student or group with the most points wins an award or a small prize.

Extensions

- Assign categories to small groups and ask students to sketch images or clip pictures from magazines to make category posters or collages.
- Encourage students to compose a silly song or brief skit featuring the items they listed in a given category.

Category Suggestions

- Jobs that require talking
- Jobs that require walking
- Kinds of music
- Kinds of sports
- Kinds of vehicles
- Things made of wood
- Things that are black
- Things that are bigger than a car
- Things that are in the sea
- Things that are orange
- Things that are round
- Things that are white
- Things that can be used as containers
- Things that did not exist 100 years ago
- Things that fit in a cup
- Things that fit in a thimble
- Things that have lights
- Things that have numbers
- Things that have wheels
- Things that make a mark
- Things that make a sound
- Things that roll
- Things you read

"Discovery consists in seeing what everyone else has seen and thinking what no one else has thought."
– Albert Szent-Gyorgi

Grade Level: 2 through 6
Participants: Individuals or teams of two
Objectives: Exercise flexibility, tactile awareness, tactile discrimination, and mental visualization
Time: Approximately ½ hour

Quick View

Students sketch a visual representation of an object that they have observed through their sense of touch alone. Blindfolded and seated, students touch their item to form a tactile memory that will serve as the inspiration for their drawing.

Example

See illustration.

Take Home
Original sketches and enhanced visualization skills

Materials
- Soft cloth for blindfolds
- A variety of objects to serve as subjects for students' drawings (see sidebar, "Guidelines")
- Pencils
- Paper
- Large bag for hiding objects

Getting Ready
- Gather all the materials.
- Make sure that the objects you will use are hidden from sight prior to the activity.

Activities and Procedures

1 Explain the activity to the class, and ask for one or two volunteers to begin the activity.

2 Seat the students at a table or in their desks, and blindfold them. (Some students may be reluctant to be blindfolded and should not be pressured.)

3 Hand the volunteers an object. Make sure they do not see it.

4 Ask the students to observe their objects' characteristics by feeling its shapes and surfaces. When they have created clear mental images, put the objects back in the bag and remove the blindfolds.

5 Now, have students sketch their objects from tactile memory only. When they have completed their sketches, show them the objects and compare them to the finished drawings.

6 Display the sketches alongside the objects as a testament to the power of mental visualization.

Extensions

- *Do a Second Sketch:* Have students do another sketch while looking at their objects. Note the sensitivity and detail in this second sketch as a result of the students' prior tactile experience with the subject matter.
- *Dual Touch and Draw:* Have two or more students touch and draw the same object and compare their varying interpretations.
- *1000 Words Is Worth a Picture:* A blindfolded student holds an object and describes it in detail to other students who are positioned so they never get to see it. The describing student must not name the object or tell what it does. The other students sketch the object based on verbal descriptions, such as "It is long, thin, and flat on top. It has smooth surfaces,…" It is amazing to compare final sketches.
- *Blindfold Option:* Put an object inside an opaque bag, so that neither the describing student, nor the sketching students get to see it.

Guidelines

Choosing Objects:

1 Objects should not have sharp edges.

2 They should not be easily identifiable by their shape (e.g. a ball or book).

3 There should be some complexity to the form, such as eyeglasses or a tape dispenser.

4 The more unusual the shape of the object, the better.

Examples of Objects that Work Well:

- Costume jewelry pieces
- Eyeglasses
- Garlic press
- Handbag, backpack, or wallet
- Hole punch
- Keys and keychain ornaments
- Toys
- Parts of toys
- Pieces of packaging
- Rolodex
- Shoes or boots
- Small figurine
- Stapler (remove staples)
- Tape dispenser
- Unusual cooking utensils
- Unusual hardware items
- Unusual pieces of metal, wood, or plastic

Whatsit Brushes

Grade Level: 2 through 8
Participants: Individuals
Objectives: Exercise flexibility, originality, brainstorming skills, imagination, chart making, and visual awareness
Time: 1 to 1½ hours

Quick View

In this exercise in artistic experimentation, students stretch their imaginations by brainstorming, testing, and finally employing a variety of items that can be used to apply paint. By creating and implementing a number of "outside the paint box" possibilities, students practice their creative thinking skills while expanding their artistic vision as well.

Examples

Whatsit Brushes

- Tuft of grass
- Rubber bands
- Bunch of yarn ends
- Cooking utensils
- Cloth, cut in fringes
- Cotton swabs
- Facial tissues, cut in fringes

- Feathers
- Flowers, real and artificial
- Hairbrushes
- Leaves
- Mops
- Scraps of bread
- Carpet samples

- Scrub brushes
- Shoelaces
- Sponges
- Strips of paper
- Toothbrushes
- Whisk brooms
- Curly gift wrap ribbons
- Crumpled cellophane

TIP: Browse through a craft store, tour your back yard, look through your junk drawers, check out hardware stores, grocery stores, rummage sales, and dollar stores for Whatsit Brush possibilities.

Take Home

An enhanced artistic vision and a highly original and perhaps unusual painting to share with family and friends

Materials

- Tempera paint or watercolors
- Heavy paper
- Boxes of possible Whatsit Brushes
- Pencils

- Scissors
- Glue sticks
- Soap, water, and paper towels for cleanup
- Chalkboard and chalk or equivalent

Getting Ready

- List a few Whatsit Brush possibilities on the board as idea-sparkers. You can use some of the items listed here as examples or come up with your own.
- Ask students to bring in disposable things from home to use as their own Whatsit Brushes.

Activities and Procedures

1 Invite students to brainstorm for other Whatsit Brush ideas, and add their responses to the list on the board.

2 Next, ask students to pick at least three ideas that are feasible—that is, those that can actually be implemented with the resources available in the classroom.

3 Encourage students to use tempera paint and heavy paper to test their Whatsit Brushes.

4 When the paint is dry, instruct students to cut and mount the painted samples.

5 Have students label each sample, identifying what "brush" was used in each example.

6 Next, ask students to rate their Whatsit Brushes on a scale of 1 to 4, with 4 being the highest score and 1 being the lowest. Encourage students to ponder the following questions when assigning ratings:
   - Did it hold paint well?
   - Do you like the effect it produced?
   - How easy was it to use?
   - How well did it hold up for additional applications of paint?

7 Finally, invite students to paint pictures using a combination of Whatsit Brushes. Encourage them explore the effects of each technique and layer one texture on top of another.

Extensions

- Have students use traditional paintbrushes to accent their Whatsit Brush paintings.
- Conversely, invite students to use Whatsit Brushes to embellish traditionally painted artworks.
- Encourage students to experiment with other Whatsit media such as sculpting tools and stamps.
- For a related lesson plan, see "VA-13 Twenty Textures," pg. 284.

Secret Techniques

Apply imagination to your paintings with Whatsit Brushes.

By putting unlikely things to a new artistic use, you can create amazing effects. Professional artists treasure such discoveries and often keep them secret.

"Everything you can imagine is real."
– Pablo Picasso

A Game Became

Grade Level: 2 through 8
Participants: Teams of 3 - 4
Objectives: Exercise flexibility, originality, elaboration, divergent and convergent thinking, cooperation, concept development, and technical writing skills
Time: Approximately 1 hour or more

Broomball
for 2 individuals or 2 teams of 2

Object of the Game:
Use the broom to swat the apple into the basket. The first player to reach a score of five wins.

Materials:
- From List of Game Items: one broom, two basketballs, basket of apples, two yardsticks

Setting Up:
- Lay down a yardstick to mark a starting line.
- Set the basket on its side, the opening facing the starting line, about 6 ft. from the yardstick.

To Play:
- On "go," the first player uses the broom to swat the basketball into the basket.
- The opponent uses the second yardstick at the sidelines to swat apples across the basketball's path in an attempt to prevent the basketball from going into the basket.
- A point is made when a player is able to roll a basketball into the basket.
- Team members alternate between two-minute turns.

Rules:
- The yardstick is not allowed to touch an opponent's basketball directly.
- The first player to score five points wins.

Quick View

In this playful exercise, students use their prior knowledge of classic games along with their creative thinking skills to develop an entirely new game. By developing a complete and workable game using a limited amount of resources, students enrich their imaginations while honing their concept development skills as well.

Example

See "Broomball."

Take Home

Enhanced visualization and conceptualization skills as well as a fun new game idea to share with family and friends

Materials

- Game items (optional — see sidebar, "List of Game Items.")
- Paper
- Pencils
- Chalkboard and chalk or equivalent

List of Game Items

For this lesson, the items below are meant to be used through visualization, and not actually gathered. These items on the list are not difficult to find, however, and may provide an even more exciting and creative activity in the right setting.

- Ball of string
- Basket of apples
- Tray
- Broom
- Drinking straws
- Markers and paper
- Roll of tape
- Shovel
- Three cardboard boxes (any size)
- Two basketballs
- Two yardsticks
- Rubber bands
- Water

Getting Ready
- List the game items on the board for student reference.
- Gather several of the items on the list (optional).

Activities and Procedures

1 Inform the class that they will be working in small teams to develop a concept for a fun new game.

2 Discuss the basic elements of a game with your class. Over the course of the discussion, identify common game components such as opponents, objects, scoring measures, strategy, and luck. Explain that the best games are a combination of skill and luck. Some games rely more on luck than skill, and others rely on skill more than on luck.

3 Suggest that teams start brainstorming by identifying the attributes and utility of each item on the list. For example, a ball of string can be used to mark territories, a length of string can be used to swing a heavy object, the ball of string can be used as a ball, etc.

4 Encourage students to use at least 3 of the items on the list for creating a game.

Writing Instructions for a Game

Write the name of the game at the top. Under the name, indicate the minimum and maximum number of players required to play the game (e.g. 2-4 players). Next, write the actual instructions and explain the following elements:

Object of the Game
- The goal of the game and how to win

Setting Up
- What players must do to prepare to play the game

How To Play
- The procedures involved in playing the game including any special scenarios

Rules
- How much time players have
- When it is another player's turn
- Moves or actions that are not allowed
- How to keep score
- How to declare a winner

---

5 Invite students to add one other item of their choice if they wish. This object may or may not be on the game item list.

6 Give students approximately 15-20 minutes to work out the details of the game including materials, object, procedures, and rules as well as the name of the game.

7 After the basic elements of the game have been developed, invite students to take about 10 minutes to write instructions (see sidebar, "Writing Instructions for a Game").

8 Then, allow an additional 15-20 minutes for each team to present their games to the class, explaining the object of the game and teaching their classmates how to play.

9 Discuss how the students' diverse ideas and perspectives contributed to the creation of a variety of different games despite their use of the same or very similar materials.

Extensions
- Have students rate one another's games in terms of challenge and fun-factor.
- Invite students to design an advertisement for their new game and write a sales pitch to introduce it to consumers.
- Connect this lesson to any unit of study by including elements of the current subject matter (e.g.. a math game in which problems are solved to advance on the board, or a social studies game in which the course of history may be changed according to what path players take, etc.).

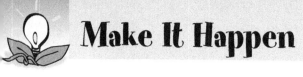

Make It Happen

Grade Level: 2 through 8
Participants: Teams of 2-4 or individuals
Objectives: Exercise flexibility, originality, elaboration, brainstorming, problem solving, and analytical skills
Time: 1 to 2 hours

Quick View

In this exercise in hypothetical problem solving, students use a limited and seemingly non-related list of items to solve a randomly-assigned problem. By looking at their resources in new ways and analyzing their various attributes, students enhance their observation and conceptualization skills while challenging their ability to make things happen.

Examples

Items: an orange, a brick, and a telephone book.

Free Choice: a potato masher

Challenge: Create a Painting

1 The team pulls several pages out of the telephone book, tears them into strips, and weaves the strips together to form a large surface on which to paint.

2 Next, they peel the orange and smash the segments with the brick. They use the masher to apply the orange juice to their surface. The grid of the masher makes pretty patterns of orange color on the absorbent paper of the telephone book.

3 Students then use pieces of orange peel, which adhere to the sticky juice, for accenting their painting. They name their masterpiece "The Orange Pages."

Items: a boot, a sponge, and a pumpkin.

Free Choice: a fork

Challenge: Dig a Hole

1 Students press the fork into the ground until the top dirt is loosened.

2 Next, they smash the pumpkin with the boot. They then use the sponge to absorb the gooey parts of the pumpkin, and use the dry curved pieces of pumpkin shell to scoop out the loosened dirt.

3 They widen and deepen the hole by using the boot itself as a digger and scraper.

4 They use the fork again to loosen the dirt at the bottom of hole, and repeat the procedure until the hole is deep and wide.

Take Home
Enhanced visualization and conceptualization skills as well as a new creation or idea to share with family and friends

Materials
- Scrap paper
- Blank or lined paper for notes and sketches
- Pencils
- Chalk and chalkboard, or equivalent
- Object Cards (see *Reproducibles,* pg. 320)

NOTE: To make your own Object Cards, ask each student to write the name of one item per scrap of paper. Sketches are optional. (See sidebar, "Ideas for Object Cards" for a list of possibilities.)

Ideas for Object Cards

• Bag of marbles	• Poster board
• Ballpoint pen	• Pumpkin
• Beach ball	• Rolling pin
• Block of ice	• Rope
• Boot	• Rubber glove
• Butter	• Screen door
• Elastic hair tie	• Shoebox
• Gears	• Skateboard
• Lipstick	• Stickers
• Loaf of bread	• Sunglasses
• Lollipop	• Tea cup & saucer
• Mug	• Telephone book
• Orange	• Tube of toothpaste
• Paintbrush	• Wheel

A full set of 50 reproducible Object Cards is available starting on pg. 320

Make It Happen *continues* ➜

continued from previous page

Getting Ready

- Engage your class in a discussion about assessing an object's attributes and utility. Encourage them to consider an object, identify its parts, and visualize what the parts can do. For example, think of a box of crayons not in the way it was meant to be used (for coloring something), but rather, think of it abstractly, as a container of shapes and materials. Keep in mind that the crayon box is a shape and material as well. (See sidebar, "A Box of Crayons.")

- For practice, ask your students to name all the characteristics they can think of for an item. Write the list on the board. This will help your students be aware of the assets they have for meeting their challenge.

- Make a list of "Free Choice" items for the class from the list below. Each team may select one of their choice to add to their combination of items.

Free Choice Items

- Bag of marshmallows
- Bar of soap
- Beach towel
- Box of straws
- Bucket of water
- Can of soda
- Chest of drawers
- Coffee cup
- Crayons
- Eggs
- Fork
- Hairbrush
- Jar of peanut butter
- Old CDs
- Pair of socks
- Potato masher
- Roll of toilet paper
- Spiral notebook
- Sponge
- Sunglasses
- Tape dispenser and tape
- Tennis racquet
- Window shade
- Yardstick

- Shuffle the Object Cards and distribute them, three per team or individual.

- Explain that any Object Card item or "Free Choice" item may be considered as multiples of ten (e.g. ten bags of marbles or ten rolling pins).

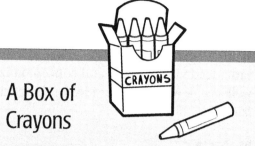

A Box of Crayons

Object Attributes of Crayons

- The crayons are 12 cylinders in a cardboard box
- The cylinders are uniform in size
- The cylinders are made of a waxy material
- Each cylinder is a different color
- The cylinders have paper labels that can be removed
- The labels have names of colors printed on them
- The cylinders can roll
- The cylinders break easily
- The cylinders can be crushed
- The cylinders can be melted
- The cylinders make colorful marks, even when melted

Object Attributes of Box

- It is cardboard
- It has lettering and designs printed in color
- The inside of the box is plain gray
- The inside of the box can be colored with crayons
- The box can hold things
- The box can be open or closed
- The box can be torn into pieces
- The box can be pulverized
- The box can be folded
- The box can be crumpled
- The box can be reshaped
- The box can be burnt to ashes
- Ashes make marks

Activities and Procedures

1 Have teams or individuals pick three Object Cards at random.

2 Next, randomly assign one challenge to each team. You can choose from the examples below or create your own.

Challenges

- Climb over a smooth, high fence
- Create an instrument for making music
- Create a painting
- Create a bin for storage
- Dig a hole
- Disguise yourself
- Get a toy down from the top of a tree
- Hide a piano
- Invent a game
- Make a hat
- Make a popcorn bowl
- Make a blanket
- Make a swing
- Make a wagon
- Protect yourself from the rain
- Write and send a message

3 Invite teams to consider their challenge as well as the resources they have available to them, and use this information to select one item from the "Free Choice" list.

NOTE: Students are not required to use all of their four items, but they should use at least two.

4 Encourage students to brainstorm ways to use the materials they have in order to meet their challenge. Suggest that they sketch and take notes as they formulate their ideas.

5 When each team has met its challenge, allow students to present both the challenges and solutions to the class. Invite students to explain their trials, errors, and the thinking processes that led them to "Make It Happen."

6 Encourage the class to discuss each solution, considering its creativity, cleverness, and feasibility.

Extensions

- Give each team the same challenge, but different items to use in achieving the goal. Then, have fun comparing the results and considering many ways of achieving the same goal.
- Give each team the same items, but different challenges. Then, compare the results and ponder the various ways materials can be used.
- To increase the challenge level, restrict teams to the use of only one of each item rather than multiples.
- Conversely, to expand the possibilities, allow the use of unlimited multiples of items, and encourage students to generate outrageous solutions.

"Creativity is the power to connect the seemingly unconnected."
– William Plomer

Outside the Box Clocks

Grade Level: 2 through 6
Participants: Individuals or teams of two to three
Objectives: Exercise originality, flexibility, elaboration, brainstorming techniques, and temporal concepts
Time: Approximately 1 hour

Quick View

In this inventive activity, students learn about the history of clocks and other time-telling devices while simultaneously inventing new and novel ways to measure time.

Examples

- As tea drips into a teacup, the overflow sets off an alarm.
- Gumballs slide through a giant tube like sand in an hourglass.
- A roof sundial casts large shadows across the yard.
- A miniature automatic ping pong game marks beats, like a metronome.
- A tiny digital clock on an eraser fits over a pencil top.
- A contemporary cuckoo clock has a hip-hop artist emerge every hour and "rap" the time out loud.

Take Home

Enhanced brainstorming skills and a creative sketch for a new time-measuring invention

Materials

- Pictures of clocks and other time-measuring devices
- Pencils
- Plain paper, several sheets per team
- Large sheets of colored paper, one sheet per team
- Crayons or markers (optional)

Getting Ready

- Gather books, magazines, and pictures of clocks and display them for student reference.

Activities and Procedures

1 Show and discuss pictures of devices used throughout history to measure time. Display pictures of time measuring devices such as:

- Alarm clocks
- Analog clocks
- Atomic clocks
- Cuckoo clocks
- Digital clocks
- Grandfather clocks
- Hourglasses
- Metronomes
- Motion clocks
- Pendulum clocks
- Sundials
- Water dripping devices
- Wind-up clocks

2 Discuss with your class the definition of time-telling: measuring the passing of time in regular intervals coordinated with the Earth's rotation or the phases of the Moon.

3 Discuss what man-made parts or natural phenomena can be used to create or mark time intervals.

4 List some ideas on the board, and invite students to contribute their own ideas to the list. You can use the examples below or come up with your own:

- Ball bearings
- Bells
- Electrical pulses
- Gears
- Gumballs
- Heat
- Light
- Magnetic motion
- Melting ice
- Notched metal
- Notched wood
- Sand
- Springs
- Water
- Weights
- Whistles

5 Divide the class into small teams, and ask students to brainstorm new and novel ways to measure the passing of time.

6 Explain to students that their team may meet the task objective in one of two ways:
 1 By inventing a new way of measuring time such as the gumball example; or,
 2 By inventing a novel approach to a traditional way of measuring time such as the cuckoo clock example.

Outrageous, outside-the-box ideas are always welcome, but teams must be able to explain how their clocks display the passing of time.

NOTE: Teams do not need to resolve the actual, mechanical workings of the clock, but they should have a general idea of how it might work. For example, "as a spring unwinds, it releases a little bird figure" is acceptable. "A magical dragon disappears and returns every hour," however, is not an acceptable explanation because it is too vague. "A hologram dragon on a timer disappears and returns every hour," is acceptable because it offers a specific explanation of how the device works.

7 Encourage teams to use the S.C.A.M.P.E.R. techniques to help them brainstorm (see *Creativity: Mysteries Revealed,* pgs. 9–10).

8 Invite teams to sketch and name their time-measuring devices. The product should include:
- A final, titled drawing of the time-telling device
- A sketch of the time-telling device with labels and descriptions
- Close-up sketches of details and small parts

9 Have teams paste their drawings and sketches on large pieces of colored paper.

10 Allow teams to present and explain their time-measuring devices to the class.

Extensions
Curriculum Connections:
- Coordinate this lesson with a unit on telling time.
- Tie-in this lesson with a unit on astronomy and calendars.
- Integrate this lesson into a unit on the calendars of ancient cultures.
- Connect this lesson with a science unit on mechanics (i.e. gears, levers, etc.)

A Cuckoo Idea:
- Have students work individually to design unusual cuckoo clocks featuring sports figures, animals, vehicles, hamburgers, or any theme the designer dreams up.
- Ask students to think about the different parts of their clocks and what actions they will perform. For example, a basketball theme might feature a revolving disk on which players emerge from a door, dribble a ball across the front the clock with an up and down arm movement, and retreat through another door as the disk continues to spin.

Shopping for Ideas

Grade Level: 2 through 6
Participants: Individuals
Objectives: Exercise fluency, flexibility, and originality
Time: Approximately ½ hour

Quick View

In this imaginative, role-playing activity, students "shop" for ideas by silently walking around the classroom, seeking inspiration from the visual cues in their environment. As students generate inventions and ways to improve upon the things they see around them, they jot down their thoughts on scraps of paper and literally fill their shopping bags with ideas. Any interesting, fun, or useful idea is acceptable, whether feasible or fantasy.

Examples

- Feasible Ideas: a musical pencil sharpener, a six-foot tall book, rulers made of candy
- Fantasy Ideas: desks that transport you to another school, pens that write in the air, an invisible teacher (see sidebar, "A World of Possibilities")

Take Home

A bagful of ideas to keep in a creativity journal as sources of inspiration for future writings or inventions.

Materials

- Paper or plastic shopping bags
- Small squares of paper (at least 6 per student)
- Pens or pencils

Getting Ready

- Lead your class in a discussion about the distinction between feasible ideas and those based on fantasy. Encourage students to consider the possibility that some ideas we believe to be fantasy can be made feasible through creative thinking.
- Distribute the materials.

A World of Possibilities

Perhaps a student named Jackie is looking around the classroom and notices a world globe.

She has a great idea for making the globe more useful: touch a country and a recorded voice gives you information about that country. This is a feasible idea.

Jackie has another idea for making the globe more fun—the globe comes with a set of tiny flags for every country. When you set the flag in a hole in the corresponding country, it plays its national anthem. This is a feasible idea.

Her favorite idea is this: when you touch a country you are sucked into the globe, spun around, and deposited on the land of that country. You have one hour to explore, then you are sucked back into the globe and deposited back where you started. This is a fantasy idea.

Activities and Procedures

1 Ask students to line up with their materials and silently walk around the room, looking for visual cues to spark their imaginations.

2 Invite students to ponder the following thought-provoking questions as they encounter objects:
   - How could this thing be changed to make it more useful?
   - What change would improve this item's appearance?
   - What else could this tool be used for?
   - What else does this remind me of that is more interesting?
   - How could this thing be changed into something that is more fun?

3 As they shop, students jot down each of their ideas on separate scraps of paper and drop them into their bags.

4 After a predetermined amount of time (between five and ten minutes is recommended), shoppers return to their desks. They may need more time to continue writing and refining their ideas.

5 Then have the shoppers divide their ideas into two piles—one pile for feasible ideas and another for fantasy ideas.

5 The teacher then asks for volunteers to share their favorite ideas with the class. Classmates are encouraged to continue brainstorming and building upon one another's ideas.

6 At the end of the discussion, shoppers may redeem any five of their ideas for a small incentive or an award.

Extensions
   - *Shop at Home:* Ask students to continue "shopping" at home and have them bring in their shopping bags on the following day for further discussion.
   - *Make a Drawing:* Sketch a favorite idea and elaborate on it with as many details as possible. Label it "feasible" or "fantasy", and give it a title or name.
   - *Language Arts Connection:* Encourage students to write a sales pitch or design a flyer touting their new invention.

"There is nothing in a caterpillar that tells you it's going to be a butterfly."
– R. Buckminster Fuller

Find the Silver Lining

Grade Level: 2 through 8
Participants: Individuals
Objectives: Exercise fluency, flexibility, originality, elaboration, optimism, and creative writing skills
Time: Approximately 1 hour

Quick View

This exercise in creativity and optimism challenges students to brainstorm positive outcomes, or "silver linings," for everyday misfortunes. As students compose short stories explaining a misfortune and how it brought about a silver lining, students discover how a shift in perspective and a little imagination can transform a negative situation into a positive one.

Example

A Reflection of Mom

My sisters depended on me to buy mom the mirror she wanted to hang on the wall. We had all saved our money to get it in time for Mother's Day.

On Saturday morning, I had it wrapped and tied with ribbons. "Mom will love this," I thought. But a terrible thing happened on the way home; I tripped and dropped the mirror. It cracked!

I walked home slowly, knowing how sad my sisters would be.

We all sat together crying.

"Mom deserves a nice gift," my sister said. "Yes," I agreed, "Mom works hard for us." "And she helps us with homework," my youngest sister said.

"She's the sweetest mom, and pretty, too." My sisters and I continued praising our mom.

Then, I had an idea.

We each wrote down compliments for mom on separate pieces of paper, and glued them to the cardboard that came with the mirror. We used bits of the wrapping paper and ribbon to accent our words.

Then we put our collage in the frame of the mirror. We titled our masterpiece, "A Reflection of Mom."

We gave her the gift on Mother's Day. She said she loved it more than anything we could have bought her, and she hung it on the wall.

Misfortune: Mom's gift is ruined.

Silver Lining: The children made something even better from the scraps.

Take Home
An original story illustrating the power of human optimism to transform misfortunes into positive experiences.

Materials
- Pencils
- Paper

Getting Ready
- Write two "misfortunes" on the board.
- Write one or two "silver linings" next to each of them. You can use the examples below or come up with your own.

Misfortune: It rains on the day of the picnic. *Silver Linings:* We need rain for our crops. We will go to the museum instead. We will not get sunburned. Frogs enjoy the puddles. We will have a mudslide contest.

Misfortune: Your best friend moves away. *Silver Linings:* It's good for your friend's family. Now you have a terrific pen pal. You have someone special to visit. You'll be open to getting to know someone new who could become a wonderful friend.

Misfortune: You drop your sandwich in the mud. *Silver Linings:* You'll find out who your true friends are by who will share their sandwich with you. You'll have to eat the veggies that you usually toss out. Now you have a funny story to tell. The squirrels will have a feast today.

Misfortune: You tear your favorite shirt. *Silver Linings:* You can sew a cool patch on it. You can use the cloth to create something else that's wonderful. You can write about the incident for an English assignment. Through introspection, you discover that material things do not bring you the most satisfaction in life. You can be proud of how well you handled disappointment.

Activities and Procedures
1 Discuss the word "misfortune" with the class. Invite students to share misfortunes that they have encountered, and write them on the board.

2 Discuss the phrase "silver lining," and ask students to recall silver linings in their own lives. Write these on the board also.

3 Choose one of the misfortunes mentioned and ask the class to brainstorm positive outcomes that could result from the misfortune. Record students' responses on the board.

4 Next, encourage each student to choose a misfortune and a corresponding silver lining. Students may use ideas from the list or make up their own.

5 Students will then compose a short story detailing how the misfortune occurred and the positive outcome that resulted from the misfortune. Students should end the story by summarizing both the misfortune and the silver lining.

Extensions
- Encourage students to write and illustrate a picture book using a misfortune/silver lining story.
- Invite students to write and perform a skit using a misfortune/silver lining story.

Notes

Dramatic Arts

Silent Movies

Grade Level: 2 through 8
Participants: At least two teams of two
Objectives: Exercise flexibility, originality, observation, teamwork, and nonverbal communication skills
Time: Approximately ½ hour to 1 hour, depending on the number of students

Quick View

In this activity which builds on the classic game of Charades, students use their creativity and nonverbal communication skills to direct and perform simple, two or three-step activities.

Example

A student "director" randomly picks a piece of paper which reads: "sweep the floor and pick up the debris with a dustpan." The director then picks a classmate to be an "actor." The actor does not know what is written on the paper. In front of the class, the director, who must stay in one spot and use only nonverbal means of communication, attempts to get the actor to perform the sweeping activity. The director points to the floor, pantomimes sweeping dirt into a dustpan, and then tries to get the actor to grab the broom and sweep. Classmates determine how successfully the director and actor work as a team by how quickly they can identify the activity.

Take Home
A fun and meaningful learning experience which reinforces students' understanding of verbal vs. nonverbal communication

Materials
- Plain paper cut into approximately 3″ Squares
- Pencils
- Paper or plastic bag

Getting Ready
- Engage students in a discussion about verbal and nonverbal communication. Invite students to think of different types of communication for each category, and list their responses on the board. Examples of verbal communication may include writing, speaking, lip reading, and signing while examples of nonverbal communication might consist of facial expressions, hand gestures, demonstrations, and pictures.
- Gather the materials and distribute a few scraps of paper to each student.
- List some examples of simple activities on the board. You may use the ones listed under "Two Part Activities" or "Three-Part Activities," or come up with your own.

Activities and Procedures
1   Ask each student to write down three simple, two or three-step activities on small pieces of paper. Students may use examples from the board or come up with their own ideas.

Two-Part Activities

- Catch a butterfly with a net and let the butterfly go
- Do a jig and twirl around the room
- Fry an egg and eat it
- Get in a boat and row
- Load rocks into a wagon and pull it up the road
- Open a huge box and lift out the heavy contents

- Paint a portrait of the director and show it to the class
- Play a game of hopscotch and jump rope
- Take off your shoes and put them on again
- Fill a glass with water and drink it
- Set and clear the table
- Sweep the floor and pick up the debris with a dustpan

Three-part activities

- Hop on one foot while waving a flag and smiling
- Fly around the room in circles, land in a corner, and fall asleep.
- Walk backwards, spin around, and sit down
- Play ping pong, jump up and down, and take a bow
- Wash a car, dry it, and drive it away

- Blow up a balloon, bat it around, and burst it with a pin
- Try on three different hats
- Play the flute, the drums, and the bass fiddle
- Dig a hole, jump in it, and jump back out
- Laugh, cry, and laugh again
- Hop backwards, hop forwards, and sit down
- Swim, dry off, and take a nap

2 Instruct students to fold the papers in half, and drop them into a bag. (Teachers may wish to do steps 1 and 2 beforehand to save time.)

3 Divide the class into two groups—one group of directors and one group of actors.

4 Discuss with students the roles that directors and actors play in movie production.

5 Select a volunteer from the director group and invite that student to draw a piece of paper from the bag at random.

6 Then, ask the director to choose a student from the group of actors.

7 The director then has two minutes to "direct" the actor to perform the activity written on their piece of paper. The director and actor must adhere to the following rules:

Director

- May use pantomime, demonstrate with real or pantomimed props, draw pictures on the board, or use any other nonverbal means of communication

- Must stay in one place while directing
- Must not touch the actor
- Must not use words or letters in any way

Actor

- Must try their best to follow the director's instructions

- Must not use words or letters in any way

8 Classmates in both groups attempt to guess the activity before time is up. The student who guesses correctly takes their turn next, picking a director or actor for their teammate.

9 Continue this process until all students have had a turn. If time permits, switch the groups, so that actors become directors and directors become actors.

Grade Level: 1 through 4
Participants: Best for a group of at least three
Objectives: Exercise fluency, flexibility, elaboration, and personal expression
Time: 15 minutes to 1 hour, depending on size of class

Quick View

In this kinetic activity, students improvise dance movements inspired by various animals. As they dance in small groups, a student calls out the name of a dance, and the dancers must then move as if they were an animal doing that dance. Students use their creativity and practice following directions as well as they move to the beat of background music, clapping, and/or singing.

Take Home
An amusing new dance to teach to family and friends

Materials
- Pencils
- Small pieces of plain white paper
- Paper bag
- Dance music of various kinds (optional)
- Chalk and chalkboard or equivalent

Getting Ready
- Gather books and pictures featuring various kinds of animals including insects, mammals, birds, reptiles, or anything living that has legs.
- Display pictures for student reference.
- Hold a class discussion about the ways different animals move and walk, asking students to offer their own observations and insights. For example, an ostrich has long, skinny legs and a distinctive way of moving. Frogs' legs are muscular and springy, and they move by leaping.
- Gather pictures of dance styles like ballet, rock 'n roll, hula, Cha Cha, tribal dances, Irish jig, folk, ballroom, square dance, and so on, offering many examples. You or student volunteers may demonstrate some dances to the classroom.
- Talk about and show pictures of various movements and rhythms.
- List the various kinds of dances on the board for students to reference.

Activities and Procedures

1 Instruct each student to write the name of one animal on each of two small pieces of paper. Have students fold the papers in half and drop them into a paper bag.

2 Now, walk around the room with the bag, allowing each student to draw an animal at random.

3 Select two students to begin and have them reveal their animals to the class.

4 Ask a third student to call out the name of any dance.

5 Invite the students to try to do the named dance as if they were their animal. For example, if the students drew the animals "elephant" and "penguin," and the dance "Irish Jig" was called out, they would dance the Irish jig, one as an elephant and one as a penguin.

6 Ask the class to clap their hands and sing to accompany the dancers, or use a musical recording.

7 Allow students enough time to create their animal dance and do a few moves (usually a minute or two will suffice). Struggling dancers may find it helpful to walk for a few seconds as if they were their chosen animal before beginning to dance.

8 After the first group of dancers has completed their performance, choose two more "animal dancers" and a new dance caller. Continue in this fashion until all students have had a turn.

NOTE: Students may dance with each other as in the Jitterbug, or side by side as in the Irish jig. Let dancers make animal sounds and the like. Be spontaneous and allow the students to be spontaneous as well; it's all in creative fun!

Extensions
- Encourage dancers to make the sounds of their animals while dancing.
- Show a video of animals running and moving to enrich this activity.
- Show a video of dances to enrich this activity.
- Play recordings of different kinds of music to enhance this activity.

Twyla Tharp: Dancer and Creative Choreographer

Combining is one of the basic ingredients of creativity. In "Zoo Dance," we combine dance movement with animal movement.

Twyla Tharp, a highly regarded choreographer, brought a unique combination to dance. She is the first choreographer to create a dance work, Deuce Coupe, that utilized both modern and ballet techniques. She is the creator of what is now known as the "cross-over" ballet. Tharp's work often incorporates classical music, jazz, and contemporary pop music.

Tharp has choreographed dances for many dance companies, Broadway plays, movies and television shows, and continues to create works and give lectures around the world.

She wrote her first book in 1992, the autobiography *Push Comes to Shove*. Twyla Tharp's second book, *The Creative Habit: Learn It and Use It for Life* was published in October, 2003 and is a great source of creative inspiration.

Grade Level: 2 through 3
Participants: Small groups
Objectives: Exercise fluency, flexibility, originality, elaboration, and creative story-telling
Time: 15 minutes to 1 hour

Quick View

In this storytelling activity, each student picks a Personality Card at random (see *Reproducibles,* pg. 332). The cards reveal characters who suggest traits or moods such as giggly, sad, sweet or bossy. Going around in a circle, each student takes a turn telling part of a familiar story such as Chicken Little with just one change: students must voice their part in a way that represents the character of their Personality Card.

Examples

Narrator: (Student #1 in a funny voice) "Once upon a time Chicken Little was walking in the woods. Suddenly, PLUNKERS, an acorn fell on her head."

Chicken Little: (Student #2 in a high voice) "Goodness me!" said Chicken Little. "The sky is falling. I must run and tell the king.

Narrator: On the way she met …

"Mr. Scuffshoe." (Student #3 says in a special voice) "I cannot go with you because I must polish my shoes."

Take Home
A funny story with a quirky twist

Materials
- Personality Cards (see *Reproducibles,* pg. 332)
- Paper bag

Getting Ready
- Make copies of enough Personality Cards for each student. Trim them and place into a bag.
- Select a simple story such as Chicken Little that is familiar to students. The story should have many characters, lots of dialogue, and a bit of narration as well.
- Make copies of the story for the students.
- Place chairs in a circle facing each other, or ask students to sit on the floor in a circle.

Activities and Procedures

1 Divide students into groups.

2 Assign the roles for Chicken Little, the Fox, and the Narrator (or other relevant characters).

3 Have each student pick a Personality Card.

4 Encourage students to name their chosen character based on their Personality Card and formulate ideas about the types of people they are. For instance, are they sweet, mean, giggly, sad, or bossy?

5 Using the panel at right "The Story of Chicken Little" as a model, instruct students to take turns telling the story, expressing the personality of their character as they read the assigned dialogue.

6 When the Narrator says, "on the way they met …," have students name their chosen characters and state where they're going or what they're doing, inventing voices and improvising dialogue to express their personalities.

Extensions
- Have students rewrite their stories independently, using characters suggested by the Personality Cards.
- Invite students to add illustrations to create their own picture books.

The Story of Chicken Little

Narrator: Once upon a time, Chicken Little was walking in the woods. Suddenly – PLUNK – an acorn fell on her head.

Chicken Little: "Goodness me!" said Chicken Little. "The sky is falling! I must run and tell the King."

Narrator: On the way, she met …

Character #1:   _____ . "I cannot go with you
                    NAME OF CHARACTER
                    because _____."
                               FILL IN THE BLANK

Chicken Little: "I beg of you. Please come with me. We must tell the King the sky is falling!"

Narrator: So they ran along, and on the way they met …

Character #2:   _____. "I cannot go with you
                    NAME OF CHARACTER
                    because _____."
                               FILL IN THE BLANK

Chicken Little: "Please come with me. We must tell the King the sky is falling!"

Narrator: So they ran along, and on the way they met …

… and so on until all the students except for Foxy Loxy have had a turn. Have the three characters below end the storytelling:

Narrator: Soon they encountered Foxy Loxy.

Foxy Loxy: "Where are you going in such a hurry, my friends?

Chicken Little: "We must tell the King the sky is falling!"

Foxy Loxy: "I know a shortcut. Follow me."

Narrator: But Foxy Loxy led them to his foxhole where he planned to gobble them up. Just then, they heard the King's dogs growling and howling and running toward Foxy Loxy. The angry dogs chased Foxy Loxy far, far away.

Chicken Little did indeed warn the King, and the King assured her that the sky was not falling. It was only an acorn that fell on her head.

From that day forward, Chicken Little carried a _____ whenever she went
                          FILL IN THE BLANK
for a walk.

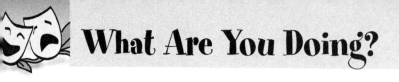

Grade Level: 1 through 4
Participants: Two or more individuals
Objectives: Exercise fluency, originality, body language, and observation skills
Time: 15 to 30 minutes, depending on number of participants

Quick View

In this fun, fast-paced game of doublespeak, students become pantomimes who say one thing but do another. Within a fifteen second timeframe, students are challenged to exercise their body language skills while simultaneously generating ideas for new activities.

Example

The first student pretends to engage in an activity such as hammering a nail. The second student asks, "Hey buddy, what are you doing?" The first student then answers by stating any activity other than the one they are pretending to do. For example, student 1 may say, "I'm catching a fish," or "I'm flying a kite," but may not say, "I'm hammering a nail." The second student must then pretend to perform the activity that the first student said they were doing (i.e. catching a fish, flying a kite, etc).

The third student then asks the second student, "Hey Buddy, what are you doing?" The second student answers, "I'm playing the piano." The third student must then pantomime playing the piano. This process continues with each student enacting what the previous student has answered.

Take Home
A fun new game to play with friends and family and a memorable learning experience

Materials
- A timer
- Chalkboard and chalk or equivalent

Getting Ready

- List a few activities on the board for idea starters. You can use the ones listed below or come up with your own.

Familiar Activities

- Batting a ball
- Catching a fish
- Drinking tea
- Flying a kite
- Hammering a nail
- Playing golf
- Playing soccer
- Playing tennis
- Playing the piano
- Running
- Swimming
- Washing dishes

Unusual Activities

- Chasing a kangaroo
- Eating a sour lemon
- Flying like a bat
- Laughing like a baby
- Playing in a one-man band
- Looking for a four-leaf clover
- Painting stripes on an elephant
- Riding a pogo stick
- Riding on a bumpy bus
- Scaring a monster
- Sinking in quicksand
- Walking on a tight rope

- Write the following definition on the board:

pantomime – (v.) to pretend through the use of body language

- Engage students in a discussion of pantomiming by asking if they have had ever pantomimed or witnessed someone else pantomiming. Allow students to demonstrate some examples.

Activities and Procedures

1 Explain the game to your class and choose volunteers to demonstrate a couple of rounds.

2 Encourage students to think of new activities for their classmates to pantomime. Add these ideas to the list on the board.

3 Ask players to line up and take their turns. Using a timer, allow fifteen seconds maximum per turn. Students may use ideas from the board, but they may not repeat activities that have already been used.

4 If a player cannot pantomime the activity (any attempt is acceptable) or cannot think of an activity to name for the next player to pantomime, the player is out.

5 Keep playing the game until each student has had a turn, or until all but one student has been eliminated from the game.

Extensions

- Shorten the allotted time to ten seconds to heighten the fluency requirement.
- To make the game more challenging, require students to use only activities other than those listed on the board.
- For a more creative challenge, have players try to stump the next player by answering the question, "What are you doing?" with an outrageous activity for them to pantomime such as putting lipstick on a giraffe, skiing uphill, or waltzing with a mouse.

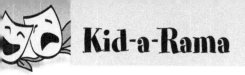

Grade Level: 1 through 8
Participants: Six or more students
Objectives: Exercise fluency, originality, elaboration, imagination, visualization, and body language
Time: Approximately ½ hour

Quick View

In our version* of this exercise in creative body language, students act as the subjects of a diorama by using their bodies to illustrate parts of a picture. By spontaneously creating and "becoming" additions to the scene, students stretch their imaginative muscles and enhance their visualization skills as well.

Example

One person skips into the space, freezes their body into a pose and declares who or what they are: "I'm an apple tree."

The next person runs on stage and freezes their body into a pose of something else near the first thing in the picture: "I'm a swing under the tree."

The next person hastens on stage and poses: "I'm a baby on the swing."

The next person enters the picture, "I'm an apple on the ground."

Another, "I'm a dog eating the apple."

And another, "I'm the boy walking the dog."

And another, "I'm a cloud in the sky."

Play continues until each student has become a part of the scene.

Materials
- A space that can be designated as a performance area
- Six or more players
- A box of props (optional)

Getting Ready
- Divide six or more students into two teams.

* *Kid-a-Rama is based on a young actor's improvisation game called "The Martha Game," the origin of which is unknown.*

Activities and Procedures

1 Inform students that they will each be contributing to a human diorama.

2 Have students stand in a line outside the designated performance area.

3 Explain the following rules of the game:
   - Each student must become something different from the others.
   - Students should take their turns promptly in order to keep the game progressing rapidly and spontaneously.
   - Students should pose as people, animals, or objects that are related in some way to the "subjects" that have already been placed in the scene. For example, an apple-picker would be an appropriate addition to the example scene, but an astronaut would not.
   - For additional rounds, a different student should start the picture.

4 The first child skips into the space must freeze their body into a pose, and declares who or what they are.

5 The next person enters and poses, declaring their role, followed by the rest of the group in succession.

6 When each student has taken a turn, another student begins the next round with an idea for a new scene.

Extensions
   - After all the parts of the "picture" are in place, declare it a motion picture and have students act out their specific roles.
   - Declare the scene a talking picture and have students speak or make sounds appropriate to their various roles.
   - As an optional enhancement, invite students to choose from a box of props including old clothes, scarves, hats, artificial flowers, discarded household items, etc.
   - For an added challenge, require kids to use a prop from the box.
   - To foster teamwork and cooperation, encourage teams of two to "become" something together such as a chair or an animal.

> "Creativity is inventing, experimenting, growing, taking risks, breaking rules, making mistakes, and having fun."
> – Mary Lou Cook

The No "No" Game

Grade Level: 3 through 8
Participants: Pairs
Objectives: Exercise flexibility, elaboration, and verbal skills
Time: Approximately ½ hour to 1 hour depending on the number of participants

Quick View

In this exercise in diplomacy, pairs of students conduct mock interviews with a "hold your tongue" caveat: the student playing the role of a public figure must not use any form of the word "no" in their responses. As the interviewer tries to embarrass and discredit the official by asking tough questions and making strong accusations, the public figure is challenged to defend their image while choosing their words cautiously.

Example

See example at right, "Interview with the World's Best Pizza Maker."

Take Home

Enhanced verbal skills and an exciting new game to play with friends and family

Materials

- Pencils
- Paper
- Chalkboard and chalk or equivalent
- A microphone prop (e.g. water bottle, ruler, ball of crumpled paper, etc.)

Interview with the World's Best Pizza Maker

Interviewer: Do you sometimes use rotten tomatoes in your sauce to save money?

Pizza Maker: I use only fresh ingredients.

Interviewer: There is evidence that you stole your famous anchovy pizza recipe from an Italian fisherman. Please explain.

Pizza Maker: The Italian fisherman is confused. The evidence is phony. I created the recipe last year for the Queen of Vermicelli.

Interviewer: Do you use pig fat in your pizza crust?

Pizza Maker: Only if I run out of rhinoceros fat.

Interviewer: I read that you hate pizza and don't care if you burn it. Is that true?

Pizza Maker: Your statement is ridiculous and lacks truth.

Interviewer: I heard that you don't really make your pizza yourself, and that your grandma secretly helps you.

Pizza Maker: I always make the pizza myself. My Grandma lives in Iceland and does **not** have the slightest idea how to make pizza.

In this example, the interviewer wins the match since the pizza maker used the word "not" in the response.

Getting Ready

- List some examples of public figures on the board. You can use the ones below or come up with your own:
  - Politicians
  - Sports heroes
  - Television and movie stars
  - Music performers
  - Authors
  - Artists
  - CEOs
  - Inventors
  - World record holders

- Write examples of both yes-or-no questions and open-ended questions on the board.
- List several forms of the word "no" such as:
  - Naught
  - Negative
  - Never
  - No
  - None
  - Not
  - Unh Unh
  - Contractions ending in "n't"
  - The prefix "non-"
  - The prefix "un-"
  - The suffix "-less"
  - Foreign language words meaning "no"
  - Head shaking (and other nonverbal gestures indicating the word "no")

Activities and Procedures

1 Divide the class into pairs.

2 Tell students that they will be participating in a mock interview with a public figure.

3 Discuss the difference between "yes-and-no questions" and "open-ended questions" and inform students that they will be using both in their interviews.

4 Ask teams to decide who will play the role of the interviewer.

5 Invite the other team member to choose an identity as a fictitious public figure, giving himself a name and a claim to fame.

6 Tell the interviewer to take on a jealous and mean-spirited persona and try to embarrass and discredit the public figure by asking tough questions and making false and incredulous accusations.

7 Instruct the public figure to try to protect their image by answering the questions and denying the accusations without using any form of the word "no."

8 Encourage the interviewer to ask a total of five questions and include both "yes-or no-questions" and "open-ended questions."

9 Hold a class contest according to the following guidelines:
  - Have teams stage their interviews in the front of the classroom.
  - If the interviewer gets the public figure to use a form of the word, "no," the interviewer is the winner of the match.
  - The public figure wins the match by avoiding using a form of the word "no" in their answers.

10 Hold several matches if time permits, and award a small prize to each team's overall winner.

Extensions

- Have students lengthen the interview by asking ten or more questions instead of five.
- Hold a mock press conference by inviting the entire class to ask questions of the public figure.

Skit-o-Matic

Grade Level: 4 through 8
Participants: Teams of two or three, or individuals.
Objectives: Exercise flexibility, originality, elaboration, understanding satire, creative writing, character development, presentation skills, body language awareness, speaking skills
Time: 1 to 2 hours

Quick View

The television infomercial is part of American pop culture. For this lesson, students write and perform skits spoofing infomercials as they pitch their new inventions in the style of Ron Popeil, Billy Mays, and others. *"But wait, there's more!"* Students become familiar with presentation techniques while they create and bring to life their own pitchman character, too.

Ron Popeil, the Amazing Mr. Ron-o-Matic

Ron Popeil, born in 1935 in New York City, is an inventor and marketing personality. He is famous for his appearances in television infomercials for cooking gadgets and more, such as the Veg-O-Matic, Chop-O-Matic, and Pocket Fisherman. It was Popeil who first used the phrase, "But wait, there's more!" as early as the 1950's.

Ron Popeil's success in infomercials, his memorable personality, and his inventive gadgets have made him a well known figure in American popular culture.

Popeil and the pitchmen who follow him are often targets of satire. Hilarious parodies of Popeil's infomercials have been performed by comedians Dan Akroyd, Eddie Murphy, Gallagher, and others.

BUT WAIT, THERE'S MORE!

Example

Product:	**Homework-O-Matic**
Opening Line:	Boys and Girls, I'm going to show you the greatest homework helper ever made.
	It's the awesome Homework-O-Matic Pen and Scanner set.
	(show it to the audience)
Demonstration:	• Simply write your name with the special Homework-O-Matic Pen. Now your handwriting style is programmed into the pen.
	• Plug the pen into our Smart-Scanner, and place the Smart-Scanner onto any book.
	• Place the pen upright over your notebook paper. The pen will copy down the important information in your own personal handwriting! Your teacher will think you wrote it yourself!
Slogan:	"Do your homework while you sleep or play. Just do nothing and get an A."
Testimonial:	"I don't have to miss my favorite TV shows because of homework anymore. Homework-O-Matic does my homework while I goof off."
	— Chris, age 12, third grade
Pitch And Price:	You'll get the:
	• Homework-O-Matic Pen
	• A special pen stand
	• The Smart-Scanner
	• An instruction booklet
	All for just six easy payments of $15.00 per month.
	That's less than your allowance!
Free Offer:	But wait, there's more! Act now, and get:
	• A free ream of lined notebook paper.
	This offer is not available in stores.
	Call, D-O-H-O-M-E-W-O-R-K.
	Operators are standing by.
	Call now, while supplies last.

Skit-o-Matic *continues* ➜

continued from previous page

Take Home
A original comedy script for entertaining family and friends.

Materials
- Pencils
- Paper
- Props as needed

And That's Not All! The Vocabulary of Infomercials

The pitchman grabs the viewer's attention and uses persuasive language to describe the product and its benefits.

PRODUCT CATEGORIES:
- Cleaning products
- Crafts
- Education products
- Fitness products
- Hair styling products
- Kitchen gadgets
- New toys
- Pet care products
- Sports equipment
- Unusual backpacks
  and more; anything can work

INFOMERCIAL TERMS
- Call to action
- Demo
- Direct marketing
- Entertain
- Infomercial
- Limited supply
- Marketeer
- Opening line
- Persuasive language
- Pitchman
- Pricing
- Sales pitch
- Slogan
- Tell a story
- Testimonial

PRODUCT NAME PREFIXES AND SUFFIXES
- Amazing-
- Dream-
- Easy-
- Miracle-
- Mr.-
- Ultra-
- Wonder-
- Wow-
- -Bliss
- -Magic
- -Maker
- -O-Matic
- -Quick
- -Styler

SKIT VOCABULARY
- Body language
- Character type
- Comedy
- Format
- Mannerisms
- Parody
- Satire
- Speech idiosyncrasies
- Spoof

INFOMERCIAL PHRASES
- Act now
- As seen on TV
- But wait, there's more!
- Call now
- First time ever
- Ladies and gentlemen, I'm going to show you the greatest_____ever made.
- Low price of _____.
- Miracle product
- New and revolutionary
- Not available in stores
- Operators are standing by
- Pick up the phone
- This special offer
- While supplies last

Getting Ready

- Invite your students to watch a TV infomercial, and to study the way the pitchman talks and acts. QVC and Home Shopping Network are typical TV sources.
- Infomercials featuring legendary greats Ron Popeil and Billy Mays are available online.
- Many infomercial spoofs can also be seen online.

Activities and Procedures

1. Explain to the class that they will be writing a short skit (approximately 3 minutes) as a TV infomercial.

2. Divide the class into teams of two or three.

3. Teams brainstorm ideas for a unique new product they will sell. It can be silly or serious. Name the product. (See sidebar, "*And That's Not All!* The Vocabulary of Infomercials," to spark ideas, or come up with your own.)

4. Find props or make something to represent your new product.

5. Teams brainstorm and make notes, writing down everything they want to say and do in their skits.

6. Organize your notes into an infomercial format. (See Example, "Homework-O-Matic," pg. 81)

    This should include:
    - The opening line introducing the product to the audience
    - A demonstration of how the product works
    - A slogan for your product (a memorable phrase about your product)
    - A testimonial (someone claiming they used the product and why they liked it)
    - The pitch and price (what they get and how much it costs)
    - A free offer when they buy the product (what they get for free)
    - Tell them the offer is available only from you
    - How to buy it (phone numbers, order online, etc.)
    - Motivate the audience by telling them the supply is limited, so they must act fast

7. Team members decide who will be the pitchman, who will be the testimonial giver, and who else will speak on their infomercial. Each speaker develops their character's personality through their look, their tone of voice, and their body language. Props like hats and scarves can help, but are optional.

8. Teams perform their skits for their classmates. The pitchman can wear an attention-getting accessory such as a goofy hat, big bow-tie, or bright flower.

Extensions

- Coordinate this fun activity with a study of marketing principles and writing serious TV commercials.
- Coordinate this activity with a unit on creative writing.
- Coordinate this activity with a unit on literature and understanding satire.

Notes

Language Arts

Grade Level: 2 through 6
Participants: Small or large groups
Objectives: Exercise flexibility, originality, elaboration, imagination, verbal skills, and brainstorming
Time: 15 to 30 minutes

Quick View

In this original twist on storytelling, students work in succession to transform a story into an entirely new and imaginative oral tale. As the story is "passed" from one author to the next, students "morph" the original tale by adding new characters and events inspired by Personality Cards (see *Reproducibles,* pg. 332).

Example

Three Bears and Many Friends

Storyteller 1: One day The Three Bears, Mama, Papa, and their baby (Personality Card) went for a walk in the woods.

Storyteller 2: A minute after they left home, Goldilocks and her best friend (Personality Card) walked by and knocked on the door. There was no answer, so they went in.

Storyteller 3: They ate breakfast and took a quick nap. Then they invited some friends (Personality Card) over for a wild party.

Storyteller 4: By now The Three Bears had started for home. A neighbor (Personality Card), who knew the bears' routine, heard the party music coming from their house and knew that something was not right.

Storyteller 5: To avoid trouble, the neighbor ran over to the bears' house and warned Goldilocks and her friends that The Three Bears were coming homo.

But there wasn't enough time to clean up the mess and get out of the bears' house before they returned. Luckily, the neighbor's child (Personality Card) had an idea.

Storyteller 6: "Let's make a big sign that says, 'Welcome Home' and turn this wild party into a surprise party for The Three Bears." "And I'll make just-right porridge for everyone," said the neighbor's grandma (Personality Card), and that's just what they did.

Storyteller 3: When the bears got home they were delighted to find the party. Everyone had fun. A news reporter living nearby (Personality Card) came and took pictures for the newspaper.

Storyteller 4: The Three Bears became famous. A TV station created a reality show about them, titled, "Bear With Me." Goldilocks met a nice cameraman (Personality Card) and got married. They have dinner with The Three Bears every Sunday.

Take Home

An original story to share with their families or use as a basis for further creative writing

Materials
- Personality Cards (see *Reproducibles*, pg. 332)
- A bell or other sound device to prompt transitions (optional)

Getting Ready
- Make copies of Personality Cards and cut them out, or to make them yourself follow the instructions in the sidebar, "Make Your Own Personality Cards."
- Select a familiar story or a simple picture book to use as the foundation of a story.
- Discuss the art of storytelling with your class. Explain the anatomy of a story including character, plot, and conflict.
- Explain the Personality Cards to your students and discuss how they might be used in the writing of a story. Encourage them to breathe life into the characters by giving them names and personalities and deciding what part they will play in the story.

Make Your Own Personality Cards
- Teachers distribute 2½" x 5" vertical cards. Each student should receive five cards.
- On each card, the student will sketch a person, either real or imaginary. The image can be a cartoon, a famous person, or a stereotypical personality (e.g. fireman, doctor, mother, baby, etc.). The drawings need not be realistic as long as they are recognizable.
- Students may also wish to clip pictures from magazines as an alternative way of making Personality Cards.

Activities and Procedures

1 To begin the activity, students sit in a circle with the "Personality Cards" placed in a stack inside the circle. The first student begins the story by narrating the first two sentences of the base story. The student then "passes" the story around the circle.

2 The next student draws a "Personality Card" from the stack and has ten seconds to weave the new character into the story in two or three sentences.

3 The teacher then prompts the next student in the circle to pick a "Personality Card," show it to the class, and incorporate that character into the story.

4 Students continue around the circle, adding two or three sentences each, and adding more characters as indicated by the "Personality Cards."

5 When the story reaches the end of the circle, the last student will choose a "Personality Card" and use this character to end the story.

Extensions
To extend the activity, encourage students to:
- Create your own "phrase" cards or "action" cards and provide them to students to use in their story circles along with the Personality Cards.
- Provide Object Cards (see *Reproducibles*, pg. 320) to use in their story circles in addition to the "Personality Cards."
- Create a children's book based on their group story. Individuals may select a part of the story to write and illustrate.

My First Visit to Earth

Grade Level: 3 through 8
Participants: Teams of two to four
Objectives: Exercise fluency, flexibility, originality, elaboration, personal expression
Time: 1 to 2 hours depending on the number of participants

Quick View

Student teams explore the classroom from the point of view of beings from another planet, who are visiting Earth for the first time. They make notes about their observations and present skits to the class.

Example

We are The Twips. We come from the planet Twippus, in a far away galaxy. We communicate by beeping, but we are so smart that we learned English in one minute. This is our report about planet Earth. (Water Faucet) A shiny tube has clear liquid pouring out. Sometimes it makes whistling sounds. Could it be sending messages? We wonder what the clear liquid is for. (Light Switch) When you move the small lever, why do those stars in the fake sky flicker on and off? (Pencil Sharpener) This box has a hole in it. Is the box a device for humans to recharge the batteries in their fingers?

Earth is fun to visit but we don't want to stay on this strange planet. We want to go home where the sky is pink and the ground is covered with bubbles.

Take Home

Amusing skits and a new way to look at their world!

Materials
- Pencils
- Paper
- A classroom or yard to explore

Getting Ready
- Discuss ideas for imaginary beings from outer space. What do they look like? How do they communicate with each other? and so on.
- Ask students to name some common objects in the classroom like a chair, a pencil or a light switch.
- Now ask them to imagine that they are beings from outer space and are seeing things in the classroom for the very first time.

  NOTE: When looking at objects in the room, don't think about how we use them. Think of each object in an abstract way: What shape and color is it? What happens with it? What could another kind of being use it for?

Activities and Procedures

1 Divide your class into teams of two to four students.

2 Each team chooses a leader, and decides what kind of outer space beings they are. They choose a name for themselves.

3 Now the teams of outer space beings explore the classroom. Everything is strange to them. The leader keeps notes on team members' observations and theories about Earth and Earthlings.

4 Each team writes and acts a short skit portraying their visit to Earth, from the point of view of beings from another world.

5 Teams present their skits to the class.

Extensions
This lesson plan can be used with other fun substitutions:
- *People from the Past:* Famous characters from the past explore our classroom today. "Amazing! A moving horseless carriage with children sitting inside!"
- *Children from the Future:* Students from the year 3015, are sent back in time to explore our quaint classroom." Back in the 21st Century children had to use their legs because they hadn't invented instant molecular transport yet. How exhausting their lives were!"
- *Animals Explore a Human Environment:* Squirrels enter a classroom filled with desks and chairs. "What funny looking trees. Some parts are good to chew on, but the shiny silver parts are hard to split with our teeth."

> "Creativity involves breaking out of established patterns in order to look at things in a different way."
> – Edward de Bono

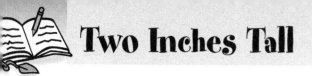

Grade Level: 2 through 5
Participants: Individuals
Objectives: Exercise fluency, flexibility, originality, elaboration, visual metaphors, and imagination.
Time: ½ hour to 1 hour

Quick View

This exercise in creative writing invites students to imagine what life would be like if they were only two inches tall. Using visual metaphors and lots of imagination, each student composes a short story describing their daily activities as a tiny human.

Example

My Big Small Life

Yesterday, I went for a walk with my big sister, Annie. When I say "big sister," I don't mean that she is older. She is actually a year younger, but compared to me, she is huge. You see, I am only two inches tall.

I walked outside with Annie, but after running along for three of her steps, I was out of breath. So, I rode on her sneaker instead, using the shoelace for a seat belt.

When Annie stopped to pick a flower, a hairy bug that was as big as me, spit in my face. "Let's go home, Annie," I shouted. As she ran home, I hung onto the shoelace for dear life!

For lunch, I ate a sliced grape, two Cheerios, and drank milk from a bottle cap. Mom offered me some mashed potatoes, but I was afraid I would fall in.

Next, I took a nap. My bed is a sponge covered with a hanky, and my pillow is a cotton ball. I cover up with a nice fuzzy sock.

When I wake up, I will go swimming in a dish of water. I like to use a popsicle stick for a raft, and sliding down a tape dispenser is great fun!

Later, I will crawl under my brother's bedroom door and spy on him. Being teensy does has its advantages after all.

Take Home
An original and creative narrative describing life from a whole new perspective

Materials
- Paper
- Pens or pencils
- Crayons, colored pencils, or markers (optional)

Getting Ready
- List some questions on the board to help stimulate creative thought. Here are some that are sure to incite students' imaginations. If you were two inches tall:
  - What could you do for fun?
  - What would you eat?
  - Where would you sleep?
  - Who could you play with?
  - What pets would you have?
  - What might scare you?
  - How would you brush your teeth and hair, and bathe?
  - What would you wear?
  - What would you not be able to do if you were tiny that you can do now?
  - What could you do if you were tiny that you cannot do now?
- Discuss the meaning of the term "visual metaphor." Explain that a visual metaphor is something that resembles something else. In the example story, for instance, the sponge is a visual metaphor for a tiny bed, a tape dispenser is a visual metaphor for a playground slide, and a dish of water is a visual metaphor for a swimming pool. Encourage students to list visual metaphors of small scale things acting as normal-sized objects.

Activities and Procedures

1 Have students pretend that their fingers are legs and "walk" around the room, imagining that they have been diminished to a mere two inches tall.

2 Lead the class in a discussion of what life would be like from this perspective. Invite students to brainstorm some answers to the questions on the board.

3 After the discussion is complete, encourage students to write their own stories describing at least three activities or insights from a two-inch tall point of view. Invite students to bring the story to life by including as many visual metaphors as possible.

4 Students may also wish to include illustrations to enhance their narratives and show how a two-inch person may look in a world of large people, creatures, and objects.

Extensions
- Have students work individually or in pairs to create an illustrated picture book. Encourage them to give it a creative title such as "It's a Large World After All" or "Wee Me."
- Ask students to write another story from the perspective of a giant.

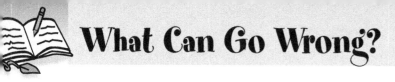

Grade Level: 3 through 8
Participants: Individuals or teams of two or three
Objectives: Exercise fluency, flexibility, originality, elaboration, brainstorming, understanding sequences and cause and effect, storyboards, book structure, and script format
Time: Approximately 1 to 2 hours

Quick View

In this exercise in humorous pessimism, students create storyboards demonstrating a sequence of events gone wrong. These creative and amusing mishaps then become the basis for an original picture book or skit.

Example

A Cookie Catastrophe

1. Your little brother drops soap into the batter. What would happen next? Bubbles might fill the oven as the cookies bake. If you ate a cookie and then talked, soap bubbles might pour out of your mouth. What if you brought the cookies to a classroom party and everyone had bubbles gushing out of their mouths?

2. The roof leaks onto the pan of cookies as they are cooling. The cookies are now runny and gooey. You try to dry the cookies with a paper towel, but pieces of towel stick to the cookies. So, you pour sugar over the cookies to hide the pieces of paper towel. What could happen next?

3. A squirrel steals half the cookies as they are cooling on your windowsill. You chase the squirrel. While you are chasing the squirrel, your dog gobbles up the rest of the cookies. But you don't know it, and you invite your friend over for cookies and milk. What happens next?

4. You make some more cookies, but you accidentally put salt in the batter instead of sugar. What happens?

5. Grandma's hairnet falls into the batter. What happens?

6. The cat jumps onto the cookies before they are baked. What happens?

7. The oven isn't working, so you put the unbaked cookies in the toaster. What happens?

And the saga continues...

Take Home

Storyboards or skits demonstrating creative thinking at its worst!

Materials

- Pencils
- Markers, crayons, or colored pencils
- Heavy white paper, 8½″ x 11″ or larger
- Plain paper
- Scissors
- Washable glue stick
- Chalkboard and chalk or equivalent

Getting Ready

- Make a list of familiar activities such as these:
  - Baking cookies
  - Walking the dog
  - Spending a day at the beach
  - Having a picnic
  - Babysitting
  - Riding on your scooter
- Distribute materials to individuals or teams.

Activities and Procedures

1   Explain to your students that storyboards are sequential drawings that reveal the plot of a story or a script. Tell them that professional writers who create movies, TV commercials, animated cartoons, and books use storyboards to organize their ideas.

2   Invite students to consider a few of the activities listed on the board, and ask them to think of things that could go wrong during each activity. Write the ideas on the board as examples.

3   Have students fold their heavy paper into eight sections according to the following instructions: fold in half left to right, half the paper again from top to bottom, and then half it one more time to create eight even sections.

4   Direct students to turn the paper horizontally, flatten it out, and number each section from one through eight using small numbers at the bottom right of each section.

5   Tell students to designate an area across the top of the paper for the storyboard title.

6   Ask students to choose an activity and list "things gone wrong" on the plain sheet of paper. Encourage students to think about sequencing and cause and effect when brainstorming for mishaps. Students may use ideas from the board or come up with their own.

7   After students have finished their list, invite them to choose a few of their best ideas for further development.

8   Have students sketch a drawing in each section of the storyboard to illustrate how things went wrong. Assure students that stick figures are fine; it's the ideas that matter.

9   Instruct students to add captions under each illustration to help explain what's happening.

10   Encourage students to think of creative titles, and write them in large letters at the top of their storyboards.

Extensions

- Have students make picture books inspired by their storyboards
- Encourage students to create skits based on their storyboards

Grade Level: 3 through 6
Participants: Individuals
Objectives: Exercise flexibility, elaboration, understanding words
Time: Approximately 15 minutes to 1 hour

Quick View

Students combine a root word with a common noun to create a new word. The new word defines a person, place, or thing. Students draw, name, and define their word-ventions.

Examples

Combine "cow" with "tele" for "telecow." What is it? A cow that moos the Morse code.

Combine "sonic" with "crayon" for "sonicrayon". What is it? A crayon that hums when you use it.

My Sonicrayons

Take Home
Word-Vention drawings that tell a story

Materials
- Pencils
- Paper
- Dictionary or lists of root words and nouns

Getting Ready
- List root words and their meanings on the board. Here are a few:
  - Tele (distant)
  - Aquatic (water)
  - Sonic (sound)
  - Auto (involuntary)
  - Bi (two)
  - Sol (sun)
  - Mega (large)

Activities and Procedures

1 Ask students to mention as many nouns, (names of persons, places, and things) as they can. Write the nouns on the board.

Think in categories to come up with many nouns. Categories like animals, geographic features, household items, foods, articles of clothing, and toys will spark ideas for nouns: dogs, cats, elephants; rivers, mountains, a beach; lamps, toasters, chairs; apples, candy bars, potatoes; shoes, jackets, backpacks; blocks, balls, rubber ducks.

2 Explain root words to your students, showing them the list on the board.

3 Students combine a root word with a noun to coin a word for something new. They may use the words listed on the board or use different words.

4 Each student writes the name of their Word-Vention, draws it, and writes its definition on the paper.

5. Display these around the room or compile a classroom dictionary.

Extension
- Some students may want to try more challenging Word-Ventions by combining one root word with two nouns.

Grade Level: 3 through 8
Participants: Individuals or small teams
Objectives: Exercise flexibility, originality, elaboration, brainstorming, vocabulary, phonemic awareness, and dictionary use
Time: ½ hour to 1 hour

Quick View

In this lesson in creative naming, students learn the power of great names, their distinct characteristics, and techniques for creating their own. Using a rhyming dictionary, thesaurus, and some teacher-provided examples, students will learn skills for naming inventions, games, stories, pets, places, procedures, recipes, events, companies, plays, songs, stores, works of art, and anything else in need of a great name.

Examples

I have an imaginary pet that is half puppy and half kitten. My unusual pet needs a name. My favorite choices are Meowmutt, Double Trouble, Fluffy-Ruffy, Doc, and Puppycat. (See sidebar, "Naming an Imaginary Pet.")

Glossary of Creative Naming Methods

What's in a Name?

"A rose by any other name would smell as sweet," but it might not be as beloved. If we call a rose by its botanical name, Rosaceae Thaurnus, or call it Thorny Redbloom or Flower # 627, its emotional effect on us changes dramatically.

Try These Methods

Approach naming using one or more of the following. Not all of these will result in final names that are usable or become your favorites, but they may offer words that spark new name ideas..

Acronyms: a word formed from the first letters in the words of a short phrase (e.g. SCUBA, Self-Contained Underwater Breathing Apparatus, or DIY, Do It Yourself)

Alliteration: words that begin with the same sounds

Common phrases: well-known phrases such as good night, hungry as a bear, and jump for joy

Puns: words that have double meanings

Rhymes: words that begin with different sounds, but end in similar sounds such as cat and hat, kitty and pretty, etc.

Prefixes and suffixes: a prefix is letter group at the beginning of a word; a suffix is a letter group at the end of a word.

Thesaurus: a book of subject-related vocabulary including synonyms and antonyms

Word analogs: a list of ideas related to a subject

Word combos: combining part of one word with part of another

Word substitutions: substitute a new word for a word in a common phrase

Alternate spelling: spelling a word in an nontraditional way

Meanings and origins of names: Most first names have an original meaning.

Foreign language words: the word in another language

Ancient language references: names and ideas from mythology and ancient recorded history.

Naming an Imaginary Pet

My imaginary pet is half puppy and half kitten. It needs a name. I'll use the Glossary of Creative Naming Methods to invent a name for it.

Acronym: DOC (Dog Or Cat)

Alliteration: Catty-Canine, Purry Puppy, Meow Mutt, Pet Peever, Play Pet, Cute 'n' Cuddle.

Common Phrases: It Takes Two, Two In One, Easy Come-Easy Go, On the Double, Share & Share Alike, Double Play

Pun: Paws-ible, Purr-sonality Pups, Furever Yours.

Rhyme: Double Trouble, Creature Feature, Sharing & Caring, Fluffy-Ruffy

Suffix: Cat Barker

Prefix: Meow Dog

Thesaurus words, phrases, and word elements:

- *Cat* – kitty, kitty-cat, feline, kitten, alley cat, tomcat, mouser, pussycat, tomcat, housecat
- *Dog* – pup, puppy, doggie, canine, hound, mutt, bow-wow, pooch, Rover, man's best friend
- *Two* – double, twins, duo, dual, both, bi, ambi-, half and half, pair, couple, mates, soul mates, buddies, buddy-buddy, combo, shared, partners, odd couple, side by side, heart to heart
- *Critter* – pet, animal, house pet, creature, beast, fauna, four- legged friend, mammal, living thing, living being, animal kingdom, wildlife, animal life
- *Pet* – beloved, precious, darling, adored, cherished, spoiled, dear, won my heart, my loved one, my child, affection, my baby, little one, delight, apple of my eye, favorite
- *Companion* – pal, buddy, friend, chum, best buddies, best friends, buds, palsy-walsy, buddy-buddy, shadow, inseparables, side-kick, faithful friend, loyal friend, trusted friend, dependable friend, confidante, fellow creature, playmate, soul mate, BFF, forever yours

I also consider words for "unusual," "imaginary," or other relevant characteristics of my imaginary pet.

Analog words:

- *Cat* – claws, feline, fluffy, furry, kitten, kitty-cat, meow, nine lives, paws, purr, pussycat, puss, stripes, tail, whiskers, etc.
- *Dog* – best friend, bow wow, bark, bone, companion, canine, dig, dog tags, fur, hot dog, hound, leash, pal, pup, puppy, wag, etc.

Word combos: K for kitten + Puppy = "Kuppy,"

- Bow for bow wow + Meow = "Bow Meow" or "Meow Wow,"
- Meower + Barker = "Meowker," Dog + Feline = "Dogline," Pussycat = Puppy = "Puppycat"

Word substitutions: man's best friend = man's best feline, copy cat = puppy cat

Alternate Spellings: cat = Katte, dog = Dawg, Buddy = Buddee

Meanings and origins of names: Katherine (nickname: Kat) means "pure," Wolfe means "canine" = Purican

Words in foreign languages: Cat = Katze (German), Dog = Hund (German) = Hundikatz

Words in ancient languages: Mau (ancient Egyptian cat goddess) Ibezan Hounds (ancient Egyptian) = Maubezan

Conclusion: The names that are my favorites are Meowmutt, Double Trouble, Fluffy-Ruffy, Doc, and Puppycat.

Name Us Famous *continues* ➜

continued from previous page

Characteristics of Great Names

Easy to Read and Say
- Phonetic or familiar spelling is best.
- One or two syllables is an ideal length, but more syllables can work also.
- Pepsi, Coca Cola, and 7-Up are good examples of names that are easy and fun to say.

Easy to Remember
- Names that create a visual image tend to be easiest to remember.
- The names Apple, Foot Locker, and Jelly Bellies are easy to remember.

Fits Its Category
- "Fluffy" is a suitable name for a toy bunny, but not for a sporting goods line.
- Somehow "Fluffy Surfboards" doesn't conjure up a serious surfer image. Try for a name that imparts the feeling you want to give your the audience. The names iPhone and Sizzler Restaurant are good examples.

Describes the Benefit You Get
- Cozy Comfort Pajamas, Yum and Some Cupcakes, The Game of Laughing Silly, and Speedway Skates are good examples.
- Names like Water Wayz Backpacks (they're waterproof), Kool-Keepers Backpacks (they're insulated), My Tunes Backpacks (they're musical) are more good examples.

Tells What Is Different
- Include a word or prefix that distinguishes the item from others like it.
- Payless Shoes, Mini Markers, and Featherlight Bowling are good examples.

Ways to Name an Invention

The name you give your invention can help you sell it. When brainstorming a name, ask yourself if you want people to associate your invention with:
- *Your name* such as Martin's Hydro-skates
- *Part(s)* of your invention such as Water Jet Skates
- *A special feature* of your invention such as Power Burst Skates
- *An acronym* of a short phrase that describes your invention such as "HUMS," Hydro-Ultra-Magnetic-Skates
- *Prefixes and suffixes* to help create catchy names. Include a familiar prefix or suffix to the name of your invention such as Hydro-Skates (prefix), or Skate-matics (suffix).

Familiar Prefixes and Suffixes

Prefixes

Bi-	Hydro-	Poly-	Ultra-
Dyno-	Hyper-	Roto-	Uni-
Electro-	Magna-	Tele-	Vege-
Extra-	Multi-	Tri-	

Suffixes

-arama	-ical	-onic	-tech
-atric	-izer	-pedic	-tron
-boost	-matic	-power	-way
-flex	-ocity	-sonic	

Poorly Chosen Names

- Consider Gerolke Khriegeische Hairstylers. I actually tried to make an appointment with them, but gave up when I couldn't track them down; I could neither spell, nor say their name, so I went to "Haircut Champs" instead. When I mentioned that their name made them difficult to contact, they explained that Gerolke Khriegeische is the owner's name. In my opinion, the owner should have used "G.K.," or his middle name, Edwin, instead.
- Certified Plumbing is another bad name for a different reason. I had been satisfied with this service, but could not recall their name when I needed it because it's generic and does not distinguish them from other plumbers.
- I used to live near a restaurant named Belle Acres. The food was awful; it became known as "Belly Achers." Be careful not to use an unintentional pun. Had Belle Acres chosen a better name (and offered better food), they might still be in business.

Materials
- Pencils
- Paper
- Thesaurus, Rhyming Dictionary, etc. (optional)

Getting Ready
- Display reference books such as a dictionary, a rhyming dictionary, and a thesaurus for student use.
- Discuss and/or list some naming techniques such as the ones provided here.
- Invite students to share some of their favorite names for restaurants, clothing items, electronics, and other common items. Discuss how these names might have been created and what purpose they serve.

Activities and Procedures

1 Ask students to select something to name: a restaurant, a sports team, a pet, or a product, for instance. Or, have them draw Object Cards. (See *Reproducibles,* pg. 320.)

2 Suggest that students use three different techniques to come up with at least six different names. See sidebar, "Glossary of Creative Naming Methods." Consider making the activity more interesting by randomly assigning techniques to students or teams.

3 Invite students to select their favorites out of the results and share them with the class. Have students identify the techniques they used to generate those names. If time allows, students could share the possibilities they didn't use as well.

4 Provide a *Jr Imagination* "Award of Creative Excellence" for each participant. (See *Reproducibles,* pg. 341.)

Extensions
- Create a list of names that are familiar to your students such as brand names, book titles, movies, songs, businesses, or products. Have students evaluate the names by answering these questions:
  - Is the name memorable?
  - Is the name easy to say and read?
  - Does the name fit its product or service?
- Invite students to create a television or radio commercial featuring their newly-created name.
- If your class has recently read a story, they may give it a new title.
- United States Patent and Trademark Office: Teachers and students can learn more about trademarks, copyrights, and patents, by visiting http://www.uspto.gov/kids/

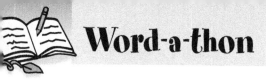

Word-a-thon

Grade Level: 2 through 6
Participants: Individuals
Objective: Exercise fluency, flexibility, and phonics.
Time: 15 to 30 minutes

Quick View

In this fun, phonetic activity, students race to locate as many hidden words as possible from a "Master Word" written on the board. As they consider vowel combinations and consonant clusters, students lengthen their word lists while simultaneously strengthening their phonetic skills.

Example

Master Word: ORIGINAL

- Vowels: a, i, i, o.
- Consonants: g, l, n, r.
- Vowel combinations: ai and oa.
- Consonant clusters: ng and gr.
- Rhyming words: nail, rail, gal, and more
- Words spelled frontwards and backwards: gal and lag

Derivative words: a, I, an, in, or, go, ago, lag, gal, oar, loan, groan, goal, girl, ail, air, lair, lion, oral, nail, rail, railing, long, ring, rang, rain, gain, grain, grin, organ, origin, and more.

Take Home

Increased word analysis skills and a fun new game to share with family and friends

Materials

- Pens or pencils
- Paper
- Chalkboard and chalk, or similar
- Timer

Getting Ready

- Select a word from the Master Words list and write it on the board. You can choose one from the suggestions below or make up your own.

    Master Words Suggestions

    - Dictionary
    - Dinosaur
    - Earthling
    - Friendship
    - Machines
    - Original
    - Playground
    - Planets
    - Shakespeare
    - Wildflowers

- Decide on a time limit for the challenge. Five minutes is usually sufficient, but you may wish to lengthen or shorten the allotted time in accordance with your student's ages and abilities.

Activities and Procedures

1 Show the class the Master Word and have them write it at the top of their papers.

2 Explain the following Word-A-Thon Rules to the class:

Rules of Play
- Words may be any length.
- Proper nouns do not count.
- Letters cannot be used more often than they appear in the Master Word.
- Words may be used only once.

- A word and its plural are allowed as two words.
- Misspelled words do not count.
- One point is awarded for each correct word.

3 Explain the Strategy Tips to the class.

Strategy Tips
- Note which vowels you see. Do you have more than one of any vowel?
- Note which consonants you see. Do you have more than one of any consonant?
- Start with 1 letter words, 2 letter words, 3 letter words, and so on. Two and three letter words are the easiest to find.
- Look for vowel combinations. For example, in the word, ORIGINAL, the vowels are a, i and o. The most common vowel combinations are ai and oa, as in rail and loan.
- Look for consonant clusters, like ng: ring, long, railing or gr: grin, grail, grain
- Look for words by changing one vowel: lag to log or ail to oil.
- Look for words by changing one consonant: ail to air or rail to rain.
- Look for rhymes by changing the first consonant: gain to rain, or nail to rail or nag to rag to lag.
- Try spelling words both forwards and backwards: on and no, rail and liar, and gal and lag.
- If there is an "s" in your word, use both singular and plural forms of words.

4 Set the timer and begin.

5 Students will enjoy comparing words and word counts after time is up.

Extensions
- Award extra points for vowel combination words.
- Award extra points for consonant cluster words.
- Award extra points for each word that no one else has.
- Tell students that here are five animals hiding in the phrase, ANIMAL KINGDOM (dog, dingo, lion, koala, mink).

- Have students compete to find the most words within this phrase in five minutes, and award extra points for each animal name found.
- Find words with four or more letters.
- Find words whose second letter is a specific vowel.
- Find words whose second letter is any consonant.

Grade Level: 3 through 6
Participants: Individuals
Objective: Exercise fluency, understanding relationships, vocabulary, grid making.
Time: Approximately ½ hour to 1 hour

Quick View

Students create their own word-find puzzles by brainstorming words that relate to their animals and designing illustrated grids for their Animal Analogs.

Example

Animal: Tiger

Analogs:

  1 beautiful

  2 carnivorous

  3 cat

  4 claws

  5 cub

  6 fangs

  7 feline

  8 predator

  9 hiding

10 jungle

11 mammal

12 prey

13 stripes

14 tail

15 watching

16 wild

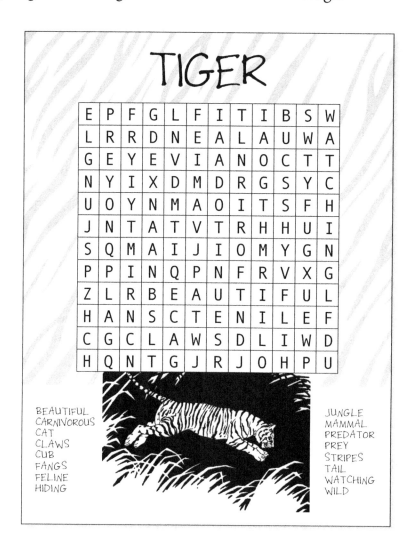

Take Home

An original word-find puzzle to share with friends and family

Materials

- Pencils
- Scrap paper
- Heavy white paper, 8½″ x 11″ or larger

- Rulers
- Crayons or markers
- Books and pictures of animals for reference

Getting Ready

- Write the following definition on the board:
  Analog – (n.) something related to or pertaining to something else
- Display animal reference for student use

Activities and Procedures

1 Ask each student to choose an animal and make a list of ten or more analog words. Students may refer to the animals resources to generate more analog word ideas.

2 Instruct students to use a ruler to draw a 6″ square, leaving some room above and below the square.

3 Then, have students divide the square into 12 half-inch squares across and 12 half-inch squares down. Fill in with lines for a total of 144 grid squares.

4 Direct students to write the name of the animal in large letters across the top of the paper.

5 Have students lightly fill in the grid squares with analog words from top to bottom, bottom to top, left to right, right to left, or diagonally in any direction. Encourage students to intersect letters crossword style whenever possible. Remind students to begin with large words first and use each word only once.

6 When students have inserted all of their words, invite them to add extra letters at random in the spaces around the words to camouflage them.

7 Then, have students darken the letters to complete the grid.

8 Instruct students to list all of their analog words under the grid.

9 Students may wish to decorate their puzzles with drawings and designs related to their animals.

10 Allow students to make copies of their puzzles if possible. Encourage them to switch puzzles with a classmate and solve their new puzzle by finding and circling the hidden analog words.

Extensions

This is a fun project to coordinate with many lessons. Here are some theme suggestions:

- All About Me Analogs
- Ancient Cultures Analogs
- City Analogs
- Dinosaur Analogs
- Events in History Analogs
- Holiday Analogs
- Inventions Analogs
- People in History Analogs
- School Analogs
- Sea Life Analogs
- Season Analogs
- Weather Analogs

There Once Was a Lesson in School

Grade Level: 3 through 8
Participants: Individuals or teams of two
Objectives: Exercise flexibility, originality, elaboration, imagination, understanding rhymes, and writing skills
Time: ½ hour to 1 hour

Quick View

In this lesson in imaginative nonsense, students learn about the rhyme scheme, structure, and meter of limericks. After exploring a few classic examples, students try their hand at writing their very own limericks. In doing so, they learn about a new literary form while practicing their creative writing skills as well.

Examples

Original limerick:

There was a young fellow from Crete
Whose homework was never complete.
He came to class late
And said his dog ate
The homework he thought was a treat.

From Edward Lear's "Book of Nonsense."
See sidebar, "History of Limericks":

There was an old man with a beard,
Who said, 'It is just as I feared!
Two Owls and a Hen,
Four Larks and a Wren,
Have all built their nests in my beard!'

Take Home

Enhanced creative writing skills and an original limerick to share with family and friends

Materials

- Pencils
- Paper
- Chalkboard and chalk or equivalent
- Rhyming dictionary (optional)
- Crayons or markers (optional)

There was an Old Man with a beard,
Who said, "It is just as I feared!
Two Owls and a Hen,
Four Larks and a Wren,
Have all built their nests in my beard!"

Edward Lear

History of Limericks

There is a city in Ireland named Limerick. Some people believe that the poems originated there centuries ago and spread through oral tradition as people shared tall tales and poems for entertainment. Classic limericks usually introduce a character or a place. British poet Edward Lear (1812 – 1888) is best known for his nonsense verses and limericks and is generally considered the "father of the limerick."

Illustration from "John Martin's Book, The Child's Magazine," originally published October 1922

Getting Ready

- Read the two sample limericks aloud to the class.
- Write one limerick on the board for students to see.

There Once Was a Lesson in School *continues* ➜

continued from previous page

Activities and Procedures

1   Explain to the class that a limerick is a nonsense verse with a special structure:
Limericks have five lines:
- The rhyme scheme is A, A, B, B, A
- Lines 1, 2, and 5 rhyme. They each have 8 syllables.
- Lines 3 and 4 rhyme. They *usually* each have 5 syllables.

Rhyme Scheme
1   There was an old man with a beard,   (A)
2   Who said, 'It is just as I feared!   (A)
3   Two Owls and a Hen,   (B)
4   Four Larks and a Wren,   (B)
5   Have all built their nests in my beard!'   (A)

2   Read the limerick on the board aloud, underlining the stressed syllables as you read.

3   Read the limerick aloud again, this time verbally emphasizing the meter as you recite it:
Meter of the Limerick (stressed syllables are in boldface)
There **was** an old **man** with a **beard,**
Who **said,** 'It is **just** as I **feared!**
Two **Owls** and a **Hen,**
Four **Larks** and a **Wren,**
Have **all** built their **nests** in my **beard!**

4   Explain that limericks often follow a specific formula, starting by introducing a character or location. For instance, in Lear's example, we are introduced to an old man in the first line:
There was an old man with a beard

In the other example, the beginning of the limerick identifies a place:
There was a young fellow from Crete

The middle of the limerick usually tells a story:
He came to class late
And said his dog ate

The ending is usually silly or has a funny twist:
The homework he thought was a treat

5   Inform students that they will be writing their very own limericks on a topic of their choice. To get them started, invite them to consider the following subject possibilities:
- A city, real or imagined
- A holiday
- A person in history
- A sport
- A vehicle
- An animal or pet, real or imagined
- An imaginary character
- An invention

Faces and Places

One-Syllable Names		One-Syllable Places	
Ann	Jade	Bern	Mars
Bill	James	Bronx	Nome
Bob	Jane	Chad	Perth
Brett	Joe	Crete	Prague
Burt	Joy	Earth	Rome
Cam	Kate	Flint	school
Cole	Lil	France	Seoul
Dan	Lynne	Greece	Spain
Dirk	Nick	Guam	Troy
Fred	Sue	home	Wales
Grace	Tess	Kent	work
Jack	Tim	Maine	York

6 Write some one-syllable names and places on the board that are easy to rhyme. (See sidebar, "Faces and Places.")

7 Have the class brainstorm a list of rhymes for these words, and ask students to jot them down.

8 Invite students to use these or other rhymes to compose their own limericks. Remind your class that their limericks do not have to make sense, but they do have to rhyme, and they must follow the prescribed meter and formula.

9 If time allows, invite students to add illustrations to their limericks.

10 When the limericks are complete, encourage students to read their limericks aloud to their classmates and comment on one another's work.

Extensions
- Have students work together to create a Classroom Book of Limericks. Encourage them to create a cover design, make copies, and bind the pages together.
- Have all students write limericks on the same subject and compare their varying perspectives.
- Invite students to create large artworks illustrating the stories told within the lines of their limericks.

Grade Level: 4 through 8
Participants: Teams of two or three
Objectives: Exercise flexibility, originality, elaboration, substitution, imagination, phonics, parts of speech, and origins of language
Time: 2 to 3 hours

Quick View

In this exercise in verbal expression, students work in small teams to create their very own languages. As they explore the range of human vocal sounds, students create an alphabet and a lexicon—the building blocks for their new language.

Examples

Using English as a foundation for the development of a new language, these are just some of the many possibilities. These are achieved by replacing vowels or consonants, or replacing words with made-up words. (See "Activities and Procedures," Step 3.)

English Sentence:

    I saw a cow jump over the rainbow.

New Language Sentences:

    O sow o cow jomp ovor tho roonbow.
    I sag a cog jump over the rainbog.
    Zeep saw zeep cow jump over zeep rainbow.
    I saw a lactula jump over the slooxa.
    I shleggum a cow shleggum over the rainbow.

We Speak Our Minds

A spoken language is a system of human vocal sounds for communicating thoughts to others who use the same system of sounds. Every human culture has a spoken language.

Who Spoke First?

Nobody knows for sure when the first languages were spoken because we have no records of them. We know the Sumerians and Egyptians had written languages as early as 3200 B.C., but linguists believe that many other languages began around the world tens of thousands of years earlier.

Everyone Has an Old Mother

Several of the languages we speak today were derived from earlier languages called "mother tongues." For instance, French and Spanish are both descended from Archaic Latin, a language with origins that can be traced back to between 400 and 700 A.D.

The English language emerged from ancient Germanic tongues around 100 A.D.

Languages are continuously evolving over time, and most speakers of modern languages would need training to understand their earlier forms. In fact, speakers of modern English have difficulty with Shakespearean English from just 500 years ago.

New Worlds, New Words

If Shakespeare could visit us today, he wouldn't understand how we speak either. Even President Teddy Roosevelt, who lived until 1919, would have trouble decoding many of our everyday words such as software, email, texting, DVDs, cell phones, video games, energy bars, bottled water, and track shoes.

Language is fascinating. As Shakespeare would have said, "Leorner, enjoy thy Engliscgereorde," or as we might say, "Student, enjoy the English language."

Take Home
Enhanced verbal skills and an imaginative new language to teach to friends and family

Materials
- Pencils
- Paper
- Chalkboard and chalk or equivalent

Getting Ready
- Write some of the most common English words on the board such as:
  a, and, be, have, he, I, in, it, of, she, that, the, to, was, you
- Invite students to think of sounds apart from the English language that could be used as components of a new language. Write some ideas on the board and have students add to the list. You can use the ones below or come up with your own:

Some Non-English Sounds:
- Clicks
- Clucks
- Giggles
- Grunts
- Hisses
- Hums
- Stomps
- Toots
- Whistles

- Divide the class into teams of two to three students.

Speaking Imaginese *continues* ➜

continued from previous page

Activities and Procedures

1 Write the following definition on the board and discuss its meaning with the class:

   language: a system of sounds used to communicate thoughts to others who use the same system of sounds

2 Inform students that their teams will create their very own language.

Explain the following requirements that students should adhere to when creating their new languages:

3 *Foundation:* Base the new language on English (or another system of sounds). Apply one or more of the following techniques:

   Technique: *Replacing Letters*
   - Replace all vowels with one vowel:
     O sow o cow jomp ovor tho roonbow.
   - Replace one consonant with a different consonant:
     I sag a cog jump over the rainbog.

   Technique: *Replacing Words*
   - Replace common words "I," "a," and "the" with a made-up word:
     Zeep saw zeep cow jump over zeep rainbow.
   - Replace nouns with made-up words.
     I saw a lactula jump over the slooxa.
   - Replace all verbs with one made-up word:
     I shleggum a cow shleggum over the rainbow.
   - Replace each verb with a non-English sound. Design characters to represent the sounds:
     I (click) a cow (whistle) over the rainbow.

4 *Vocabulary:* Develop a vocabulary of twenty words or more; five of them should be nouns and five should be verbs. The other ten may be any other part of speech.

5 *New sounds:* Add three new sounds that are not part of the English alphabet and design alphabet characters for those sounds. For example, the sound made by clicking with your tongue could be represented by three triangles, one above the other.

6 *Name:* Name your language

7 *Write:* Use your language to write at least two paragraphs of a short story or a familiar poem. You can use the examples below to spark ideas or come up with your own.

   Cow Chasing
      I saw a cow jump over the rainbow. Then I heard a moo.
      So I ran across a large grassy field to see where she had landed.
      I found her standing at the end of the rainbow, holding a pot of gold.
      She offered the pot of gold to me, but when I grasped it, the gold turned to buttermilk.
      Nevertheless, it was a delicious ending to a lovely afternoon.

Cow Chosong

O sow o cow yulah ovor tho roonbow. Thon O hoord o (hum sound).
So O scunn ocross o lorge grossy panna to soo whoro sho hod plunkott.
Sho wos vablungee ot tho ond of tho roonbow, gratchim o pot of gold.
Sho offorod tho pot of gold to mo, bot whon O grospod ot tho gold tornod to bottermolk.
Novortholoss, ot bottz o dolocooos onding to o lovoly neelleena.

In the above example the Cow Chasing story is translated into the "Jombo" language by replacing all vowels with the letter, "o," using new nouns and verbs, and including new sounds not found in the English alphabet, which are shown in parentheses.

8 Invite teams to present their languages to the class by reading their stories aloud.

9 Encourage students in the audience to ask the presenting team questions.

10 Instruct the team to answer the questions using their new language.

Extensions

- Have students speak in hums and grunts only, using intonation and body language to get ideas across.
- Ask students to use only hums and grunts to perform short skits featuring situations such as playing a game or eating a picnic lunch. Encourage students in the audience to attempt to identify the subject of the skit.
- Have students create three new words that do not exist in the English language, but should. For example, create a word that means the act of hopping and falling simultaneously such as "hoppelsplat."

"Creativity is the type of learning process where the teacher and the pupil are located in the same individual."
– Arthur Koestler

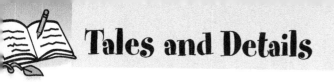

Tales and Details

Grade Level: 2 through 6
Participants: Individuals
Objectives: Exercise flexibility, originality, elaboration, creative writing skills, and plot structure
Time: Approximately 1 hour

Quick View

In this exercise in creative writing, students demonstrate their powers of imagination and elaboration by composing unique narratives. Starting with identical story structures, students breathe life into their individual tales through the use of original description and detail.

Examples

Bugsy's Garden Adventure

Main Character – Bugsy
Bugsy seeks adventure – explores the garden
Bugsy meets others – a snail, a grasshopper, a beetle
Bugsy visits other places – other parts of the garden
Bugsy finds fortune, adventure, or happiness – appreciates what she has at home

(Beginning)

Bugsy was bored because nothing interesting ever happened on her leaf.

There were no juicy berries or big colorful flowers nearby, so Bugsy set off on a long hike to explore the garden.

(Middle)

It was almost noon before she passed the row of tulips, and Bugsy's tiny legs were tired. She hitched a ride on the back of a snail, but an hour later she was only three inches along. She thanked the snail and got a ride from a grasshopper who hopped her through the garden in four seconds.

Bugsy landed in an exciting spot. Bright colors and berry smells were everywhere! Bugsy wanted some strawberry juice, but a giant beetle chased her away. When she stopped to look at a beautiful flower, it tried to trap her and swallow her up!

Bugsy tasted a pansy, but it was too bitter. "I'm hungry and I want to go home", Bugsy said to herself.

(End)

Bugsy got home just before dark. She noticed how pretty her leaf was, with its silvery green veins and little purple dots. Her friends and family were there, and they all shared a meal of sweet grass salad, played tag, and sang songs in the moonlight. "I'm glad to be home. I discovered that we live in the best part of the garden," Bugsy told everyone.

Just Imagine

Main Character – Azure

Azure seeks happiness – dreams of being on another planet

Azure meets others – Plumo and his friends

Azure visits other places – Plumo's planet

Azure finds fortune, adventure, or happiness – learns she has a special ability, so she feels happy on her own planet.

(Beginning)

Azure was named for the blue sky, and she had a skylight in her bedroom ceiling. Every night, Azure would lie in bed and look out her skylight window, dreaming of better places. She wished she could go to another planet, where kids might be nicer.

(Middle)

She was fast asleep when a sound awakened her. A teenage alien was tapping on her skylight. "Good evening. I'm Plumo. I invite you to visit our planet." Azure reached through the skylight, grasped his nine-fingered hand, and away they soared to a planet hidden among the stars.

Plumo showed Azure the strange beauty of his planet, and he introduced her to his amazing friends. They went to a "rocket concert." Plumo told Azure that for his birthday, his parents let him have a date with an Earth girl.

"Why did you choose me?," Azure asked Plumo. "I'm not the prettiest girl on Earth, and many kids get better grades than I do."

"I chose you because you have imagination," said Plumo. "Without imagination, this night would not be possible." Azure had a wonderful evening, but she was ready to go home.

(End)

The next day at school, Azure held her head high. She knew she was special on Earth. She had something important; she had imagination.

Tales and Details *continues* ➜

continued from previous page

Take Home
An original story demonstrating the transforming effect of detail and elaboration

Materials
- Pens or pencils
- Paper
- Chalk and chalkboard, or equivalent

Getting Ready
- Write the following story structure on the board:
  - Beginning: Main Character leaves home to seek fortune, adventure, or happiness. (state the motivation)
  - Middle: Main Character meets others along the way (add some characters)
  - Middle: Main Character visits other places (describe the setting)
  - Middle: Main Character wants to go home (show or explain the conflict)
  - End: Main Character finds fortune, adventure, or happiness at home. (show or explain the resolution)
- List some of the following story components on the board:

  Examples of Main Characters – students may select from these characters or make up their own:
  - Animal (any)
  - Brother
  - Bully
  - Dad
  - Fairy
  - Giant
  - Magician
  - Mom
  - Princess
  - Robot
  - Rock Star
  - Sailor
  - Scientist
  - Sister
  - Skateboarder
  - Teacher

  Character Details:
  - Who are they?
  - How do they look?
  - How do they talk?
  - What are their personalities?
  - What do they believe?
  - What do they want?
  - Are there other important details about the characters?

  Settings – students may invent their own settings or use one on this list:
  - Amusement Park
  - Ancient City
  - Big City
  - Castle
  - Desert Island
  - Fairyland
  - Forest
  - Ghost Town
  - Jungle
  - Mountains
  - Ocean
  - Outer Space
  - Prehistoric Land
  - Rocket Ship
  - Rural Town
  - School

  Setting Details:
  - When did the story take place?
  - What are surrounding details such as sounds, sights, smells, tastes, and touch?
  - Are there other important details about the setting?

Activities and Procedures

1 Explain to the class what "plot" means. Show them the story structure, and tell them that they will each be working with the same story line (plot).

2 Show the class the lists of character and setting possibilities, and ask them to choose settings, characters, and details for their stories.

3 Have students begin composing their stories, using the story structure as their outlines. Encourage students to add unique characters, settings, and details to bring their story to life.

4 Encourage writers to think of creative titles for their stories, and have them write these titles on the top of their manuscripts.

5 Invite students to enhance their stories with illustrations of characters, settings, and/or events.

6 When students have completed the writing process, ask volunteers to read their stories aloud to the class. Discuss how the author has made each story different unique through elaboration.

Extensions

- Have students create picture books based on their stories.
- Have students randomly select their main character from the Personality Cards (see *Reproducibles*, pg. 332), and build their story around their selection.

"Laughter is an instant vacation."
– Milton Berle, comedian

Grade Level: 3 through 8
Participants: Individuals
Objectives: Exercise flexibility, originality, elaboration, cause and effect, and writing skills.
Time: A few minutes every day; ½ hour for the writing activity

Quick View

This exercise in creative thinking encourages students to make imaginative brainstorming a part of their daily activities. By pondering What Ifs associated with everyday life, students open their minds to new possibilities (and impossibilities). After generating and collecting What Ifs, students compose original cause and effect narratives based on their inquiries.

Example

Fact: People can talk.

What if: People had no voices?

Speechless

I awoke to the sounds of birds chirping. How I envy the birds. It's not that I want to fly. I am perfectly happy walking or running. But I would give the world to sing.

When I feel happy, when I see a scary movie, or when funny things happen at school, I react in silence. Ever since the Purple Ozone Incident, we Earthlings have had no vocal sounds.

I walked into the kitchen and wrote "Good Morning, Family" on the wall. All our walls are made of dry erase material. We wear markers attached to ribbons around our necks.

There was a knock at the door. I pushed a button that made our "Who's there?" sign pop up outside.

Someone slid a note under the door. "This is not a Knock Knock joke. Our puppy, Barkover, is missing. We are organizing a neighborhood search. If you have a whistle or a horn, please help us call him home."

All morning we heard whistles and horns. By midday, fourteen dogs, three cats, a billy-goat and a raccoon showed up. Happily, the missing puppy was among them.

All is well, but if only we had had voices to call "Barkover," we wouldn't now have eighteen extra critters making a mess on our street.

My friends will be amused to learn about today's events on Text-Radio.

Take Home
A personal treasure trove of idea-starters for stories, skits, artwork, and more

Materials
- Pencils
- Paper
- Journal (optional)
- Chalk and chalkboard or equivalent

Getting Ready
- List a few What Ifs on the board. You can use the suggestions below or come up with your own:

What if... candy grew on trees?
What if... cats made the laws in your town?
What if... dogs could do housework?
What if... it snowed every day?
What if... our houses turned upside down?
What if... people all became the size of ants?
What if... there were no cars?
What if... we could breathe under water?
What if... we didn't need to sleep?
What if... you had a dinosaur for a pet?
What if... you traveled back in time 100 years?
What if... you were a giant?
What if... you were invisible for one hour each day?
What if... you were the principal of Silly School?
What if... your hands were powerful magnets?
What if... a child was enrolled in dog obedience school?
What if... dogs made the laws in your town?
What if... it snowed rainbow colors?
What if... people all became the size of hamsters?

What if... it was illegal to do homework?
What if... we had no voices?
What if... you could change your face into a famous face?
What if... you could plant an inanimate object and make it grow?
What if... you made the rules at school?
What if... you won $40 million dollars?
What if... everything in the room became round?
What if... people had the keen sense of smell a dog has?
What if... the Earth were square?
What if... electricity didn't exist?
What if... your feet had brains and could talk?
What if... your school became a school for creativity?
What if... there was no written language?
What if... there was no such thing as math?
What if... we had sounds of musical instruments instead of voices?
What if... we had wheels for feet?
What if... there was no such word as "yes"?

What If the Earth Were Square continues ➔

continued from previous page

Subjects of Interest

Consider using the following What Ifs that pertain to subject areas you may be studying. Ask your students to generate additional What Ifs beyond those in the lists.

Science What Ifs

What if... the Earth stopped spinning for one month?

What if... the Earth were twice as far from the sun as it is now?

What if... our oceans dried up?

What if... all carnivore animals became herbivores?

What if... all the herbivore animals became carnivores?

What if... gravity didn't exist?

Language Arts What Ifs

What if... there were no written languages?

What if... the letters "s" and "a" were eliminated from our alphabet? .

What if... there were no adjectives or adverbs? Tell about your family without using those parts of speech.

What if... only rich people could read?

What if... the words, "is", "was," "to, and "be" were eliminated from our vocabulary?

What if... we had no punctuation?

Math What Ifs

What if... there were no zeroes in our number system?

What if... multiplication had not been developed?

What if... there were no written number symbols?

What if... only rich people could do math?

What if... only dogs could do math?

What if... you had to add the number of your birth-date to the cost of everything you bought?

Social Studies What Ifs

What if... there was only one country in this world?

What if... there was no such thing as war?

What if... there were no laws?

What if... only people with red hair could own property?

What if... there were no vehicles of any kind?

What if... people lived for 500 years?

Activities and Procedures

1 Ask students to brainstorm more examples to add to the list of What Ifs on the board.

2 To generate new What Ifs, explain the meaning of the word "fact." Ask students to name some facts, such as:
   - Grass is green
   - Fish swim in water
   - School has rules

3 Then ask students to consider a reality in which these facts weren't true. For example,
   - What if… every blade of grass were a different color?
   - What if… fish swam in the air?
   - What if… school had no rules?

4 Ask students to choose a What If about which they can write a story.

   Optional: Narrow the field of choices to a subject area appropriate to your class instruction. See sidebar, "Subjects of Interest."

5 Write the Story
   - Tell your class to begin by thinking of several events, outrageous or otherwise, that could happen as a result of the What If. Encourage students to make a list of good and bad consequences.
   - Ask each student to select one or more ideas from the list for further development.
   - Then, tell students to take their imaginations a step or two further and consider the sequential consequences of these events. Ask them, "And what would happen after that? And then what?"

6 When students are finished writing, choose a few volunteers to read their stories aloud.

Extensions
   - Ask your students to keep a small journal with them at all times for recording What If ideas as they surface.
     - Ask students to think of at least five new What Ifs each week. These can be either silly or serious.
   - Make a classroom What If box with a slot at the top for students to anonymously drop in favorite What If ideas.
     - After the box is full, ask each student to randomly pick a What If and use it as inspiration for a story.

What If Consequences

Grade Level: 3 through 6
Participants: Teams of 2 to 6
Objectives: Exercise fluency, flexibility, originality, elaboration, brainstorming, understanding cause and effect, analyzing information, and team cooperation.
Time: ½ hour to 1 hour

Quick View

In this activity, students combine imagination with the logic of cause and effect to create new "realities" based on What If scenarios. As they brainstorm for both positive and negative results, students expand their creative potential while building on their analytical and cooperation skills.

Example

What if... our fingers were powerful magnets?

Good Consequences

1 You could pick up pins and paper clips quickly.
2 You could open the refrigerator door without having to grasp the handle.
3 You could hold a can of soda while also holding other things.
4 Your hands would be attracted toward the rim of a basketball net, allowing you to make more baskets.

Bad Consequences

1 You might not be able to shake the hand of someone whose magnet repels yours, causing them to think you are unfriendly.
2 It would be difficult to clap your hands at a concert.
3 You might pick up unwanted debris as you go on a walk.
4 Your fingers might interfere with your cell phone signal.

Possible Negative Effects of Good Consequences

1 It would be difficult to get the pins and clips off your hands to put them away.
2 You might accidentally open the refrigerator and not notice it.
3 You would be tempted to drink too much soda because you could always hold a can while you are doing other things.
4 Everyone would have the same big advantage, and that would take the challenge out of the game.

Possible Positive Effects of Bad Consequences

1 You could laugh with him over this.
2 You would have to learn to whistle.
3 You might find cool treasures this way.
4 You would have to communicate through letters more often, so you would sharpen your writing skills.

Take Home
A batch of new ideas ready for creative development

Materials
- Pencils
- Paper
- Chalkboard and chalk or equivalent

Getting Ready
- Write a few What If situations on the board. (For examples, see sidebar "Subjects of Interest," pg. 118.)
- Ask your class to brainstorm their own What If situations and add them to the list on the board. Assure students that their ideas may be silly (e.g. "What if… it rained soap bubbles?") or serious (e.g."What if… electricity stopped working everywhere for one year?")
- Discuss the concept of cause and effect, and define the word "consequence."
- Ask your class for some possible consequences to the What Ifs on the board. List the consequences alongside the What If scenarios.

Activities and Procedures
1 Divide your class into teams of two or more. These teams will compete to list as many consequences as they can within a predetermined amount of time (usually fifteen minutes will suffice).
  - Team one: "The Good News Giddies"
    Task: to brainstorm for positive consequences of the What If scenario
  - Team two: "The Bad News Biddies"
    Task: to brainstorm for negative consequences of the What If scenario

   Teams should be comprised of 2 to 6 members; competing teams should have an equal number of members if possible.

2 Choose team leaders to keep order and to organize a master list of consequences.

3 Instruct team members to brainstorm together and add all ideas to the master list. Give both teams the same What If scenario and have them generate as many consequences as possible.

4 When time is up, compare the lists and award one point for each consequence.

5 Invite both teams to read their lists out loud, and discuss interesting responses with the class.

6 Then, have the Biddies list ways the positives might actually be negatives, and tell the Giddies to imagine how the negatives might actually be positives.

7 Award one additional point for each "reversed" consequence they list.

8 Tally up the results and announce the winner!

Extensions
For Individual Participants:
- Ask students to select any What If from the board and independently list every consequence they can imagine.
- Have students select or make up a What If and compose a story based around the scenario.

For Small Teams:
- Ask students to select a What If and then write and perform a skit about it.

Grade Level: 3 through 8
Participants: Individuals
Objectives: Exercise originality, elaboration, brainstorming, understanding analogies and metaphors, and creative writing skills
Time: Approximately 1 hour

Quick View

In this exercise in comparison, students pretend that they belong to a family of shoes, using analogies and metaphors to describe their relatives.

Example

My Name is Sneaker

My name is Sneaker, and I love to run. I have black and white canvas skin. I look good, but sometimes I forget to change my shoelaces.

My mom is a pretty house slipper. She has pink silk skin and wears flowers across her instep.

My sister, Mary Jane, is dating a roller skate. Mom doesn't like him because he is all about fun and not very grounded. Mom is afraid he will speed off with her. I say, "At least he's not a shabby loafer like her other boyfriend."

Mary Jane's best friend, Spike, thinks she's a fine high heel. She looks down on me, but I don't care. Someday, I will be a famous basketball shoe.

We live with my Grandpa, who is a grungy old boot. He likes to tell us about his experiences at war. There were no flip-flops in those days, and only the toughest soles survived. But last year, Grandpa broke his heel and had to spend two weeks at the shoemaker's to recuperate.

Well, I've got to run now. I'm going to meet my sidekick at the track.

Take Home

An original story featuring the student's skillful use of analogies and metaphors

Materials

- Pencils
- Paper
- Chalkboard and chalk or equivalent

Getting Ready

- List some shoe styles and analog words on the board to inspire student brainstorming. You can use the ones listed below, or come up with your own:

Shoe Styles

- Army boots
- Baby shoes
- Ballet shoes
- Basketball shoes
- Beach shoes
- Boat shoes
- Booties
- Boots
- Bowling shoes
- Clogs
- Cowboy boots
- Crocs
- Dancing shoes
- Dirty gym shoes
- Dress shoes
- Elevator shoes
- Espadrilles
- Fishing boots
- Flip flops
- Football shoes
- Gladiator shoes
- Glass slippers
- Golf shoes
- Heelys
- High button shoes
- High heels
- Hiking boots
- Hockey skates
- House slippers
- Hush Puppies
- Ice skates
- Jellies
- Loafers
- Mary Janes
- Moccasins
- Mules
- Open-toe shoes
- Orthopedic shoes
- Oxfords
- Party shoes
- Penny loafers
- Platforms
- Pumps
- Rain boots
- Riding boots
- Roller skates
- Running shoes
- Saddle shoes
- Sandals
- Sling-backs
- Slippers
- Sneakers
- Snow boots
- Snow shoes
- Spats
- Spike heels
- Sport shoe
- Stilettos
- Stilts
- Tap shoes
- Tennis shoes
- Track shoes
- Wedgies
- Wing tips
- Wooden clogs
- Work boots

Shoe Analogs

- Alligator skin
- Arch support
- Boot straps
- Bows
- Buckles
- Canvas
- Heel
- Horseshoe
- Insole
- Instep
- Leather
- Lining
- Patent leather
- Pinched toes
- Reflectors
- Scuff
- Shoe horn
- Shoe polish
- Shoe store
- Shoebox
- Shoelace
- Shoemaker
- Shoeshine
- Snakeskin
- Socks
- Sole
- Suede
- Tongue

Foot Action Analogs

- Dance
- Hop
- Hopscotch
- Jump
- Just for kicks
- Kick
- Kick up a storm
- Kick up the dust
- Kickball
- Kidskin
- Left shoe
- Point your toes
- Right shoe
- Run
- Shuffle
- Skip
- Skip rope
- Stamp your feet
- Stand
- Stay on your toes
- Stomp
- Stompers
- Straps
- Stuck in the mud
- Toe-tapping

- Write the words "analogy" and "metaphor" on the board.

A Family of Shoes continues ➜

continued from previous page

Activities and Procedures

1 Have your class brainstorm a list of shoe-related words (e.g. parts of a shoe, shoe styles, shoe accessories, etc.). Add these words to the list on the board.

2 Explain the meanings of the words "analogy "and "metaphor." Write the following definitions on the board:

Analogy - a comparison that shows a similarity

Metaphor- something that represents something else

3 Explain that analogies and metaphors are important tools for creative works and are often the inspiration behind new inventions. Discuss how fine artists, song writers, screenwriters, and novelists use metaphors to express their ideas.

4 Inform students that they will be using analogies and metaphors to describe their "shoe family."

5 To inspire ideas, discuss the kinds of shoes that might make suitable metaphors for human personalities. Make up your own metaphors or use the ones below for examples:
   - Gold slipper = a glamorous woman
   - Dirty sneakers = rough and tumble boys
   - Comfortable sport shoes = old buddies
   - Tall boot = a boss or leader
   - Orthopedic shoe = an elderly school teacher

6 Encourage students to use analogies in their stories. Share examples such as the ones below to spark their imaginations:
   - A shoe being repaired by a shoemaker is an analogy for a person receiving medical care from a doctor.
   - A shoe getting a shoeshine is an analogy for someone having their hair styled.

7 Ask students to ponder the following questions as they write:
   - What kind of shoe are you?
   - What do your family members look like?
   - Where do you go for fun?
   - Where have you traveled?
   - Who are your friends?
   - What is interesting about your shoe family?

8 When students have finished writing, invite volunteers to read their stories aloud. Point out the analogies and metaphors in the stories, and invite students to discuss how these elements enhanced the narrative.

Extensions

- *Shoe Portraits* – Ask each student to remove a shoe to use as a model for drawing. Encourage students to observe and sketch the contours, scuffs, smudges, creases, and other details that give shoes character. Offer pictures of various shoes for students to use as reference for "shoe family members." Catalogs and newspaper ads are good sources of shoe references.
- *Alternative Families* – Follow the lesson plan for "A Family of Shoes," but substitute another category. Here are some category suggestions:
  - A Family of Books
  - A Family of Bugs
  - A Family of Crayons
  - A Family of Desserts
  - A Family of Musical Instruments
  - A Family of Sandwiches
  - A Family of Toys
  - A Family of Vehicles

"Life does not consist mainly, or even largely, of facts and happenings. It consists mainly of the storm of thoughts that is forever blowing through one's head."
– Mark Twain

Grade Level: 2 through 6
Participants: Individuals or classroom groups
Objectives: Exercise fluency, flexibility, imagination, phonics, parts of speech, alliteration, and sentence structure
Time: ½ hour to 1 hour

Quick View

In this fun, phonetic activity, students use their powers of creativity and alliteration to rapidly write sentences consisting of three or four words, all of which begin with the same letter.

Examples

Three Word Sentences

- Apples are awesome.
- Dogs don't drive.
- Horses have hats.
- Only oatmeal oozes.
- Ten teachers talked.
- Whiskers will wiggle.

Four Word Sentences

- An alligator ate apricots.
- Big balloons bounce beautifully.
- Chimps can catch colds.
- Green goats get grumpy.
- Mud makes me mad.
- Please pick purple pencils.

Take Home

Several whimsical sentences to serve as original story starters and a fun new game to share with family and friends

Materials
- Pencils
- Paper
- Chalkboard and chalk or equivalent
- Timer
- Dictionary (optional)

Getting Ready
- Write the entire alphabet on the board.
- Next to each letter, make a list of nouns that begin with that letter. Ask students to offer suggestions, and allow them to use dictionaries if necessary.
- Write the alphabet on the board again.
- This time, ask students to brainstorm for verbs that begin with each letter. Write their responses on the board next to each letter.
- Write the definition of the word "alliteration" on the board, and discuss its meaning with the class.
- Decide whether your class will work with three-word or four-word sentences.

Activities and Procedures

1 Instruct students to write as many alliterative sentences as they can within a ten-minute timeframe.

2 Tell students that they may choose any letters of the alphabet they wish, and may refer to the lists on the board for ideas.

3 Remind students that whether silly or serious, all sentences must be complete.

4 When time is up, invite students to read their sentences out loud. Start with the letter "A" and read all the sentences using that letter. Then, read sentences beginning with "B," and so on.

Extensions
- For lower grades, combine this lesson plan with a unit on dictionary use.
- Encourage students to write three and four-word sentences. When time is up, award one point for each three-word sentence and two points for four-word sentences. Tally the results, and announce a winner!
- Have students write sentences using the letters in their first names. Write the name from top to bottom along the left side of the page, and encourage students to write an alliterative sentence next to each letter.
- Encourage students to write alliterative sentences for the whole alphabet, add illustrations, and bind the pages into a novelty ABC book.
- Instruct students to select an alliterative sentence and use it as a "story starter." Using the original sentence as inspiration, students should write a story featuring alliterative sentences and phrases.

Slap-stick Stories

Grade Level: 2 through 4
Participants: Individuals
Objectives: Exercise flexibility, originality, elaboration, imagination, understanding sequencing, sketching, and writing skills
Time: Approximately ½ hour to 1 hour

Quick View

In this "slap-stick" activity, students create three action stick figures on separate pieces of paper which are then randomly redistributed. Students are then challenged to arrange their new stick figures in an order which portrays a silly or serious sequence of events. By creating a visual illustration of the occurrences and then composing a corresponding narrative, students hone their visualization skills while practicing the art of creative writing as well.

Examples

Go For It

Mary is running to get in line for a free concert.
She falls down from exhaustion.
She gathers all her strength and gets up again. She is determined to go to the concert.

Head Over Heels

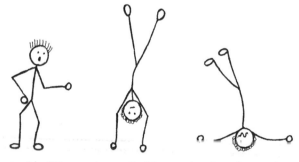

Jack's P.E. teacher tells him to do a handstand.
Jack is showing off his perfect handstand.
Ooooops. Jack falls on his head. He needs more practice.

Take Home

Enhanced visualization skills and an original story with sketches to share with family and friends

Materials

- Pencils
- Paper (one full sheet per student)
- White scrap paper or blank index cards
- Glue sticks or clear tape
- Chalkboard and chalk or equivalent
- Pictures of people in various situations or postures (optional)

Getting Ready

- List a few actions and emotions on the board. You can use the ones provided here or come up with your own.
- Draw at least one stick figure performing an action and at least one stick figure displaying an emotion. (See sidebar, "Actions and Emotions.")
- Gather pictures of people in various postures and emotional states for the class to reference (optional).

Action   Emotion

Actions and Emotions

Suggestions for Action Gestures

cartwheel	hide	reach for something	throw something
dance	hop	relax	catch something
daydream	hug	run	twirl
fall down	jump	sit	work
fly	kick	sleep	
go up or down stairs	laugh	do a somersault	
do a handstand	play	stand	

Suggestions for Emotions

afraid	excited	intelligent	shy
amused	evil	kind	sick
angry	friendly	loving	silly
annoyed	frustrated	nervous	surprised
bossy	happy	obnoxious	tired
confused	hateful	sad	worried

Slap-stick Stories *continues* ➜

continued from previous page

How to Draw a Stickman

A stickman is a great icon for demonstrating sequences of action.
In this way, they are somewhat like modern hieroglyphs.

A Stickman in 6 Steps

1 Head is a circle

2 Neck and torso line should be 2 to 3 times length of head

3 Arms start slightly below head; arms bend at elbows; hands are circles

4 Legs start at bottom of torso line; legs are a little longer than arms; feet are ovals

5 Show your stickman in action

6 Add faces, details, and props (optional)

Anatomy of a Stickman

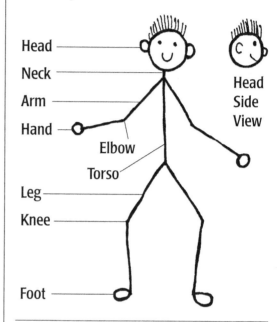

Head
Neck
Arm
Hand
Elbow
Torso
Leg
Knee
Foot

Head Side View

Make Your Stickmen Expressive

Activities and Procedures

1 Have the class brainstorm more actions and emotions to add to the list on the board.

2 Explain to your class that they will sketch three simple stick figures, each of which will show a separate action or an emotion. Students may use the examples listed on the board or generate their own ideas.

3 Instruct students to make each sketch approximately 2½" high.

4 Have students cut the sketches into separate paper cards.

5 Collect and shuffle the sketches.

6 Then, randomly distribute three sketches to each student.

7 Invite students to consider the sketches in their hand, and then strategically arrange and adhere them across the top of a sheet of paper in any sequence that tells a story.

  As students consider the task, tell them that they have the freedom to:
  • Choose any side of the paper to be the top
  • Opt to add "props"
  • Add faces and details
  • Use the three stick figures to represent the same person or different people

8 After students have glued or taped their stick figures to the paper, instruct them to number them according to the sequence of events in their story.

9 Once the sketches are complete, invite students to write stories explaining who and where the figures are, what they are doing, and why. Stories may be realistic or outlandish, but they must directly connect to the sequence of events shown in the sketches.

10 Have students number their explanations to correspond with the numbers on each sketch.

11 Instruct students to create a title for their story, and write it above the sketches.

12 Allow students to share their "stick stories" with their classmates.

Extensions
  • *Challenge* – Do not allow students to rearrange the order in which the cards were received. Then, have them stretch their imaginations to write a story based on that sequence.
  • *Back Story* – Select one of three randomly distributed sketches and explain the situation. Then write the back story: What happened beforehand that caused the events to occur?
  • *Longer Story* – Have students use more stick figures to develop a more complex storyline.

Grade Level: 3 through 6
Participants: Individuals
Objectives: Exercise originality, analogies, visual symbols, and creative writing skills
Time: ½ hour to 1 hour

Quick View

In this lesson in visual expression, students are challenged to put a new twist on the concept of emoticons. By creating unique symbols to illustrate specific feelings and ideas, and then using these symbols in their own original narratives, students practice their ingenuity as well as their creative writing skills.

Examples

My Letter to Jenny

Dear Jenny,

I hope you are well. ♡♡ I saw the sweetest puppy at the pound yesterly, ⋛♡⋚ but someone had already adopted him. ◖

Mom says we will keep looking until we find the right puppy for me. 🌈 "If you keep your grades up and do your chores every day," ☹ she said. I have a mean old teacher this year. (🍎̸) She gave me so much homework ∿.///∿ that I couldn't go skating after school for a whole month. I miss you so much, my BFF. ♡⌣♡ I hope we can go to camp together again next year. ☀

Your friend,

Isabelle

The Baking Lesson by Sam E.

I'm crazy about chocolate chip cookies, especially my Grandma's recipe. ⚡♡⚡ Last week she taught me how bake them and gave me a batch to share with the scouts at our next meeting. ♡♡ But I ate them all myself ‿ and got sick. ☹ Then, I had to stay home to bake more all by myself, instead of going to the movies with my brothers. ☾ All the scouts loved the cookies ⚡♡⚡ except for me. ☹ I don't want to eat another chocolate chip cookie for a long, long time. 🕐 Maybe Grandma will teach me to bake cupcakes for our classroom party. 🎈

Legend

♡♡	caring	☹	unhappiness	☀	fun
⚡♡⚡	love	🍎	dislike for teacher	‿	gladness
☾	sad (tear)	~//~	anger	🕐	time passing
🌈	hope	♡♡	friendship	🎈	party

Materials
- Pencils
- Paper
- Chalk and chalkboard or equivalent
- Markers or crayons (optional)

Getting Ready
- Display some common visual symbols on the board such as a heart, arrow, star, light bulb, xox, circle/slash, etc. (See illustration, "Common Visual Symbols," next page.)

Emoticon Express *continues* ➜

continued from previous page

Common Visual Symbols

Emoticon History

An emoticon is a visual expression commonly used in digital text (i.e. e-mail, text messages, and instant messages) representing the mood of the writer. The word emoticon is a blend of the words emotion and icon. Here are a few fun facts documenting the history of emoticons:

- Although commonly associated with the computer age, emoticons can be traced as far back as the 1800's as a common element of humorous letter writing.
- In 1857, The National Telegraphic Review documented the use of number 73 in Morse Code to express "love and kisses," one example among other emotional shorthand codes.
- Emoticon faces were published in the March 30, 1881 issue of *Puck* magazine. It was called "Typographical Art."

- Emoticons were in popular use among sci-fi fans in the 1940's.
- In 1963, the famous "smiley-face," a yellow button with two black dots for eyes and an upturned curved-line mouth, was created by artist Harvey Ball as part of a morale booster for employees of an insurance company. That yellow smiley-face inspired countless later emoticons, and became a classic American image.
- In the 1970's, teletype machine and typewriter operators developed a shorthand of emoticons to express themselves. These became the forerunners of digital emoticons as computers began to replace teletypes on university campuses.
- Digital forms of emoticons on the Internet were first known to be used by Scott Fahlman in a message sent on Sept. 19, 1982.

Emoticons are widely used today both on the internet and in personal correspondence. They continue to evolve as a form of contemporary personal expression.

Activities and Procedures

1 Invite students to brainstorm some familiar emotions such as anger, sadness, worry, happiness, caring. List these ideas on the board.

2 Discuss the concept of visual symbolism with the class referring to the examples on the board.

3 Ask students design at least three new emoticons that represent distinct feelings.

4 Next, invite students to write a friendly letter or short story featuring their new emoticons.

  TIP: It may be helpful to have them write their paper first, leaving space to insert their emoticons upon completing their draft.

5 When their letter or short story is complete, ask students to create a legend portraying the new symbols and their meanings.

6 If time permits, allow students to share their narratives and emoticons with their classmates.

Extensions
- Have students create cards showcasing their custom emoticons. Then, hold a class game in which students are encouraged to guess the meanings of their classmates' symbols.
- Invite students to write stories featuring symbols which represent sounds instead of facial expressions. Have volunteers read their stories aloud, adding the sound effects as they read.

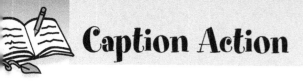

Grade Level: 3 through 6
Participants: Individuals or teams of two
Objectives: Exercise flexibility, originality, imagination, writing skills.
Time: ½ hour to 1 hour

Quick View

Students write two kinds of captions for pictures cut from magazines and comic strips. Their first caption category is a straightforward explanation of what is happening. Their second caption category is humor, making funny comments as on single cartoon panels. Wild imaginations and outrageous points of view are welcome. Classmates have fun sharing their captions.

Example

❶ Adam was in a hurry to get to his friend's house.

❷ With the invisible porcupines chasing him, Adam sped away.

Take Home
A conversation piece to tack on your bulletin board.

Materials
- Magazines and newspaper comics to cut up
- Scissors
- Glue sticks or tape
- Plain paper, 8½" x 11"
- Pencils
- Chalk and chalkboard or equivalent

Getting Ready
- Write the definition of caption on the board: A title, brief explanation, or comment for a picture or illustration.
- Gather some magazines and the comic sections of newspapers.
- Select an image with a caption to show as an example.

Activities and Procedures

1 Explain the word, caption.

2 Give each student or team a handful of pages to cut up and mount on paper, one image per paper. Existing captions and words need to be cut away.

3 Students should mount at least two images each, leaving room at the bottom of the paper for writing captions.

   TIP: Consider doing the cutting and mounting yourself, so the images are ready when the lesson begins.

   TIP: Images that show action, something unusual, or something puzzling work best.

4 Ask students to hand in the pictures. Then redistribute them at random.

5 Ask students to write captions under their images. They should decide if they will explain what is happening or add humor, and write "explanation" or "humor" on the top right of the papers.

6 Students share their pictures and captions.

Extensions
- Have more than one student or team add alternate captions to the pictures.
- All students add captions to the same picture, posted on the board. Then compare results.
- Ask students to write only humorous captions under their pictures. Have a contest by anonymous voting for the funniest.
- Cut out the existing captions separately from their pictures, and mount them, too. Ask students to match up the pictures with their captions. Add a few others to make the lesson more challenging.

Grade Level: 2 through 5
Participants: Individuals or teams
Objectives: Exercise fluency, flexibility, originality, substitution, imagination, parts of speech, reading skills, teamwork harmony, socialization.
Time: Approximately ½ hour

Quick view

This card game, adapted from an old classic for kids, is still hilarious today. Our version has updated language, and requires the players to create their own adjective-noun cards. A whimsical poem is read aloud in turns by students in a circle. When the reader pauses, the student on their left fills in the blank with words written on index cards. Through random substitution, laughter prevails.

Example

Dr. Quack

I guess you all know Dr. Quack,
Who wears a coat upon his back,
While right across his wishbone chest,
You'll find a lovely spotted vest.
And glasses, too, he wears, and spats,
and pantaloons with nifty hats.
And ties and collars, white and black,
A sporty chap is Dr. Quack.

He has _a blue crayon_ on his face,
and _a smelly fish_ in another place.
With _a rusty nail_ he combs his hair,
and uses _a hot pepper_ here and there.

And though it's such an odd technique,
He takes _a tennis racquet_ to scratch his beak,
And toenail sharp, to scratch his back,
A clever chap is Dr. Quack.

NOTE: For a free, printable copy of the full poem go to www.jrimagination.com/printables.

Take Home

An original version of a comical classic game to play with friends and family

Materials

- Pencils
- Index cards, 25 or more

- Chalkboard and chalk or equivalent
- Copies of the poem (optional)

Getting Ready

- Distribute index cards to the students.
- Write the words, noun and adjective along with their definitions on the board.

Activities and Procedures

1 Explain to your students that they will be reading a poem and filling in the blanks with adjective-noun pairs.

   NOTE: There are 48 blanks to fill. There should be at least 96 choices for each blank, but the more choices, the more fun.

2 Instruct each student to clearly write or print four nouns, top to bottom, on the right side of their cards.

3 Now exchange cards with a fellow student, who adds a modifying adjective to the left of each noun. It's ok to add "a," "an," or "the" to the left of the adjectives.

   NOTE: Challenge students to stretch their imaginations to think of interesting, absurd, or funny things, such as dirty socks, a cold potato, a broken violin, a purple giraffe, and so on.

4 Collect all the index cards. Shuffle and redistribute them.

5 Have the players form a reading circle. The first reader reads a paragraph of the poem and pauses at a blank. The player to the reader's left fills in the pause by reading aloud an adjective-noun pair on their card. Continue until the paragraph is finished, having different players fill in the pauses.

6 The next reader and players proceed in the same way… and so on. Laughter is allowed.

The History of "The Comical Game of Dr. Quack"

The game was first published in 1935, by the Russell Mfg Co., of Leicester, Massachusetts. In 1960, the game was selling for a whopping twenty-nine cents. The game is no longer in publication.

Dr. Quack is not a "game" in the typical way because there are no winners or losers. But I remember playing this game at birthday parties. Those who laughed out loud would be "out." The player's challenge was to select the funniest choice to fill a pause, in attempt to make players burst out laughing.

Kids today, despite all their electronic toys, still love laughing with friends.

Some selections from the original cards:

a ball of yarn	a green snake
a big baboon	a jumbo peanut
a big fat worm	a laughing donkey
a bottle of castor oil	a loaf of bread
a bow legged horse	a music box
a broken window	a rip in your pants
a bunch of bananas	a second-hand car
a bunch of daisies	a shaving mug
a can of beans	a sour lemon
a corn cob pipe	a string of fish
a cow bell	a three legged stool
a crowing rooster	a ton of bricks
a feather bed	an old silk hat
a glass of buttermilk	your red nose

Extensions

- Substitute Object Cards for word cards. (See *Reproducibles*, page 320.)
- *Pre-readers*: For youngsters who do not read, the teacher may read the poem, while players fill in the pauses by naming an item on an Object Card.
- *Make a Gift*: Give each student a photocopy of the poem. Have them create their own set of cards and decorate the borders and an envelope or box to hold their game.

Grade Level: 3 through 6
Participants: Individuals or teams of two
Objectives: Exercise flexibility, originality, elaboration, imagination, researching skills, cause and effect, vocabulary, and writing skills
Time: 1 to 2 hours

Quick View

In this creative writing endeavor, students write fictional, first-person narratives documenting personal discoveries or inventions. As they authenticate their stories by weaving in facts discovered through traditional as well as Internet research, students hone their research skills and reinforce their knowledge of fact vs. fiction.

Examples

See "How I Discovered Maple Syrup," and "How I Invented the Fork."

How I Discovered Maple Syrup

My sister and I were playing in the woods on the North American continent. We were shooting our bows and arrows at targets we had carved into some tree trunks.

My arrow hit a target. When I pulled my arrow out of the maple tree, I noticed that the tip of the arrow was sticky, and that something golden brown was running down the trunk.

This strange substance filled my nostrils, and it smelled good, so I tasted a very tiny bit. It was sweet and delicious!

My sister and I were getting cold, so we dripped some sticky stuff into a cup made from leaves, and headed for home.

Mom made corncakes for dinner. I dipped them into the sticky stuff, which I named "sheesheegumavvis." It means "sap flows fast" in our Objibway language.

Later, the European settlers renamed it "maple syrup." It tastes just as good, but I think "sheesheegumavvis" is a catchier name.

Researched Facts

- Maple trees grow in North America
- Maple syrup is sap from maple trees
- The Objibway were one of the Native American tribes that used maple syrup to flavor food
- Sheesheegumavvis means "sap flows fast."

How I Invented the Fork

It was October 10, 1010, my 10th birthday, and I was having a party in Sherwood Forest.

My best friends were there: Adalbert, Leofric, Brynjarr, Fedelmid, and little Meginrat. We all sat on tree stumps at a big table, set with my family's best wooden plates and silver knives.

We ate almonds, cherries, and wild turkey. Suddenly Adalbert yelled, "Ouch!" She had cut her tongue on the knife she was using for eating. Then Meginrat cried, "ouch!" too.

I didn't want sharp utensils to ruin my party.

I noticed that a fork-shaped twig was sticking out from a stump. I snapped it off and tried it for picking up my food. It worked!

We took turns, passing that twig fork around until we all finished eating. Then we used it to eat einkorn grain birthday cake.

The next day I set to work carving wood into fork-shaped eating utensils, and gave some of them to sailors to deliver to other lands. My invention caught on. I am proud of my contribution to the feeding of humanity.

Researched Facts
- Forks were first used in Europe around 1000 A.D.
- People used their fingers or knives for eating before that.
- Early forks were made of wood.
- Adalbert, Leofric, Brynjarr, Fedelmid, and Meginrat were popular first names in this era.
- Almonds, cherries, einkorn grain, and wild turkey were typical foods of this time period.
- Early sailors spread goods and ideas to other lands.

Materials
- Pencils
- Paper
- Reference books (e.g. dictionaries, atlases, encyclopedias, etc.)
- Chalkboard and chalk or equivalent
- Internet (optional)

Getting Ready
- Explain what it means to write in the "first person." Read some examples aloud and compare them to samples of text written in the third person.
- Explain the difference between the words *discovery* and *invention* and the words *fact* and *fiction*. Ask students to think of examples of each word.
- Write a list of possible titles on the board to ignite students' imaginations. You can use the ones listed in the sidebar, "Discoveries," or come up with your own:
- Gather reference materials for research.
- If necessary, explain how to use the dictionary, atlas, or encyclopedia.
- If necessary, explain how to use an Internet search engine.

Creative Imposters *continues* ➜

continued from previous page

Discoveries and Inventions

Discoveries

How I discovered **a tropical island**

How I discovered **buffalo**

How I discovered **cave paintings**

How I discovered **coconuts**

How I discovered **dinosaur fossils**

How I discovered **fire**

How I discovered **fireflies**

How I discovered **fish**

How I discovered the **Grand Canyon**

How I discovered the **Great Lakes**

How I discovered **Niagara Falls**

How I discovered the **Rocky Mountains**

How I discovered **volcanoes**

How I discovered **wheat**

How I discovered **wood**

Inventions

How I invented **erasers**

How I invented **gears**

How I invented **high heel shoes**

How I invented **hugging**

How I invented **lemonade**

How I invented **mittens**

How I invented **peanut butter and jelly sandwiches**

How I invented **pencils**

How I invented **roller skates**

How I invented **skiing**

How I invented **snowmen**

How I invented **staplers**

How I invented the **fork**

How I invented the **game of tag**

How I invented the **rowboat**

How I invented the **wheel**

Activities and Procedures

1   Tell your students to select a discovery or invention and use the reference materials provided to find at least three facts about the time and place it was discovered or invented, how it works, why it was needed, etc. Explain to students that it's best to select discoveries and inventions about things that are familiar, but which have histories that are not generally known. For example, we don't know exactly when or where the rowboat was invented, but we can assume that it was first invented by an early civilization near water, and we can find some facts about such a civilization.

2   Ask students to make a list of the facts they found and use this list for reference while writing their stories.

3   Instruct students to write their stories of invention or discovery in the first person.

4   Encourage writers to be as fictitious as they wish but to include at least three relevant facts in each story.

5 Provide the following thought-provoking suggestions for students to ponder as they write:

Tell "inventors" to imagine what problems might have arisen that would motivate them to invent things to solve those problems. For example, in "How I Invented the Fork," the problem was the danger of eating with a sharp knife. The invention of the fork solved that problem.

Tell "discoverers" to imagine what events might have led them to their discoveries. For example, in "How I Discovered Maple Syrup," the child was playing a game with a bow and arrow which led to the accidental discovery of maple syrup.

6 When all students have finished writing, allow volunteers to read their stories aloud.

7 As the stories are read, ask students to distinguish between inventions and discoveries and identify the facts and fiction in each narrative.

Extensions
- Combine this lesson with a unit on how to use various reference books.
- Combine this lesson with a unit on researching skills such as locating information, categorizing, and evaluating.
- Give students a geographic landmark to "discover" and encourage them to use an atlas or a globe to locate geographical and weather-related facts to include in their stories.
- Combine this lesson with a lesson on writing nonfiction stories which tell how, when, where, and by whom something was discovered or invented. Challenge students to use elaboration to create interesting nonfiction accounts. For example, writers might describe natural settings or mention specific clothing styles, vehicles, and dwellings.

"Be less curious about people and more curious about ideas."
– Marie Curie

Grade Level: 3 through 6
Participants: Individuals or small teams
Objectives: Exercise flexibility, originality, visual discrimination, identifying patterns, spelling, and understanding words
Time: Approximately ½ hour to 1 hour

Quick View

In this word-warping activity, students experiment with common palindromes and even generate their own by drafting short stories including as many palindrome words, phrases, and sentences as possible. As they weave palindromes into their stories and add symmetrical illustrations, students enhance their verbal skills while practicing visualization and artistic expression as well.

Example

<u>Yes, I Am Maisey</u>.

<u>Mom</u>, <u>Dad</u>, <u>Sis</u>, the <u>tot</u>, and I are The Palindromes. We all live together in a pretty house with a double door. Our <u>pup</u> is a Palindrome, too. She lives in Uncle <u>Ned's den</u>.

<u>Bob</u>, <u>Lil</u>, <u>Hannah</u>, <u>Otto</u> and their <u>Pop</u> are family members, too. They often <u>pull up</u> in a <u>kayak</u> at <u>noon</u>. They always arrive with a <u>toot toot</u>.

Aunt <u>Anna</u> is a <u>kook</u>, but Uncle <u>Pip</u> is a <u>dud</u>. They <u>did</u> get married one <u>eve</u> in <u>2002</u>. She is <u>33</u> and weighs <u>101</u> lbs. He is <u>44</u> and weighs <u>313</u> lbs. <u>Wow</u>.

They have triplets: <u>Aron</u>, <u>Nora and Edna</u>.

People call us backward, but we look forward just the same.

Take Home

Enhanced verbal skills and an illustrated palindrome story to share with family and friends

Palindrome Word List

aha	kook	refer
bib	level	rotor
civic	madam	sagas
dad	mom	sees
deed	noon	sis
did	peep	solos
dud	pep	toot
eve	pip	tot
ewe	pop	wow
eye	pup	yay
gag	racecar	
kayak	radar	

Palindrome Name List

- Anna
- Bob
- Dad
- Elle
- Eve
- Hannah
- Lil
- Madam
- Mom
- Pip
- Pop
- Sis

Materials

- Pencils
- Paper for writing
- Chalkboard and chalk or equivalent
- Crayons or markers
- Dictionary (optional)

Getting Ready

- Explain the concept of palindromes to the class:
- Palindromes are words, phrases, or sentences that are spelled the same both left to right and right to left. In palindromes, the letters appear in the same sequence, both forward and backward without regards to punctuation or word breaks. They can be just one word, or a combination of words as in "Yes, I Am Maisey." Numbers can be palindromes too.
- Invite students to brainstorm aloud to create a classroom list of palindromes. Record their ideas on the board.

Activities and Procedures

1 Tell students that they will be writing their very own palindrome stories using as many palindrome words, phrases, or sentences as possible. Stories can be silly or serious, but should have some cohesion or meaning.

2 Inform students that they may refer to the list on the board or the list of story-starters for ideas, but encourage them to generate their own palindromes as well. Any original palindrome phrase or sentence is a praiseworthy achievement.

Palindromes: Yes, I Am Maisey *continues* ➜

continued from previous page

Mara sees a ram.

A ram sees Mara

Palindrome Phrases And Sentences: Story Starters

A mama sees a papa; a papa sees a mama	Ma has a ham
A man, a plan, a canal: Panama	Ma is as selfless as I am
A tin mug for a jar of gum, Nita	Mara sees a ram; a ram sees Mara
An "it" sees Tina; Tina sees an "it"	Marta sees a tram
Aris gags Ira	Mia did aim
A Santa at NASA	Ned's den
Avid diva	No lemon, no melon
Ay, a papa sees a papaya	No pans did snap on
Bonk a knob	Pam's map
Bonk on no knob	Pots did stop
Dennis sinned	Pull up
Did I? I did	Step on no pets
Don did nod	Stop on no pots
Don't nod	Strap on no parts
Edit a tide	Spit on no tips
Enid did dine	Swap paws
Evil yams may live	Tara sees a rat; a rat sees Tara
I'm, alas, a salami	Tim's mit
I saw; Mum was I	Top level pot
Leena sees an eel - An eel sees Leena	Trap a part
Llama sees a mall	Was it a car or a cat I saw?
Liar's rail	Xona sees an ox; an ox sees Xona

3 When students have finished writing, invite them to go back through their drafts and underline every palindrome word, phrase, or sentence they used.

4 Discuss the concept of symmetry as it relates to palindromes.

5 Encourage students to illustrate their favorite palindromes by creating drawings that include some symmetrical elements.

6 Allow students to share their palindrome stories with the class and encourage open discussion.

Extensions
- Have students create a classroom picture dictionary or alphabet book of palindromes.
- Invite students to draw a scene filled with many images of palindromes, and add captions.
- Encourage students to work together to design a class mural of palindromes with captions.

Grade Level: 2 through 6
Participants: Individuals or small teams
Objectives: Exercise fluency, flexibility, spelling, vocabulary, and language skills
Time: 1 to 2 hours

Quick View

In this "punny" activity, students learn about homophones, homonyms, and puns while using their writing skills to create whimsical story panels.

Example

See next page.

Take Home

Enhanced language skills and a whimsical storyboard to develop into a picture book or skit

Materials

- Pencil
- Plain paper, 8½″ x 11″ or larger
- Chalkboard and chalk or equivalent
- Colored pencils (optional)
- "The King Who Rained" and "A Chocolate Moose for Dinner" by Fred Gwynne (optional)

Getting ready

- Write the following words and definitions on the board. You can use the examples listed or come up with your own:
  - **Homonyms** – Homonyms are words that sound the same and are spelled the same but have different meanings. *For example, the word "bark," meaning the sound made by a dog, and the word "bark," meaning the outer covering of a tree, are homonyms.*
  - **Homophones** – Homophones are words that sound the same but are spelled differently and have different meanings. *For example, the words "dear" and "deer" are homophones.*
  - **Puns** – A pun is a humorous play on words which includes terms or phrases that have multiple meanings or similar sounds. *For example, a baby bib that reads, "Peas on Earth" is a pun which plays on the common phrase, "Peace on Earth."*
- List some homonyms and homonyms on the board. Refer to the examples listed in the sidebar, "50 Homonyms & Homophones".
- Invite students to add their own examples to the list.

> ### Just For Pun
>
> Some people believe that puns are the lowest form of humor and that hearing a pun is pun-ishment for the ears. Many creative people, however, view puns as brilliant forms of humorous expression.
>
> If you write or speak in puns, you are a pun-dit. Relatives of pundits are pun-kins.

Ra**pun**zel,
Ra**pun**zel,
let down
your hair.

homophone:
hair / hare

Mom said
I had to
walk four
blocks to
school.

homonym:
blocks / blocks

A Play Date with Words *continues* ➜

continued from previous page

50 Homonyms & Homophones

Homonyms

bark/bark	fair/fair	play/play	second/second
bat/bat	fine/fine	right/right	slip/slip
box/box	light/light	ring/ring	tie/tie
check/check	pitcher/pitcher	run/run	yard/yard

Homophones

ant/aunt	herd/ heard	one /won	sun/son
bare/bear	hole/whole	pear/pair	tail/tale
beat/beet	maid/made	piece/peace	threw/through
deer/dear	meat/meet	rain/reign/rein	two/to/too
eight/ate	might/mite	red/read	wear /where /ware
eye/I	missed/mist	rowed/rode	wood /would
feet/feat	need/knead	sail/sale	write/right/rite
flower/flour	night/ knight	see/sea	
great/grate	no/know	sight/site	

Activities and Procedures

1 Discuss homophones, homonyms, and puns with the class. Be sure to emphasize the differences between these similar concepts.

2 Optional: Share "The King Who Rained" and "A Chocolate Moose for Dinner" by Fred Gwynne with the class.

3 Inform students that they will be creating their own "punny" scenarios using homonyms, homophones, and puns.

4 Instruct students to divide their papers into four sections to create two double panels.

5 Have students use scrap paper to brainstorm some quirky situations in which characters experience misunderstandings as a result of homophones, homonyms, and puns.

6 Ask students to write at least two sentences each using a homophone or homonym. Encourage students to sketch out 'word play' concepts on scrap paper based on their sentences. The sketches should show the other meaning of the homophone or homonym.

7 Once students have decided on a few ideas, have them fill in the double panels with sentences on the left and illustrations on the right.

8 Suggest that students sketch and write lightly to begin with and darken the lines in later when their ideas have been fully refined. Students may also use colored pencils to add color if they wish.

9 Instruct students to write the homophone and/or homonym pairs they use on the bottom of the sentence panel.

10 Display the finished story panels in your classroom.

Extensions
- Invite students to write and illustrate a classroom homophone book.
- Have students write short stories using five or more homophone or homonym pairs.
- Encourage student teams to create "A Play on Words" skit which illustrates the scenarios developed in their story panels.
- Invite students to read the "Amelia Bedelia" book series by Peggy Parish as inspiration for their own "wordplay" scenarios.

Illustration adapted from "John Martin's Book,
The Child's Magazine," originally published 1920

Raining Cats and Dogs Stories

Grade Level: 3 through 6
Participants: Individuals or teams of two
Objectives: Exercise originality, elaboration, imagination, understanding figurative language, and creative writing skills
Time: Approximately 1 hour

Quick View

This creative writing venture allows students to discover figurative language through the lenses of their own imaginations. Using the literal meaning of a commonly used expression, students compose a folklore story explaining the fictitious "origins" of the idiomatic expression.

Example

Put Yourself in Her Shoes

Long ago, when people owned only one pair of shoes, there was a girl named Wanda who left for school every morning but never ever got there.

She told her mother that her shoes would not move in that direction. "That's silly, you naughty daughter," said her mother. "Tomorrow, I will wear your shoes and walk you to school. You will walk barefoot alongside me."

The next day Wanda and her mother started for school.

As soon as they started out, the woman skipped down the road in the wrong direction while her daughter chased after her. Wanda's mother could not control the shoes.

That evening, Wanda's mother wrote a note. "Dear School Principal, Now that *I put myself in her shoes*, I understand why Wanda does not make it to school. From now on, I will wrap her feet with twigs and leaves to replace those unruly shoes."

And that is how the expression, *put yourself in her shoes*, came into use.

Intended Meaning: The expression *put yourself in her shoes* is used to encourage someone to view something from another person's perspective. For example, you think Joe is stupid because he doesn't ride a bike. But, if you *"put yourself in his shoes,"* you'd realize that because Joe has a sister with special needs, his family cannot afford to get him a bike. Then, instead of thinking he's stupid, you might admire Joe for being unselfish.

Take Home

An original folklore story and an increased understanding of figurative language

Materials
- Pens or pencils
- Paper
- Chalkboard and chalk or equivalent
- Drawing materials (optional)

Getting Ready
- Explain the word "idiom" to the class. Write the following definition on the board:
  Idiom- a commonly used phrase that has a figurative meaning and is not meant to be taken literally
- List some common idiomatic expressions on the board. Ask students to brainstorm more idioms to add to the list. You may use the ones in the sidebar, "Some Common Idiomatic Expressions," or come up with your own:

Activities and Procedures

1 Ask each student to select a common idiomatic expression and write it at the top of their paper. They may choose one from the list or think of their own.

2 Invite students to ponder both the literal and figurative meaning of the expression.

3 Encourage students to use the literal meaning to write an imaginative folklore story explaining how the expression came into use.

4 Suggest that students end their story with a sentence such as: *This is how the expression,*

_____

became part of our language.

5 When students have completed their narratives, ask them to write a brief explanation of the expression's *intended* meaning and give an example of how it might be used.

6 Give students the opportunity to enhance their stories with colorful illustrations (optional)

Extensions
- Have students create skits based on their folklore stories.
- Encourage students to use their stories to make picture books.

Some Common Idiomatic Expressions

- A horse of another color
- Big fish in a small pond
- Don't rock the boat
- Drive me up a wall
- Fall down on the job
- Get the ball rolling
- Get the show on the road
- Have a green thumb
- Have your cake and eat it too
- Hit the books
- Hold your horses
- Knock your socks off
- Let the cat out of the bag
- Put yourself in her shoes
- Raining cats and dogs
- Spill the beans
- The bee's knees
- The cat's pajamas
- That's the way the cookie crumbles
- Wake up on the wrong side of the bed

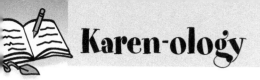

Grade Level: 3 through 8
Participants: Individuals
Objectives: Exercise fluency, flexibility, originality, phonemic awareness, understanding phonics, spelling.
Time: 15 to 30 minutes

Quick View

In this lesson in creative spelling, students learn to analyze phonetic sounds as they create as many alternate spellings for their names as they can find. Students may borrow a few unusual spellings that are found in the English language, such as the pn in pneumonia. Nancy, for example, might be spelled "Pnancy." Remember the silent "k" found in "knot" as another way to spell Knancy. The phonetic sound of the name Nancy could also be spelled Nanci, Nancee, Nansey, and so forth. Students are encouraged to explore every sound possibility found within the English language.

Example

See sidebar, "123 Ways to Spell Karen."

Take Home

New ways to spell your name, just for the phunn of it

Materials

- Chalk and chalkboard or equivalent
- Pencils
- Paper

Getting Ready

- Display the upper and lower case alphabet as reminders of letter possibilities to students.
- Review the long and short sounds of the vowels, vowel pairs, silent letters, and consonants that have more than one sound, such as "c" and "g."

Karen   Carynn   Kherrin

Activities and procedures

1 Ask students to write their first names across the top of a sheet of paper. Then add a hyphen and the suffix "ology." Explain to them that "ology" means "the study of."

2 Inform the class that they will be searching the alphabet to invent as many ways as they can to create the phonetic sound of their first names. Students who have short first names may use middle or last names if they prefer.

3 Encourage students to create a minimum of six alternate spellings for each name, and to stretch their imaginations to create as many spellings as possible.

4 Remind students that they may borrow unusual spellings for phonetic sounds that occur in the English language, such as "pn" at the beginning of the word "pneumonia." If you are Nicole, you could list "Pnicole" with a silent "p" as an alternate spelling for your name. The word, "rough" uses "ough" to represent an "f" sound. If you are Stephan perhaps you could also spell your name "Steoughan!"

5 Invite students to share their favorite and funniest alternate spellings with their classmates.

123 Ways to Spell Karen (and there are more)

1	Caerenn	32	Carrin	63	Kairren	94	Kayrynn
2	Caerhyn	33	Carryn	64	Kairrin	95	Kearenn
3	Caerhynn	34	Caryn	65	Kairryn	96	Kearin
4	Caerin	35	Carynne	66	Kairyn	97	Kearinn
5	Caerinn	36	Cayran	67	Kairynne	98	Kearren
6	Caerrin	37	Cayrann	68	Karahn	99	Kearrin
7	Caeryn	38	Cayren	69	Karahnn	100	Kearynn
8	Caerynn	39	Cayrenn	70	Karan	101	Kearynn
9	Cairen	40	Cayrhin	71	Karehn	102	Kehren
10	Cairenn	41	Cayrin	72	Karen	103	Kehrenn
11	Cairin	42	Cayrinn	73	Karenn	104	Kehrinn
12	Cairinn	43	Cayryn	74	Karhen	105	Kehryn
13	Cairren	44	Kaairin	75	Karhin	106	Kerehn
14	Cairrin	45	Kaerenn	76	Karhinn	107	Kerihn
15	Cairryn	46	Kaerhyn	77	Karin	108	Kerrehn
16	Cairyn	47	Kaerhynn	78	Karinn	109	Kerrihn
17	Cairynn	48	Kaerin	79	Karrahn	110	Kharen
18	Carahn	49	Kaerinn	80	Karrehn	111	Kharenn
19	Carahnn	50	Kaerrin	81	Karren	112	Kharinn
20	Carehn	51	Kaeryn	82	Karrin	113	Kharren
21	Caren	52	kaerynn	83	Karyn	114	Kharrin
22	Carenn	53	Kahran	84	Karynne	115	Kharyn
23	Carhen	54	Kahren	85	Kayran	116	Kharynn
24	Carhenn	55	Kahrenn	86	Kayran	117	Kharynne
25	Carhin	56	Kahrin	87	Kayren	118	Khayren
26	Carhinn	57	Kahrinn	88	Kayren	119	Khayrenn
27	Carhynn	58	Kahrren	89	Kayrenn	120	Khayrin
28	Carin	59	Kahryn	90	Kaeren	121	Khayrinn
29	Carinn	60	Kairen	91	Kaeryn	122	Kherin
30	Carrahn	61	Kairenne	92	Kayrin	123	Kherrin
31	Carrehn	62	Kairinne	93	Kayrinn		

Extensions

• Ask students to list their name spellings in alphabetical order.
• Invite students to create alternate spellings for friends and family members.

Notes

Music Awareness

Whatsit Music

MA-01

Grade Level: 1 through 6
Participants: Small or large group
Objectives: Exercise fluency, flexibility, sound and rhythm awareness, personal expression
Time: 15 to 30 minutes

Quick View

Students are given a group of objects such as sandpaper, empty soda cans, jars, or rulers. Working in small teams, students use them to create an improvised musical instrument and develop a sequence of sounds and rhythms.

Take Home

Students may decorate and name their improvised musical instruments, and take them home (optional).

Materials

Found objects that can be used for making sounds. Suggestions:

- Cardboard
- Combs
- Drinking straws
- Empty boxes
- Empty soda cans
- Erasers
- Glass jars
- Paper clips in a box
- Paper cups
- Paper towel tubes
- Pencils
- Plastic tubs of various sizes
- Popsicle sticks
- Retractable ball point pens
- Rolled up paper
- Rubber bands
- Sandpaper
- Sticks and stones
- Wax paper

Use anything that can make a sound.

Getting Ready

- Gather objects and divide them among teams of two to four students. Teams do not need to have the same items. Students should try to think of additional things for making interesting sounds.

Activities and Procedures

1 Discuss rhythm.

  Rhythms are all around us: bouncing balls, raindrops, feet jumping rope, clapping hands. Ask the class for more examples.

  Rhythm consists of sounds and silences. Sounds and silences together form patterns of sound, such as beat, silence, beat, silence, beat, beat. Tap the desk to demonstrate the pattern.

  When patterns are repeated they create what is called rhythm. Tap the desk to repeat the above pattern three times. A rhythm has a steady beat in a pattern.

  Beats can be loud or soft, long or short, and separated by silences or in quick succession.

2 Ask students to think of several word phrases, like "apple pie and cherry cola," "oh little playmate, come out and play with me," "a sailor went to sea, sea, sea," "Tarzan Jungle Man, swinging from a rubber band." Ask students to tap the beats as they repeat the phrase silently to themselves.

3 Using their objects as musical instruments, teams develop interesting rhythmic patterns by using the beats of a phrase for inspiration. Soundmakers may be used together or one at a time.

4 Teams perform rhythms for each other.

Extension

- Teams work cooperatively with each other in tapping a phrase. For example, "ap-ple-pie and" is tapped by team A and "Cher-ry-co-la" is tapped by team B.

"Music is the art
of thinking with
sounds."
– Jules Combarie

Grade Level: 3 through 8
Participants: Individuals or any size group
Objectives: Exercise flexibility, originality, new uses, sound awareness, understanding rhythm, music appreciation, manual dexterity.
Time: 2 to 3 hours

Quick View

Students are challenged to find things at home or in the classroom to adapt into percussion sound makers. They make their own "Boom-bas" and thump and jingle in time to any music played.

Example

See illustration

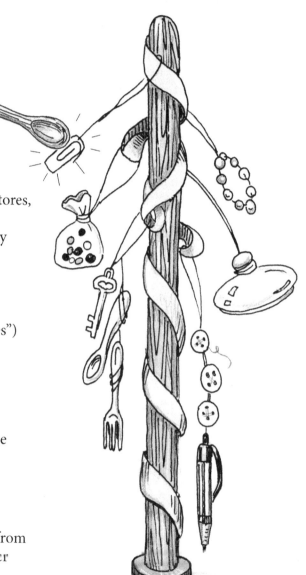

Take Home

A folk art music maker to accompany any music you hear.

Materials

- Broomstick or equivalent. Options are yardsticks, other "big sticks" found in thrift stores or dollar stores, dowels, or possibly sturdy tree branches if they're smooth. Make sure there are no splinters or pointy parts.
- Duct tape
- Rubber stool leg cap or pad of felt and glue
- Yarn, string, ribbon, or equivalent
- Jingly things to tie on (see sidebar, "All That Jingles")
- Rulers, drumsticks, or wooden spoons

Getting Ready

- Gather the boom-ba materials.
- Younger students may need help preparing the broomstick spine with tape onto which to hang the jinglers.

Activities and Procedures

1. Preparing The Boom-ba Spine
   - Use a broomstick as the spine. Either detach it from the bristles or turn it upside down. Add a rubber cap or glue a pad of felt to the bottom so it will muffle the sound and protect the floor as you stomp it. Wrap the spine with heavy duct tape. Twist parts of the tape to leave loose parts through which you can tie jinglers. (See illustration this page.)

2 Adding Jinglers
- Tie anything that makes noise to the boom-ba spine, covering it from top to bottom and all around.
- Use the loose parts of the tape to loop a string through.
- Tie jingly things to the other ends of the strings so they swing and make noise as you stomp your boom-ba or use a drumstick or ruler to strike it.

3 Musical Fun
- Play or sing any kind of lively music and ask the class to stomp their boom-bas to the beat or strike it with a wooden spoon. Country, folk, and polka music are especially good choices, but there are no rules.
- Invite each boom-ba player to show off their creation solo for a few beats, so the class can hear the differences in each other's boom-ba sounds.

Extensions

- *Make a "Hanger Banger"*: Wrap a plastic hanger with yarn or strips of cloth. Tie a fabric loop to the top of the hanger hook to use as a handle. Tie onto the bottom horizontal portion anything that jingles: spoons, paper clips, pens, bells, keys, and so forth. Thump and jingle in time to any music played.
- *Holiday Spirit*: Decorate Boom-bas and Hanger Bangers for holidays by painting some jinglers, using colored ribbons, adding colorful streamers and trims, and so forth.
- *Parade*: Treat other schoolmates to a Boom-ba and Hanger Banger parade through your school yard. Wear funny hats as well.

The Pennsylvania Beat

The Leather Corner Post Hotel in the Lehigh Valley of Pennsylvania has been famous for its "boom-ba" music for decades. Boom-bas are country music contraptions covered with cowbells, swinging bottle caps, and a clutter of other noisemakers for keeping beat to the music played. The boom-ba tradition was inspired by earlier folk instruments seen in German villages.

Boom-bas are folk art creations, and no two are ever alike. These percussion instruments are the personal expressions of the musicians who make them.

To play the boom-ba, just thump and jingle in time to the music. Boom-bas are often struck with a drumstick or wooden spoon to the beat of the music.

No two boom-bas will sound alike, and a group of boom-bas makes a unique musical feast.

All That Jingles

baby rattles	nuts & bolts
bags of beans	paper clips
bottle caps	pens & pencils
broken toys	pie plates
buttons	pot lids
chains	safety pins
clothespins	sleigh bells
coins in a sock	spools
combs	spoons & forks
cowbells	strings of beads
keys	tambourines

TIP: Look through disposable stuff at home or search dollar stores and thrift stores for interesting things that clack and jingle.

Grade Level: 3 through 8
Participants: Teams of two to four or individuals
Objectives: Exercise flexibility, originality, elaboration, team cooperation, creative writing, rhyming, and rhythm.
Time: 1 to 1½ hours

Quick View

Students write original stanzas for *The Blue Tail Fly*, an American folksong that dates back to the 1840s. Writing teams use Object Cards for generating lyric ideas, while touching on the technical aspects of songwriting, such as rhyme patterns, rhythm, meter, and repetition.

Examples

These are typical examples written by students. For traditional lyrics see, "The Blue Tail Fly: Survivor of the Civil War" on pg. 164.

My Blue Tail Fly Lyrics

Book

I read a book on Saturday,
About a worm in White Fish Bay,
What a story; it made me cry,
And wipe away the blue tail fly.

Hammer

I had a hammer in my hand,
I hammered rock down into sand,
I hammered till the sun rolled by,
And hammered on a blue tail fly.

Gumball Machine

Gumballs are yellow, green, and blue,
Good flavors make you want to chew,
And blow big bubbles so round, and high,
But don't inhale the blue tail fly.

Take Home

An original version of an American folk song

Materials

- Pencils
- Paper
- Chalkboard and chalk or equivalent
- Object Cards (see *Reproducibles*, pg. 320)
- Sound of the tune through media, voice, or musical instruments
- Rhyming dictionary (optional)

Vocabulary Words

- Folk Music
- Line
- Lyric
- Melody
- Refrain
- Repetition
- Rhyme
- Rhyming Pattern
- Rhythm
- Stanza

Getting Ready

- Write the meter for a stanza on the board.
- Write the meter for the last line of a stanza, ending with the words, "the blue tail fly" on the board.
- List some rhymes for "fly" (optional).
- Make copies of the lyrics (optional).

Activities and Procedures

1 Introduce the folksong, *The Blue Tail Fly*, to the class. Tell them that the teams are to write one or more new stanzas for the song (see Examples).
   Cadence
      The lyrics follow the cadence, da **Da** da **Da** da **Da** da **Da**.
      Four lines per stanza.
   Rhyming Pattern
      First two lines rhyme.
      Last two lines rhyme, and must end in the words, *the blue tail fly*.
   Refrain
      The refrain is repeated after each verse

2 Divide the class into teams of two to four. Randomly distribute one Object Card to each team. Tell the teams that are to use their objects for the subjects of their stanzas.

3 Each team member has a few minutes to jot down words, phrases, associations, and ideas about their object. They write independently, but combine their work when the time is up.

4 Drawing from their pool of ideas, the teams collaborate on writing the lyrics. They brainstorm lyric ideas while following the rhyming pattern and meter of the song. Inform the teams that they may need to eliminate and change many ideas as they formulate lyrics that fit the song.

5 Instruct students on how to use a rhyming dictionary, or have them brainstorm a list of words that rhyme with "fly." They may need to find other rhymes, as well, as they develop their lyrics.

   NOTE: The meaning of the lyrics does not have to be realistic, but it should make sense within its context.

6 When teams have completed their stanzas, the teacher should check them for meter and rhyming patterns, and have them make corrections as needed. Approved stanzas should be written neatly on separate pieces of paper.

New Tales of Blue Tails *continues* →

continued from previous page

The Blue Tail Fly: Survivor of The Civil War

This folksong was written in the 1840's and is still popular today. It is believed to have African American origins, but the author is unknown. Abraham Lincoln was an admirer of the tune and it is likely he played it on his harmonica.

The blue-tail fly in the song is a species of horse-fly that thrived in the American South, and carried disease. Historians debate the meaning of the lyrics, "Jimmy Crack Corn." Among the explanations, this one appeals most: In 1840 the word "Jimmy" was slang for a crow. The phrase refers to crows feeding in the cornfields. It was a slave's responsibility to keep crows out of the corn, but with the master away, the song's narrator (a slave) didn't care.

New versions of the song have been performed by Johnny and the Hurricanes, Vanessa Redgrave, Bugs Bunny, The Smothers Brothers, Burl Ives, Pete Seeger, and humorist Allan Sherman. You can hear the tune on the Internet.

When I was young I used to wait,
On the boss and hand him his plate,
And pass down the bottle when he got dry,
And brush away the blue tail fly.

Refrain (repeated each verse):

Jimmy crack corn and I don't care,
Jimmy crack corn and I don't care,
Jimmy crack corn and I don't care,
My master's gone away.

One day he rode around de farm,
De flies so numerous they did swarm,
One chance to bite him on de thigh,
De devil take de blue tail fly.

De pony run, he jump and pitch,
And tumble master in de ditch,
He died, and de jury wondered why,
De verdict was de blue tail fly.
[Traditional Lyrics Abridged]

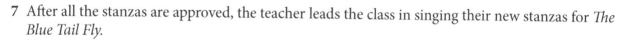

7 After all the stanzas are approved, the teacher leads the class in singing their new stanzas for *The Blue Tail Fly.*

8 Start with the whole class singing the traditional first stanza and the refrain, then a student team stanza and the refrain (whole class), another student team stanza, the refrain (whole class), and so on.

9 Collect all the stanzas and keep them together for future performances.

Extensions

- Follow the lesson plan, eliminating the Object Cards, and adapting *The Boll Weevil Song* lyrics and meter. See next page, "The Boll Weevil Song." You can hear the tune on the internet.
- Tie-in with a unit on American history.
- Tie-in with a unit on folk music.
- Tie-in with a science unit on insects.

The Boll Weevil Song: Survivor of The Great Depression

A boll weevil beetle infestation destroyed American cotton crops in the 1920's and 30's, adding to the economic devastation of the Great Depression. The origins of this traditional blues song are unclear. Carl Sandburg performed the song in the 1920's, followed by Lead Belly, Bessie Smith, Woodie Guthrie, Burl Ives, Eddie Cochran, Brook Benton, Harry Belafonte, and others. There are several versions of the lyrics. Most verses feature interaction between the farmer and the Weevil. The farmer tries to eradicate the Weevil, and the Weevil tells the farmer that he's not going anywhere. You can hear the tune on the Internet.

The first time I saw little Weevil,
He was on the Western Plain,
Next time I saw the Weevil,
He was riding a Memphis train.

He was looking for a home,
Just looking for a home.

When the farmer saw those Boll Weevils,
They were in his rocking chair,
The next time they were in his cornfield,
And they had all their family there.

Just fixing up a home,
Yes, fixing up a home.

The Boll Weevil say to the farmer,
"You can ride in that Ford machine,
But when I get through with your cotton,
You can't buy gasoline."

You won't have a home,
Won't have a home.

Well, the farmer took the Boll Weevil,
And put him in a frying pan,
Well the Weevil said to the farmer,
"This is warm and I'll take it like a man."

This will be my home,
This will be my home.

Well, the farmer took the Boll Weevil,
And put him on a block of ice,
Well the Weevil said to the farmer,
"This is mighty cool and nice."

This will be my home,
This will be my home.

Well, the farmer took the Boll Weevil,
And put him in the toxin sprays,
Well the Weevil said to the farmer,
"This will not affect my ways."

This will be my home,
This will be my home.

Well if anybody should ask you,
Who it was that sang this song,
Say a guitar picker from a down-south city,
With raggedy blue jeans on.

Just looking for a home,
Just looking for a home.

"Just fixin' up a home"

Changing Your Tune

Grade Level: 3 through 8
Participants: Teams of two to four are best, but individuals or larger teams can work, too.
Objectives: Exercises flexibility, originality, elaboration, understanding volume, tempo, and rhythm, awareness of musical moods and styles, lyric writing.
Time: 1 to 2 hours

Quick View

In this lesson in musical moods, student teams start with a well-known song and select a new style for transforming and performing the song. Students learn to vary tempo and rhythm as they create an alternate arrangement and adapt lyrics for turning a familiar song into an original musical piece.

Examples

Rap lyrics and beat:

Cha Cha lyrics and beat:

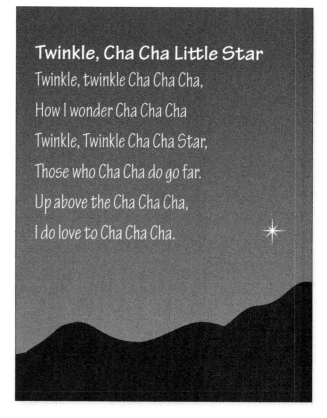

Take Home

An original arrangement of a song to perform for friends and family

Materials
- Various music styles you can play for your class using a piano, a computer, a CD player, or other device
- Chalk and chalkboard or equivalent
- Drumstick or equivalent

Getting Ready
- List a few musical styles on the board (see sidebar, "Song Styles"). Students may wish to add more.
- Gather various song style examples to play for your students.
- List some titles of songs that most students know, such as:
  - Happy Birthday
  - If I Had A Hammer
  - Oh, Susanna
  - Over The Rainbow
  - Take Me Out To The Ballgame
  - Twinkle, Twinkle Little Star
  - Who Let The Dogs Out?
  - Yankee Doodle
  - YMCA
  - You Are My Sunshine

Song Styles

50's Rock 'n' Roll	Folk	Pop
Asian Styles	Gospel	Ragtime
Ballad	Hard Rock	Railroad Songs
Big Band	Hawaiian	Rap
Bluegrass	Heavy Metal	Reggae
Blues	Hillbilly	Rondo (singing rounds)
Boogie	Hip Hop	Scat
Broadway	Improvisational Jazz	Sea Shanties
Calypso	Irish Jig	Soul
Cha Cha	Latin Beats	Swing
Chorale	Marching	Waltz
Country Western	New Age	Yodel
Cowboy	Opera	...and more
Disco	Patriotic	
Doo-Wop	Polka	

Changing Your Tune *continues* ➜

continued from previous page

And That's a Rap

Rap music is an improvisational style where spontaneously chanted rhymes are accompanied by a beat. Rappers use their voices as drums, with emphasis on the off beat.

The key to rap music is letting your emotions shape the song while using a beat to accent your words. You can be humorous, eloquent, or outrageous as long as you express true feelings. You don't need to be a master poet to be a rap artist, but you do need a message that you feel passionately about.

Sometimes rap artists find subject matter in daily activities, like walking to school. A verbal description becomes a lively rap song by adding a beat to the words. For example:

"I was SKIPping down the street, hopping to a BEAT, stamping on a CURB when a kid said HEY. I said hey, do you RAP? Do you rap, TAP or SNAP? Let's hop, bop, and flop down the street toDAY, let's rap a tap, snap a lap to school TOGETHER this WAY."

Whatever your subject matter, keep your expression highly emotional. It's great fun to rap with friends, too.

Activities and Procedures

1 Explain to your students the definitions of *volume* (loudness and softness), *tempo* (fast or slow) and *rhythm* (patterns of beats).

2 Demonstrate some types of rhythms using a drumstick.

3 Explain to your students that changing the volume, tempo, and rhythm of a song can transform it into a distinctively different song.

4 Explain that changing the lyrics adds to the transformation. Students may change the lyrics entirely or partially.

5 Divide your students into small teams, which we'll call *groups*. Ask each group to select a name for themselves, as professional music groups do. Examples are Maroon 5, Coldplay, or Fun.

6 Invite each group to select a familiar song. They may refer to the list or choose a song on their own.

7 Have each group select a song style *other than their song's original style*. They may refer to the style list or come up with their own.

8 Challenge the groups to adapt lyrics, tempo, volume, or rhythm to their selected style. They need to make some changes, but they do not need to change everything.

9 Encourage students to research their chosen style, and find out the characteristics of their style to use in their new arrangement. (See sidebar, "And That's a Rap," for an example of style research.)

10 Groups should develop their new arrangement, and practice singing it until they are ready to perform for their classmates. Groups may add percussion accompaniment of their choice.

11 Stage a classroom concert.

Extensions

- Invite musical groups to add instrumental accompaniment to their song arrangements.
- Challenge two or more groups to use the same song, but assign each group a different style to arrange. It's surprising fun to hear the variety that results.
- Challenge each group to add body language to their song performances, as if they were performing a video enactment. For further creative challenge, have the groups create their own videos of their performances.

"The poorest person
is not without a cent,
but without a dream."
– Anonymous

Grade Level: 1 through 6
Participants: One or more teams of four or more
Objectives: Exercise flexibility, originality, imagination, and awareness of sounds
Time: 15 to 30 minutes

Quick View

This lesson in creative sound making relies on every student's participation and cooperation as they each sing a note that other students use to compose simple melodies.

Taking turns, three or more students create a human xylophone that another student "plays" as they write an original song.

Take Home
An imaginative new game of sounds to play with friends and family.

Materials
- Xylophone or piano, or equivalent (optional)

Getting Ready
- Divide your class into teams of four to eight.

Do   Re   Mi   Fa

Activities and Procedures

1 Ask the students in each team to stand side by side in line with one hand outstretched in front of them.

2 Select one student of the team to be the player/composer.

3 Each remaining student represents a note on the xylophone. Ask the first person to sing a low note and remember it. Then ask the next student to sing a little higher note and remember it, the next sings an even higher note, and so forth. The progression should be balanced depending on how many student-notes the xylophone has.

4 Now ask the students to sing Do, Re, Mi, Fa, So, La, Ti, Do using their note.

5 When the player/composer taps an outstretched hand, that student must sing their word-note. Each student must continue singing their note for a long as their hand is touched. It can be a long continuous sound, or short staccato sounds.

6 The player composer creates a melody by "playing" the classmate xylophone, repeating notes and choosing the rhythm.

7 Students rotate turns being the player/composer and being a note on the xylophone.

Extensions

- Challenge students to sing the letters of the musical scale: A, B, C, D, E, F, G. Make sure the pitch is correct.
- Students may sing their names.
- Students may sing "scat" vocal sounds.
- Students make animal sounds instead of notes.
- In a large class, have two classmate xylophones playing in harmony with each other.

"Happiness lies in the joy of achievement, in the thrill of creative effort."
– Franklin D. Roosevelt

Grade Level: 1 through 8
Participants: three or more
Objectives: Exercise fluency, flexibility, originality, and recognizing and remembering rhythm patterns
Time: Approximately ½ hour

Quick View

In this lesson in musical amusement, each classmate invents sounds by using their hands and voice, and participates in a round-robin circle of sound making and rhythm repetitions and creations. Students copy each participant before them, and add an original sound and rhythm, as well.

Example

Soundmaker I

Clap, clap, whistle. Clap, clap, whistle.

Soundmaker II

Clap, clap, whistle. Clap, clap, whistle.
Croak, whistle. Croak, whistle. Croak, whistle.

Soundmaker III

Clap, clap, whistle. Clap, clap, whistle.
Croak, whistle. Croak, whistle. Croak, whistle.
Wa, wa, wa, slap, wa. Wa, wa, wa, slap, wa.

Soundmaker IV

Clap, clap, whistle. Clap, clap, whistle.
Croak, whistle. Croak, whistle. Croak, whistle.
Wa, wa, wa, slap, wa. Wa,wa, wa, slap, wa.
Beep, wa, wa. Beep, wa, wa. Beep, wa, wa.

And so on…

Take Home
A noisy fun game to play with friends that exercises sound awareness

Materials
- None needed

Getting Ready
- Have three or more participants sitting in a circle or across from one another.

Activities and Procedures

1 Explain to the class that each participant will invent sounds by using their hands and voice. They may slap, snap, clap, tap, whistle, snort, gurgle, or sing, making any sound or sound combination.

2 Invite the participants to sit in a circle. The first sound-maker creates a rhythm pattern from their sounds. The next sound-maker copies the sound/rhythm pattern, then adds their own new sound and rhythm. The third copies the first two, then adds their sound and rhythm, and so forth.

3 Continue on until there are too many rhythm patterns for the participants to remember. Participants who forget the rhythms, may drop out, until the last sound-maker is left to perform.

Extensions
- Challenge to use animal sounds only to create their rhythm patterns.
- Challenge students to use machine and vehicle sounds only to create their rhythm patterns.
- Challenge students to use weather sounds, such as wind, rain, waterfalls, and so forth to create their rhythm patterns.
- Challenge students to sing the letter name of their note, such as "a, b, c, d, e, f, or g."

Notes

Math Explorations

Grade Level: 3 through 6
Participants: Groups
Objectives: Exercise fluency, flexibility, math facts
Time: Approximately 15 to 45 minutes

Quick View

This is a fun math contest, with a creative thinking component. Teams of three students are given a short amount of time to come up with as many different ways as they can of reaching a three digit number.

Example

If the number is 256:

$$250 + 6 = 256$$
$$250 + 3 + 3 = 256$$
$$269 - 13 = 256$$
$$768 \div 3 = 256$$
$$64 \times 4 = 256$$

Take Home
A lot of math facts that equal the same number

Materials
- Paper
- Pencils
- Markers
- Clock or timer

Getting Ready
- On 3″ squares of paper, using a marker, write numbers from 0 to 9, one number per square.
- Create at least three sets or as many as needed to account for the number of students in the class.

Activities and Procedures

1 Organize students in teams of three.

2 Each student on the team picks a number from 0 to 9. The teams line up and reveal their numbers, creating a three-digit number. They may choose any arrangement of their three numbers. Each team does this at the same time.

3 Teams have three minutes to come up with as many different ways of reaching the number as they can. Students may use paper and pencils for working on this.

4 Teams must include at least one or two examples each of addition, subtraction, division, and multiplication.

5 When the time is up, the team who found the most correct equations, wins.

Extensions
- Higher grades may use combinations of addition, subtraction, multiplication, and division in one equation.
  Example: $31 + 993 \div 4 = 256$
- Lower grades may be limited to addition and subtraction.

"Don't let what
you cannot do
interfere with what
you can do."
– Anonymous

Math Cousins

ME-02

Grade Level: 3 through 8
Participants: Small or large groups or individuals.
Objectives: Exercise flexibility, finding connections, understanding numbers
Time: Approximately 15 to 30 minutes

Quick View

Each student picks a number from 0 to 20. In teams of three, students find relationships between the numbers they picked, looking for as many things in common as they can find. There will be some surprising results.

Examples

Team 1 picks 9, 3, and 15.

Things in common:

- The numbers are odd numbers
- The numbers cannot be divided by two
- The numbers can be divided by three
- The numbers are found on the calendar
- The numbers make pitiful bowling score totals

Team 2 picks 10, 13, and 20.

Things in common:

- The numbers are two-digit numbers
- The numbers are found on a yardstick
- The numbers end with a curved-line number shape
- The numbers can be multiplied by four and still remain two digit numbers
- The numbers begin with the letter "t" when spelled

Take Home
Some new points of view about numbers

Materials
- Pencils
- Paper
- Chalkboard and chalk or equivalent

Getting Ready

- On small squares of paper write number each from 0 to 20. You may need to number higher depending on the size of your class.
- Discuss "thinking outside the box." Numbers can be looked at from many points of view beyond the quantity they represent:

   Numbers are shapes, they have syllables and phonic sounds, they have spelling, they can be written in more than one writing system, they're associated with items like clocks, scales, and tape measures. They're associated with games, like cards and baseball scores. Numbers come to mind in many ways.

- Show some groups of numbers and what they have in common.

Activities and Procedures

1 Each student randomly picks a number from 0 to 20.

2 Students work in teams of three. Teams lay their three numbers side by side.

3 Teams spend ten to fifteen minutes collaborating on one master list of everything they can think of that their three numbers have in common.

4 Teams share their lists with the classroom.

Extensions

- *Have a Contest:* The team who lists the most relationships among their numbers, wins.
- Use only two numbers, or use more than three numbers.

"My right brain is dominating."

Grade Level: 1 through 4
Participants: Groups of twelve or more
Objectives: Exercise flexibility, addition, subtraction, organization, sequencing, and teamwork
Time: Approximately ½ hour

Quick View

This activity puts math in motion as students race against the clock to create human equations. While using their bodies to represent components of mathematical equations, students hone their cooperation skills as well as their knowledge of mathematical concepts.

Example

- Student 9 is the equation leader.
- The teacher calls out the number 22.
- Student 9 has one minute to choose students whose numbers and/or symbols can be combined with hers to create an equation resulting in the number 22.
- For example, the student might pick a student holding the number 7, one holding the number 6, as well as two students who hold the symbol +, and one student with the symbol =.
- Student 9 lines up with the others in front of the class and leads them in the act of arranging their numbers and symbols to solve the human equation.
- When the equation is complete, students announce their numbers and symbols in succession: 7 + 9 + 6 =" … After the student with the equal sign announces their symbol, the teacher asks the whole class to call out the number 22 together.

Take Home
Enhanced cooperation skills and a sensory memory of fundamental mathematical concepts

Materials
- Paper, approximately 8½″ x 11″, 25 sheets or more
- Black marker or similar
- Timer or equivalent

Getting Ready
- Using a dark-colored marker and plain paper, write the numbers 0-9 as well as the plus (+), minus (-), and equal (=) signs on individual sheets of paper. Be sure to make the characters large enough so that students can see them from afar, and make at least two sets.
- Give each student a number or symbol paper to hold. If you have a small number of students, give each student more than one paper to hold.

Activities and Procedures

1 Explain to students that they will be working in teams to create human equations.

2 Have students line up in number order, holding their numbers out in front of them. Instruct students holding symbols to take their places at the end of the line.

3 Choose a student to be the "equation leader" and call out a random number to represent the solution of the equation.

4 When the equation leader hears the number, they have one minute to walk up and down the line, pick one or more students whose numbers will combine to equal the number that was announced, and organize the numbers and symbols to create a feasible equation.

   NOTES:

   If a student is holding more than one number, the equation leader should choose one number and tell the student which one. The student should then place that number in front of the other numbers.

   The equal sign (=) and plus sign (+) or minus sign (-) will appear in every equation. Consider rotating these assignments with other players.

5 When the equation is complete, each student announces their number or symbol. After the equal sign is announced, the teacher leads the whole class in announcing the solution in unison.

6 Repeat the process until all students have had the opportunity to be the equation leader.

Extensions
- Have students complete the activity using multiplication or division equations.

Tell Sum Stories

Grade Level: 1 through 3
Participants: Groups of four or more
Objectives: Exercise originality, elaboration, storytelling, and mathematical skills
Time: 15 to 30 minutes

Quick View

In this fast-paced game of mathematical mayhem, students spontaneously generate word problems while passing a ball from one classmate to another. In doing so, students heighten their capacity for creativity while practicing both language and math skills.

Examples

Simple Stories:

- I have 4 erasers and 8 cookies equaling 12 things I like.
- I have 9 friends and 3 cousins equaling 12 people.
- I have 2 pencils and 2 violins equaling 4 things.

Elaborate Stories:

- I have 5 dogs and 2 bones equaling 5 things, but only 2 happy dogs.
- I have 10 books and 3 snakes equaling 13 things I keep in my room. Who wants to borrow a book?
- I have 7 cans of soup and 6 magnets equaling 13 pieces of metal. I can build a wall.

Take Home
Enhanced mathematical and language skills and a fun game to play with family and friends

Materials
- Paper, 8½″ x 11″, at least one per student
- Black marker
- Tape
- Chalkboard and chalk or equivalent
- Music or timer (optional)

Getting Ready
- Crumple paper to make three or more balls.
- Write several single-digit numbers on scrap paper and tape one number to each ball.
- Create number signs by using a black marker to write each of the numbers 0 to 10 on separate sheets of 5½" x 8½" paper. For a large class, make two sets or continue numbering up to 20.

Activities and Procedures

1 Explain to your class that they will be playing a game of addition, using equations and their sums to tell a story.

2 Have students sit or stand in a circle.

3 Distribute number signs randomly to students and have them hold the signs out in front of them.

4 Begin playing music or clapping your hands to a beat and have students pass their number signs from left to right to the rhythm.

5 At the same time, have students pass one of the crumpled paper balls in the opposite direction.

6 When the music/clapping stops, instruct the student holding the ball to add the number on the ball to the number they are holding.

7 Then, give the student fifteen seconds to tell "sum" story (either simple or elaborate) using the newly created equation. For example, the student might say "I have 3 socks and 2 shoes, making 5 things to wear on my feet. I hope to find my other sock."

8 Write the two objects used in the story (i.e. socks and shoes) on the board and instruct students not to use those words in their own stories.

9 Repeat the procedure, using a ball with a different number.

10 Eliminate those students who: cannot think of "sum" story within the time limit, use the words listed on the board, or add incorrectly.

11 Continue the game until only a few students are remaining, or until time runs out.

12 Award small prizes to the winners!

Extensions

- To make the game more challenging, have students create stories using double and triple digit numbers.
- Have older students complete the activity using subtraction, multiplication, or division instead of addition.

"I haven't failed.
I've found ten
thousand ways
that don't work."
– Benjamin Franklin

Magic Potion Recipes

Grade level: 2 through 6
Participants: Individuals
Objective: Exercise originality, elaboration, imagination, standard measurements, creative writing, and adding fractions
Time: 1 to 2 hours

Quick View

In this exercise in creative concocting, students practice math and measuring skills while developing imaginative recipes for magic potions. As students decorate jars to hold their potions, create recipe cards and make labels that describe their potions' powers, they heighten their capacity for creative thinking while strengthening their basic math skills as well.

Example

Magic Math Potion

This potion will triple your speed for completing math homework:

- one t (teaspoons) of silver beach sand (1 teaspoon)
- four T (tablespoons) of blue fairy wings (1/4 cups)
- three cups of muddy water (3 cups)
- 16 oz. self-rising stardust (2 cups)
- one quart imagination (4 cups)

Mix all the glittery ingredients together.

Add muddy water and imagination, and stir until blended.

Yield: 9 and ¼ cups plus one teaspoon total volume

Doubled recipe

- two t (teaspoons) of silver beach sand (2 teaspoons)
- eight T (tablespoons) of blue fairy wings (1/2 cups)
- 6 cups of muddy water (6 cups= 1 quart plus 1 pint)
- 32 oz. self-rising stardust (8 cups= 2 quarts)
- 2 quarts imagination (8 cups= ½ gallon or 2 quarts)

Double Yield: 18 ½ cups plus two teaspoons total volume = 1 1¼ quarts plus two teaspoons. Pour into jars.

A spoonful per day will increase your math skills.

Potions remain good for several decades.

Take Home

- Enhanced mathematical and creative thinking skills and a "magic potion" in a jar

Materials

- Pencils
- Paper
- Examples of recipes
- Index cards
- Markers or colored pencils
- Glue sticks
- Empty plastic jars
- Hole punch
- Ribbon or string
- Measurement chart (optional)

Ingredient Suggestions

- Beach sand
- Bee stingers
- Beetle fruit
- Blue apples
- Boggle flakes
- Boiled slime
- Chocolate songs
- Creature toes
- Creeping lizards
- Critter eyes
- Crushed fossils
- Crust of earth
- Dragon claws

- Dragonflies
- Dried hootberries
- Dried laughter
- Dried water
- Electric eels
- Fairy wings
- Fireflies
- Fly juice
- Fried tulips
- Giggle flakes
- Gingerweed
- Glow worms
- Green cheese

- Honey drops
- Jellyfish
- Lilly pads
- Liquid moonbeam
- Muddy water
- Music sprinkles
- Purple lemons
- Rainbow by the foot
- Rose petals
- Seaweed
- Sillyseeds
- Snake steak
- Sparkling lava

- Spider web
- Spiderfruit
- Stardust
- Starfish
- Summer breeze
- Sun pebbles
- Sunflowers
- Tiger teeth
- Toads
- Volcanic ash
- Wazzenmelon seeds

Magic Potion Recipes *continues* ➜

continued from previous page

Getting Ready

- Gather empty plastic jars, or ask your students to bring them in.
- Gather some recipes for student reference.
- Remind students of standard measurements such as teaspoons, tablespoons, cups, ounces, pounds, pints, quarts, gallons, and more. Display a measurement chart, or make a list on the board and write the appropriate abbreviations alongside each measurement.
- List some ideas for interesting ingredients on the board. You can use the ones in the sidebar, "Ingredient Suggestions," or come up with your own. Have students add their own ideas to the list as well.

Activities and Procedures

1 Explain to your students that they will create magic potions using standard measurements for the ingredients in their recipes.

2 Have students begin by brainstorming a list of magic powers they would like to have themselves or that they wish they could give to others.

3 After a few minutes of brainstorming, instruct students to choose one power from the list to use as the basis for their recipe.

4 Tell students to begin planning their recipes by choosing their ingredients and measurements.

5 Encourage students to select interesting and imaginative ingredients for their recipes. They may come up with their own or choose some from the list on the board.

6 Instruct students to include at least four ingredients and several different measurements, one of which must be a fraction.

7 When the recipe itself is complete, ask students to calculate the total yield and provide instructions for doubling the recipe as well.

8 Next, have students create recipe cards by transferring their instructions onto index cards. Allow students to decorate the borders and give their recipes creative titles.

Use either 3˝ x 5˝ or 5˝ x 7˝ unlined index cards

9   After the recipe cards are complete, invite students to design labels for their jars. Each label should feature the name of the potion in large letters and should be glued to the side of the jar.

10   You may also allow students to fill their jars with sand, mud, stones, leaves, tinted water, soap bubbles, or anything else you have on hand. Students may also wish to decorate their jars with acrylic paint or stickers to make them even more interesting and visually appealing (optional).

11   Have students fold the recipe cards in half, punch a hole in the cards, and tie them to the jars with ribbon or string.

12   Display all the magic potion jars together on a shelf and give students the opportunity to comment on one another's work.

Extensions

- Invite students to create a story featuring a character who is transformed by their newly created magic potion.
- Have students create word problems by combining their magic potions to create even more powerful concoctions.

Creative Currency

Grade Level: 2 through 6
Participants: Teams of two to four
Objectives: Exercise originality, elaboration, basic math skills, understanding monetary systems, social studies, and visual arts
Time: Approximately 1 hour

Quick View

In this exercise in creative money-making, students devise their own financial systems by designing original coins and paper certificates. Through the process of establishing denominations, issuing parties, and tangible storehouses, students practice their creative thinking and mathematical skills while learning more about our own monetary system.

Example

The Students of the 7 Seas

This monetary system is based on the number 7.

- Their money is secured by a storehouse of fish bones kept in seven "Financially Fish" buildings around the world.
- They call their coins "sots".
- They have five sots: 1s, 7s, 14s, 28s, and 70s (the lower case "s" is used as a symbol for "sots")
- They call their paper notes "fins."
- They have three fins: ^^^1.40, ^^^14.00, and ^^^35.00 (^^^ is the symbol for fins and is equal to dollars ($))
- Sots that will equal a ^^^1.40 fins are:
  - Two 70s
  - Five 28s
  - Ten 14s
  - Twenty 7s
  - One hundred and forty 1s
  - Three 14s, one 28s, and one 70s
  - Two 28s, one 14s, and seventy 1s
- Fins:
  - Twenty five ^^^1.40 equals ^^^35.00
  - Two ^^^14.00 plus five ^^^1.40 equals ^^^35.00

Take Home
Enhanced mathematical skills and a bundle of custom designed money as a priceless keepsake

Materials
- Pencils
- Paper
- Pens
- Markers or colored pencils
- Pictures of coins and bills, both ancient and contemporary
- Chalkboard and chalk or equivalent

Dollar Symbols

The U.S. Seal
- The back of the U.S. dollar bill has a seal—an official design that represents the United States.
- On the seal is an eagle with wings outstretched. The eagle was chosen as a symbol because it is fearless in a storm and smart enough to soar above the storm.
- The eagle wears no crown, representing a non-monarchy. Above the eagle's head is a "glory," or a burst of light. The glory has 13 stars, one for each of the original colonies.
- The eagle's right claw holds an olive branch, symbolizing peace. Its left claw holds 13 arrows, symbolizing war. The eagle's head is intentionally turned toward "peace."

- The eagle grasps a shield with 13 stripes, symbolizing a united nation.
- The eagle holds a ribbon in its beak with the Latin words, E Pluribus Unum (13 letters), which means "Out Of Many, One."
- Other symbols on the back of the dollar bill include a pyramid, representing strength and endurance. The

pyramid is unfinished, to represent our continued pursuit toward perfection. The eye above the pyramid represents a higher, spiritual presence.

U.S. Treasury Seal
Found on the front of the U.S. dollar bill, the U.S. Treasury Seal shows scales for a balanced budget, a carpenter's square for an even cut, and a key to the U.S. Treasury.

Creative Currency *continues* ➜

continued from previous page

Old Money

The practice of bartering goods and services dates back 100,000 years or more. The first use of a term for money came from Mesopotamia circa 3000 B. C.

The first metal coins came from China, circa 1500 B.C. where people traded pieces of bronze for goods. The Lydians, an ancient Greek culture, were the first people to have stamped and minted gold and silver coins around 650 – 600 B.C.

By 1637, the Massachusetts Bay colony declared wampum (beads made from shells) to be legal money.

Early in American history, colonies issued their own paper money. This caused problems for those who traveled among the colonies and made the value of the money uncertain.

New Money

In 1792, the United States Congress adopted legislation that regulated the design and value of coins and currency for all of the United States. The first paper dollar bill was issued in 1862. The $100 dollar bill is the largest paper currency in circulation in the United States today.

Getting Ready
- List some names of foreign coins and dollars on the board as well as their approximate equivalents to the U.S. dollar.
- Ask teams to bring in some things to become their "storehouse" of goods for securing the value of their money. A bag of hard candies, a box of pebbles, a pile of paper clips, a bunch of drinking straws, or multiples of anything solid is acceptable (optional).

Activities and Procedures

1 Write the following definition on the board and discuss its meaning:

money: any object that is generally accepted as exchange for goods and services

2 Divide the class into teams of two to four.

3 Instruct students to use their imaginations and basic math skills to devise a unique monetary system.

4 Suggest that students follow these steps to create their original monetary systems:
- Choose a number from one to ten to use as the basis for both coin and paper values.
- Create three or more coin denominations and three or more paper certificate denominations.
- Show some equivalents within your money system by adding and subtracting the values of your coins and paper certificates. (See Example, "The Students of the 7 Seas.")

- Decide upon a storehouse of valuable goods that your currency represents. For example, painted pebbles, hard candies, wire coat hangers, seashells, or anything else the society considers valuable can act as the "gold standard."
- Construct a mathematical equation which demonstrates the numerical relationship between the money and the chosen storehouse of goods. For example, 1 Fin =7 fishbones.

5 Once students have devised their monetary systems, encourage them to name the coins and certificate as well as the issuing parties. Students may use the thesaurus to locate ideas or refer to the slang examples in the sidebar, "Makin' Bacon."

6 Then, have students sketch images of their certificates and coins (both front and back views) onto heavy paper.

7 Briefly discuss the visual symbolism used on United States currency, and encourage students to include visual symbolism on their money as well. (See sidebar, "Dollar Symbols".)

8 Instruct each team to include the value, the year of issuance, and the issuing party on both coins and certificates.

9 Invite students to color the sketches, cut them out, and paste them onto a surface for display.

10 Direct students to title the display with the name of the people issuing the money (e.g. "The Money of the Green Straw Culture").

11 Have students indicate which number the monetary system is based on underneath the title.

12 Ask students to label the coins and paper certificates with creative names such as "Greenits" and "Straw-notes."

13 Display the finished products around the classroom and invite students to comment on one another's work.

Extensions
- Have students sculpt coins from self-hardening clay, and then paint them.
- Connect this lesson with a social studies unit on cultures and their financial systems.
- Use this lesson as a starting point for a unit about the U.S. monetary system and the changes it has undergone throughout our history.
- Integrate this lesson into a visual arts unit on symbolism.
- Use this activity as part of a visual arts unit on design.

Makin' Bacon

Terms for Money
- Bacon
- Beans
- Bread
- Buckaroos
- Bucks
- Chips
- Clams
- Dead Presidents
- Doubloons
- Dough
- Folding Green
- Frog skins
- Greenbacks
- Jack
- Loot
- Moolah
- Scratch
- Smackers
- Wampum

Notes

Social Awareness

My Best Friend Moved Away

Grade Level: 2 through 6
Participants: Individuals and group discussion
Objectives: Exercise fluency and flexibility in problem solving
Time: Approximately ½ hour to 1 hour

Quick View

This activity gives students a sense of personal responsibility and power over their own lives. Students are told a situation that makes them unhappy. By thinking creatively, they find ways they can make life better. This activity involves classroom discussion, brainstorming, and writing.

Example

The Situation: "You have had the same best friend since kindergarten, someone you've played with at recess every day. Now your friend has moved away, and you are lonely at school. What can you do to make life better?"

Possible solutions, resulting from brainstorming:

- Accept your situation and get used to being lonely.
- Keep hoping that someday another friend will come to you.
- View this as a chance to make great new friends.
- Get to know another friend better.
- Invite some classmates to your house after school.
- Call someone after school to start getting to know them better.
- Join an after school club to get to know more students.
- Get involved in school activities like band or student council.
- Ask a teacher who might need a friend, too, and introduce yourself.
- Volunteer to help a teacher at recess. At least you won't be lonely.
- Go to the library at recess and do your homework. Then you'll have more time to make friends outside of school, like at Church or soccer practice.
- Who needs friends anyway? Spend more time with your dog.
- Beg your parents to move to the city your friend moved, so you can be schoolmates again.
- Smile and say hello to everyone you see at school. If you are friendly to others, someone will be friendly back.

Take Home
An optimistic attitude and maybe a nice new friend

Materials
- Pencils
- Paper
- Chalkboard and chalk or large paper and marker

Getting Ready
- Tell your classroom the situation:

  "You have had the same best friend since kindergarten, someone you've played with at recess every day. Now your friend has moved away, and you are lonely at school."

- Ask these questions:

  What can you do to make life better? Is there a great opportunity in this situation?

Activities and Procedures

1 Through classroom discussion, brainstorm some things students can do to solve the problem. There will be various points of view.

2 List all ideas on the board. Add more for balance, if needed. Students will see that they have choices to make for improving a situation.

3 Each student picks the best solution (their opinion) and writes two paragraphs. The first paragraph states the problem and the second paragraph describes a way to solve it. Writing helps clarify one's thoughts.

4 Students may want to share their solutions with the classroom.

Extensions
- The possibilities are many for problems your students may be facing, and need to solve. Here are a few.
- Something embarrassing happened to you at school. Now you think everyone is laughing at you.
- Someone you thought was a friend didn't invite you to their party.
- Your schoolmates formed a club and didn't ask you to be a member.
- You flunked a subject and now you are ashamed.
- You think your teacher doesn't like you at all.
- Nobody ever notices you.
- There is a bully at school who makes your life miserable.
- A obnoxious kid keeps hanging around you at school and interfering with your friendships.

  NOTE: This activity helps students see that they can't always control what happens in their lives, but they can control how they respond to what happens.

Grade Level: 3 through 8
Participants: Individuals
Objectives: Exercise flexibility, originality, elaboration, evaluating cause and effect, identifying personal values, writing skills
Time: Approximately 1 hour

Quick View

In this exercise in social problem solving, students write their own advice columns. Each student asks a question of a "Classmate Advisor." Each question is then answered by two separate classmates, who are chosen randomly.

The class will discuss and vote on the best of the two answers to each request for advice. Students get in touch with their own sense of values when offering personal advice, and again when deciding the best solution between two answers others offered.

Examples

Problem 1

Dear Classmate Advisor,
All the kids at my school play softball at recess. I hate that game, and I'm bad at it. What should I do?
Bad-Batter

Advice A
Dear Bad-Batter,
Even though you don't love the game, if you got better at it, you would like it more. Ask your dad, a friend, or the coach to practice with you until you get better.
The Classmate Advisor

Advice B
Dear Bad Batter,
There are probably some other kids who don't like softball. Do something else with them, like going to the library. Or start a different game with other kids at recess.
The Classmate Advisor

Problem 2

Dear Classmate Advisor,
My best friend, Shaylee, stopped hanging out with me and I don't know why. She and Nancy are together all the time and they both ignore me. What should I do?
Best-Friendless

Advice A
Dear Best-Friendless,
Ask Shaylee if you did something to make her stop being your friend. Tell her from your heart that you are hurt and wish she could make room in her life for both you and Nancy. If she is still cold to you, then forget her and find better friends.
The Classmate Advisor

Advice B
Dear Best-Friendless,
Be sweet and friendly to Shaylee anyway. Maybe Shaylee will be your friend again when the novelty of her new friendship wears off. Also, try to become friends with Nancy. Shaylee may include you if she knows you will get along with Nancy, too.
The Classmate Advisor

Problem 3

Dear Classmate Advisor,
I saw Aiden cheating on a test. He has an unhappy home life, and I don't want to cause more trouble in his life by telling on him. What should I do?
Cheater Spy

Advice A
Dear Cheater Spy,
Mind your own business. Aiden's parents might punish him severely if they find out, so don't create a bigger problem for him. Besides, nobody likes a snitch.
Classmate Advisor

Advice B
Dear Cheater Spy,
Tell Aiden that you saw him cheat, and it's not fair to anyone, including himself. Offer to study with him for the next exam, and tell him if you see him cheating again you will tell the teacher.
Classmate Advisor

Take Home
Deeper thought about your own values

Materials
- Pencils
- Paper

Getting Ready
- Read the examples to the class.
- Encourage discussion about the answers, to get students' minds working. Allow students to offer additional solutions to the problems other than the two answers given in each example.
- Explain to your class that there is often more than one right answer to a question. Sometimes there is no perfect solution and you must weigh several factors to find the best solution, even with its flaws.

Activities and Procedures

1 Assign each student a random number, from 1 to the number of participants. Student should write their number on the top right of their paper, instead of their name.

2 Tell you students that they will be asking for advice from the "Classmate Advisor" regarding a pretend social issue.

3 Instruct your students to each write down a question, at the top of the page, asking for advice about a situation regarding friendship, ethics, or school issues. It should begin with "Dear Classmate Advisor." If a name is used in a question it should be fictitious. Make up a signature that shows emotion or state-of-mind, such as "Lonely 5th Grader" or "Jealous Juniper."

4 Distribute the questions randomly to other classmates. These classmates write a few sentences offering their best advice. They should label their answers, Advice A. They should answer in letter format, starting with "Dear Lonely 5th Grader," and signing with The Classmate Advisor.

5 Randomly distribute the papers again, asking different classmates to offer their best advice. It can be entirely different or slightly different from Advice A., but it must differ. The second advice should be labeled Advice B.

   NOTE: Allow approximately 15 minutes each for writing questions and advice.

6 Collect all the questions with the two answers and read them to the class. Take a vote on the answers the class prefers: A or B. Encourage open and lively discussion about the issues and solutions to the problems. Continue as time permits.

Extensions
- Connect this activity with a unit in language arts and writing skills.

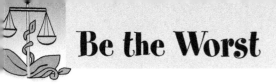
Grade Level: 3 through 8
Participants: Individuals
Objectives: Exercise flexibility, originality, elaboration, understanding opposites
Time: Approximately 1 to 2 hours

Quick View

This thinking and writing activity focuses on students' values about friendship. The activity uses the concepts of opposites, sarcasm and satire to express a student's point of view, as they write a humorous essay on what it takes to be a very bad friend.

Examples

How To Be A Very Bad Friend

- A bad friend lets you know when your hair looks stupid, but only if you can't do anything about it.
- Another way to be a bad friend is to not show up when you say you will, and don't apologize.
- Always use your friend when you need their help with something, but never have time to help them.
- A bad friend tells mean lies about you behind your back, but smiles to your face.

Take Home

A humorous essay

Materials

- Pencils
- Paper
- Chalkboard and chalk or large paper and marker

Getting Ready

- Discuss the concept of friendship with your class. Talk about important values. Students brainstorm the qualities and behaviors of a true friend. List them on the board.
- Discuss the meaning of "opposites" with the class. Sometimes looking at something from an opposite point of view deepens your insights.
- Discuss *sarcasm* with the class: *Sarcasm* is a use of words in which apparent praise conceals another, scornful meaning. In sarcasm ridicule or mockery is used harshly for destructive purposes. "I replied, 'I can always count on you,' when he said he couldn't attend my birthday party."
- Discuss *satire* with the class: *Satire* is the use of humor through exaggeration, incongruity,

opposites, and parody to expose and criticize people's stupid actions or bad habits.
Here are some techniques of satire:

- Exaggeration – to represent something to a ridiculously increased level
- Incongruity – to present something that is so out of place as to become ridiculous
- Opposites – to present something that is out of the normal order, or the opposite of what you believe
- Parody – to imitate the behavior or characteristics of a person, place or thing

Activities and Procedures

1 Students review the list on the board of the qualities of a true friend, then imagine the opposite. Give some examples like "caring." The opposite would be a bad friend who will purposely hurt your feelings.

2 Students write a short essay titled "How To Be The Worst Friend," or "My Worst Friend." They can write about either being a bad friend, or having a bad friend (who is imaginary).

3 Students may enjoy reading their essays to the class.

Extensions

The possible topics for satirical essays are many. Here are a few:

- Be a Bully
- Be the Worst Citizen
- Be the Worst Student
- How to Be Unhealthy
- How to Be Unsafe
- How to Pollute the Environment
- How to Waste Water

"If at first the idea is
not absurd, there is
no hope for it."
– Albert Einstein

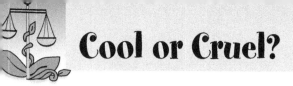

Cool or Cruel?

SA-04

Grade Level: 3 through 8
Participants: Individuals and classroom participation
Objectives: Exercise flexibility, elaboration, identifying values, and persuasive writing skills
Time: 1 to 2 hours

Quick View

This exercise in values and friendship enables students to identify their own value systems, establish criteria for choosing friends, and problem-solve solutions to social problems. By grappling with an issue involving a close friend, choosing a solution, and writing about their beliefs, students solidify their values while honing their analytical skills and persuasive writing abilities.

Example

See "Cruel in School" on next page.

Take Home

Enhanced problem-solving skills as well as a better understanding of the student's own values and the perspectives of others

Materials

- Pencils
- Paper
- Chalkboard and chalk or equivalent

Nice or Nasty?   Cool or Cruel?   Friend or Foe?

Cruel in School

Issue:

My friend is nice to me, and lots of fun, but she is cruel to someone else at school.

Choices:

- Gather my courage and ask her to stop being cruel.
- Ask her what personal problems cause her to be so cruel to another person.
- Stop being her friend.
- Mind my own business and ignore the situation.
- Get several friends together for talking to her about changing her unkind behavior.
- Tell her that if she doesn't stop being cruel, I will discuss it with a teacher.
- Send flyers around my school about cruel behavior (no names) so classmates become aware and sensitive to others' feelings. This might put peer pressure on my friend to stop.
- Befriend the person who is the target so they won't feel so rejected.
- Make new friends and forget the cruel friend and her target.
- Beg my parents to move to another city or let me transfer to another school.
- Pretend I am sick and not go back to school until the situation changes.
- Do something mean to her to teach her a lesson.

Concerns:

- Other friends will stop liking me if I confront her.
- The cruel friend will start being cruel to me too.
- Others will think I'm not cool for caring.
- I lack courage to confront people.
- I'm not used to confronting people.
- I'm afraid of retaliation from the friend.
- If I turn my back on the situation, and do nothing, I will not respect myself.
- The person who is the target of the cruelty is nice, but lacks social skills anyway.

The Best Thing to Do:

If my friend is being repeatedly cruel to someone on purpose, I wouldn't feel ok about her anymore. I would not want her cruel ways to rub off on me. The right thing to do is ask her to consider the feelings of the other person, and to stop being cruel. I would also tell her I don't want to be her friend until she apologizes to the target. It's important to stay safe. I could ask an adult to help me talk to her, or I could talk to her at her house when her parents are at home.

Cool or Cruel? *continues* ➜

continued from previous page

Getting Ready
- Write the following issue on the board: *Your friend is nice to you, but is cruel to another classmate.*
- Write this question on the board: *How do you choose your friends?*
- Allow students to share their responses with the class. Some possible answers may include: *popularity, cool factor, ability to have fun, attractiveness, common interests, trustworthiness, kindness, intelligence, helpfulness, generosity, etc.*
- Ask students to consider what it means to have good character and whether they believe it is an important thing to consider when choosing friends.

Activities and Procedures

1 Explain the following situation to your class: *Your good friend, who has always been nice to you, is doing something you think is wrong—saying cruel things to another student and treating this student unkindly.*

2 Through classroom participation, brainstorm some solutions to the problem. List some potential solutions on the board and have students add their own ideas as well.

3 After the brainstorming session is complete, review the list with the students and invite them to discuss the merits and downfalls of each suggestion.

A Variety of Values

- How a friend treats someone else is none of my business as long as they are nice to me.
- I don't think about it; I'm just grateful that nobody picks on me.
- My friend is popular, and I want to be in her crowd. If I criticize her, she'll reject me.
- Stop being judgmental about my friend. I'm not perfect, either. Until I'm perfect I have no right to judge others.
- Kindness matters, but being a fun person is more important. Some kids are nice, but they're boring. I'd rather be friends with someone who I have fun with no matter how they treat others.
- Maybe the target deserves cruel treatment in some way.
- If my friend can be cruel to someone else, it's likely I will be treated mean someday. I don't want to take a chance on being hurt.
- If my friend is cruel to someone, even while treating me nicely, I can't feel ok about it, and I must tell my friend I don't like that behavior.
- If my friend is cruel to someone, it needs to be stopped, but not by me because but I'm afraid of what might happen.
- I should try to stop my friend's behavior. I'll ask an adult to help me, because I want to stay safe.
- I'll tell the target to stick up for him or herself and do something mean back to my friend.
- I'd rather be alone than have a friend who is cruel to others.
- I'd rather find new friends than have a friend who is cruel to others.

> VALUES: A person's belief system, including ethical boundaries, and what one believes to be important in life.

4 Write the following definition on the board and discuss its meaning with the class:

Values: A person's belief system, including ethical boundaries, and what one believes to be important in life.

5 Discuss how a person's values might influence the way they deal with issues such as the one in question. Ask students to review the list in the sidebar, "A Variety of Values." Discuss how each perspective reflects a different set of values:

6 Instruct your students to write the issue at the tops of their papers, and list five or more choices, and the concerns that follow, for responding to the issue.

7 Ask each student to write two to four paragraphs explaining the best way of dealing with the issue. The essay should be an argumentative piece demonstrating the reasons why this strategy is the most effective choice.

8 Allow students to share their completed essays with the class. Take advantage of opportunities to acknowledge the positive aspects of varying points of view.

Extensions
- Integrate this activity with a discussion about school bullying.
- Connect this lesson with a discussion about how friends can influence one's behavior.
- Use the procedures in this lesson to explore the following topics with your class:
  - Cheating On Tests
  - Vandalizing Or Stealing Property
  - Being Disrespectful Toward Parents and/or Teachers
  - Using Bad Language

Notes

Science Explorations

"To raise new questions, new possibilities,
to regard old problems from a new angle
requires a creative imagination and marks
the real advances in science."
– Albert Einstein

205

Animobiles

Grade Level: 1 through 3
Participants: Individuals
Objectives: Exercise flexibility, originality, elaboration, animal studies
Time: Approximately ½ hour to 1 hour

Quick View

Students learn about the animal kingdom and invent vehicles based on any creature's ability to move. They write descriptions of their Animobiles, then name and illustrate them.

Examples

The "Penguin Car" could navigate snow and icebergs. The car might have features similar to a penguin's, such as wide, flat feet instead of wheels. It might stand tall and upright so it doesn't drag in the snow.

The "Fish Car" could have fins as well as wheels, so it can go from land to the water.

The "Caterpillar Train" would move like a caterpillar. Its series of back cars would bunch up in a high arch, then flatten out as the front cars move forward. Caterpillar Trains don't need tracks.

Roadswimmer Fishcar

Take Home

Concept sketches for an imaginative vehicle that might someday be a popular mode of transportation

Materials

- Pictures of animals
- Pencils
- Paper

Getting Ready

- Gather pictures of many kinds of animals for the students to use as reference, including dinosaurs, insects, sea creatures and more.
- On what kinds of surfaces do some animals move: sand, snow, air, water, grass, rocky cliffs?
- Discuss many ways animals move: swimming, hopping, running, flying, waddling, slithering, and more.

Activities and Procedures

1 Ask your students to pick an animal that moves in an interesting way, and to find out the environment in which it transports itself.

   Determine what gives it the ability to move, such as powerful flippers that push water, or agile legs with sticky feet that adhere to walls.

2 Students create sketches of imaginary vehicles, based on the way their animal moves. Technical realities are not important, but the sketches should clearly show the concept.

3 Using clean paper, students draw their Animobiles.

4 Students then name* their Animobiles and write descriptions of how their Animobiles move. They should explain why their Animobliles are useful or fun.

   NOTE: See lesson plan, "Name Us Famous," pg. 96, for tips on creative naming.

5 Animobiles are fun to share with the classroom.

Extensions

Many of our best inventions and new technologies were inspired by nature. Here are some interesting examples for discussion.
- The helicopter was inspired by bees' wings, which allow them to hover in the air.
- The shape of the submarine was inspired by a sharks' streamlined shape.
- Velcro fasteners were developed in the 1950's by Swiss inventor George de Mestral. He was curious one day when he was out walking his dog and noticed that burs stuck tenaciously to his wool pants and his dog's fur. When he examined the burs under a microscope he discovered that each bur consisted of hundreds of tiny hooks. Mother Nature had designed an amazing fastener.
- Higher grades may do more in-depth research and development for nature-inspired inventions.

Rube Goldberg Machines

Grade Level: 3 through 8
Participants: Individuals or teams of two
Objectives: Exercise flexibility, originality, elaboration, creative problem solving and sketching as well as understanding simple mechanisms, energy, cause and effect, and sequencing
Time: ½ hour to 1 hour

Quick View

In this exercise in imaginative expression, students pay homage to the great cartoonist, Rube Goldberg, by creating original Rube Goldberg-style cartoons. By sketching complex contraptions that use ordinary objects to accomplish simple tasks, students practice their creative problem-solving skills while also revisiting the concepts of cause and effect and sequencing.

Examples

Visit the website www.rubegoldberg.com

Take home

Enhanced creative problem-solving skills and an original Rube Goldberg-style cartoon

Materials

- Pencils
- Paper
- Chalkboard and chalk or equivalent
- Examples of Rube Goldberg cartoons

Keeping It Complicated

Rueben Goldberg was born in 1883 in San Francisco, California. As a boy, he loved art and creativity, but his parents discouraged such interests.

He graduated from the University of California at Berkeley in 1904 with a degree in engineering—a field which eventually inspired his unique cartoon machines.

By 1915, he became a popular newspaper cartoonist while living in New York. A special cartoon character he created, Professor Lucifer Gorgonzola Butts, brought him enduring fame. He used the professor to illustrate extremely complex machines designed to perform simple tasks. These cartoon contraptions came to be known as "Rube Goldberg Machines." Commenting on his work,

Rube was quoted as saying, "The machines are a symbol of man's capacity for exerting maximum effort to achieve minimal results."

The National Cartoonists Society named the Rueben Award in his honor. This award is granted to the "Cartoonist of the Year."

Contests

Today, Rube Goldberg contests are held at high schools and universities around the world. These competitions challenge students to design intricate machines to execute simple tasks.

Find out more about Rube Goldberg and his cartoons by visiting www.rubegoldberg.com.

Getting ready

- Gather and display copies of Rube Goldberg cartoons from websites for student reference.
- Discuss the concept of *simple mechanisms* with the class and list some examples on the board such as levers, springs, gears, pendulums, pulleys, etc.
- Discuss various *sources of power* such as steam, wind, electricity, water power, animal power, magnets, gravity, etc. List these on the board as well.

Activities and Procedures

1 Introduce students to Rube Goldberg and show some examples of his cartoons.

2 Explain to the class that their creative challenge is to create a cartoon machine that will demonstrate many steps that work in sequence to accomplish a simple task.

3 Ask the class to brainstorm a list of simple tasks. To stimulate ideas, you can suggest some of the following examples or come up with your own.

4 Invite students to review their list and choose one idea as the basis for their contraption.

5 Encourage students to brainstorm complex and imaginative contraptions that will execute at least three different steps in order to achieve the desired result.

6 To facilitate the brainstorming process, suggest that students think about the concept of cause and effect as well as the sequence of events that will occur as the contraption is set in motion.

7 Other Idea Sparkers: Refer students to the lists of simple mechanisms and power sources for ideas. Tell them to consider assembling ordinary objects such as boots, books, or chairs for their contraptions as well.

8 Have students sketch the contraptions lightly in pencil.

9 Once the contraption is complete and both teacher and student are satisfied with the results, have students reinforce the sketch with a darker pencil line.

10 Instruct students to write a description of how the contraption works, explaining each mechanism and procedure in detail.

11 Finally, invite each student or team to give their invention a unique title and write it across the top of the page.

12 Allow students to present their cartoons to the class and explain how they work.

Extensions

- Connect this lesson with a science unit on physics and mechanisms.
- Integrate this activity with a language arts unit on writing descriptions.
- Super challenge: Have students use their sketches to create an actual model of a Rube Goldberg machine. Visit www.rubegoldberg.com for examples.

Some Simple Tasks

- Boil water
- Bring in the mail
- Brush your teeth
- Butter your toast
- Crack an egg
- Feed your fish
- Make your bed
- Make a sandwich
- Open a door
- Paint a fence
- Put on your socks
- Sharpen a pencil
- Shovel snow
- Turn on a light
- Ring a doorbell from five feet away
- Catch a cat
- Peel an apple
- Wake yourself up
- Water the flowers

Grade Level: 3 through 6
Participants: Individuals
Objectives: Exercise flexibility, originality, elaboration
Time: Approximately ½ hour to 1 hour

Quick View

Students make postcards to send home to friends and family from their vacations on the Moon. Students illustrate the fronts of their postcards and design special Moon Postage Stamps. On the backs they write a description of the landscape and tell the activities they do for fun. They include some interesting Moon facts, too.

Example

See illustrations

Take Home

A postcard from the Moon

Materials

- Index cards, blank/blank or lined/blank (one per student with some extras)
- Pencils
- Crayons
- Paper
- Pictures of the moon, both close up and distant
- Pictures of our solar system

Hi Mom and Dad,

I'm having a great time here at Camp Moon. The mountains and Milky Way are beautiful. I can see Mars from my bunk window.

Mom, I'm so glad you made me bring my heavy jacket. It gets very cold at night, down to −153 degrees. We've been moon rock skiing in the highlands and we play crater-ball.

See you in 27.3 days unless our space shuttle is delayed.

Love,
Anthony

MOM AND DAD
17341 SOLAR LANE
EARTHBOUND, CA 90236
PLANET EARTH

Getting Ready

- Gather pictures of the Moon and our Solar System and spread them out for use as reference.
- List some basic facts about the moon. Read and display the list for the class to use a reference. Some facts could include temperature, the terrain, revolutions around the Earth, and heavenly bodies that are visible from the moon.

Activities and Procedures

1 Ask students to write a first draft of their postcard message.

   It should be one or two paragraphs mentioning some facts about the moon, but pretending they are visiting there and telling folks back home what they see and do. They may tell about imaginary structures or creatures—if what they imagine is woven with facts.

2 Students sketch and color a picture on the blank side of the index card, using the pictures for reference. They may use high degree of creative license, as well.

3 On the opposite side, divide the card in half with a pencil line as shown:

4 Students copy their drafted messages onto the left side of the cards, and write addresses on the right sides.

5 On separate pieces of paper students sketch rectangular Moon Postage Stamp designs, color them, cut them out, and paste them onto the upper right corners of the postcard backs.

Extensions

- Students can send postcards from anywhere in our Solar System. They could choose any planet, or a moon from another planet such as Titan, Europa, or Io.

Solar System Travel Brochures

Grade Level: 3 through 6
Participants: Individuals, pairs, or small teams
Objectives: Exercise originality, elaboration, imagination, brainstorming, astronomy knowledge, creative writing, persuasive techniques, and visual design.
Time: 1 to 3 hours

Quick View

Students combine their knowledge of astronomy with creative thinking to design galactic travel brochures. The brochures describe "astro-tours" of our solar system and highlight visits to various planets and heavenly bodies.

Examples

See illustration

Take Home

An enticing travel brochure for places far, far from home

Materials

- Sample travel brochures
- Books and pictures about astronomy
- Paper—letter size or larger.
  Heavy paper works best.
- Pencil
- Crayons, markers, or
  colored pencils

BACK COVER

FRONT COVER

INSIDE

The Solar System AS YOU'VE NEVER SEEN IT BEFORE!

Getting Ready

- Gather travel brochures from travel agencies or web sites, and bring them in to share with the class. Read a few destination descriptions aloud and encourage discussion of audience, tone, and persuasive techniques.
- Collect and display books and pictures related to astronomy for student reference.
- List some astronomy words and facts on the board to inspire students. Start the list by naming the planets, constellations, comets, moons, and other astronomical objects.

Activities and Procedures

1 Students begin brainstorming to decide on the locations for their astro-tours. Once the locations have been determined, students should list facts and details related to their travel destinations. They may also wish to sketch or write a visual description. Below are some of the questions students should consider while brainstorming:
   - How will the visitors reach their destination(s)?
   - What activities will they engage in once they arrive?
   - What supplies should they bring?
   - What types of clothing should they wear/pack?

2 To begin designing the brochure, students will position their paper horizontally and fold it in half on the long side. The right side panel becomes the front cover panel.

3 On the front panel, students should compose a catchy heading to promote their astro-tour. Some examples include: *Passport to the Galaxy, The Solar System As You've Never Seen It Before, View Earth From 93,000,000 Miles Away,* and *Let's Go Planet Hopping.* The front panel should also feature a colorful and inviting illustration.

4 Students will use the materials you've provided to research their travel destinations.

5 On the inside of the brochure, students should combine scientifically accurate information with their own imaginations to create interesting and descriptive details intended to make the trip seem exciting and pleasurable. The brochure will address all of the details and information found on real travel brochures including cost, duration, meals, sleeping accommodations, and other important information.

Extensions

To create more fact-filled, fictional brochures, students can research other time periods and locations such as:

Terrains
- Himalayan Mountain Top
- Rainforest
- Sahara Desert
- Under The Sea

Periods in History
- Ancient Egypt
- Ice Age
- Medieval Era
- Prehistoric Era
- Stone Age

Astro Pen-Pals

Grade Level: 2 through 5
Participants: two or more individuals
Objectives: Exercise originality, elaboration, imagination, astronomy facts and vocabulary, and letter writing skills.
Time: Approximately 1 hour

Quick View

In this science fiction-inspired writing activity, students pretend to be either "Earthlings" or Otherlings" and write pen pal letters to each other. By using reality and fantasy -based details to describe their planets, students learn about astronomy while honing their creative writing skills as well.

Examples

David Bernard
902 Main Street
Kedzie, Illinois 60600
United States of America
Planet Earth, Solar System of the Sun
The Milky Way Galaxy

September 23, 2310

Dear Rukululu,

My name is David, and I am in third grade at Lincoln Elementary Sc[hool] in Kedzie, Illinois.

We have a cold winter in this part of the United States. Sometim[es] it stays below freezing for days. When it is cold, we enjoy ice ska[ting] in the park. In the spring, it gets much warmer—about 75 deg[rees] Fahrenheit. Then, we play ball games outside.

Do you play games on your planet?

We eat fruits and vegetables, chicken, fish, and hamburgers. [What do] people eat on your planet? Please describe a meal to me.

I look forward to hearing from you.

Your Earthling Friend,
David

Rukululu Wawawawawa
7 Crooked Canal
29th Latitude, Flat Territory
Planet Thoosa, Telaxa Binary System
Andromeda Galaxy

October 1, 2310

Dear David,

Thank you for your letter. I study "Planet Earth Languages" at my school. I can read and write only 43 of your languages, but I will learn more Earth languages in 4th grade.

We have two winters every orbit. Planet Thoosa winters are colder than yours, but our springs are hotter as we pass between two suns. In the winter, we play games swinging between icicle formations. In the spring, we go solar sailing on airstreams.

We eat one meal every three rotations here. We dine on sun petal plants and sweet stardust pudding, and we drink melted icicles. We do not eat animal life.

Someday, I would like to visit you, and taste an Earth apple. My aunt visited Earth during your Bronze Age and still talks about your tasty apples. What is your favorite star? Mine is Alpha Centauri.

Your Otherling Friend,
Rukululu

For full-size printable copies of these Astro Pen-Pal letters, visit www.jrimagination.com/printables

Take Home
Extraordinary pen-pal letters to share with family and friends or to use as inspiration for other creative works

Materials
- Paper
- Pencils
- Envelopes
- Chalkboard and chalk or equivalent
- Crayons or markers (optional)

Getting Ready
- Create an example of a letter and envelope format on the board. Discuss the letter format: writer's address, date, opening, body, salutation, and signature. Explain how to address an envelope as well.
- List astronomy vocabulary words such as solar system, orbit, galaxy, moon, sun, planet, star clusters, and stratosphere.
- Gather and display astronomy-related reference materials.

Activities and Procedures

1 Divide the class into two groups: Earthlings and Otherlings.

2 Invite the Earthlings to write the first pen-pal letters to the Otherlings who live on other planets in real or imaginary solar systems.

3 Ask Otherlings to then write back to the Earthlings.

4 Instruct Earthlings to include at least three facts describing their planet and its characteristics (e.g. percentage of water, continents, atmosphere, distance from the sun, rotation, etc.).

5 Encourage Otherlings to invent or select a home planet and include at least three real or imaginary facts describing it.

6 Both Earthlings and Otherlings should describe their homes, their families, and their lives.

7 Each pen-pal should end their letter with a question, so that the recipient has a writing prompt to use as a basis for beginning their letter.

8 Repeat this process so that students exchange at least two letters each.

9 Allow students to illustrate their letters if they wish.

Extensions
- Have writers switch groups so that Earthlings become Otherlings and vice-versa.
- Encourage students to include full-page illustrations.
- Limit Otherlings to known planets in our solar system.
- Limit Otherlings to imaginary planets in imaginary solar systems.
- Use this lesson as an opportunity to teach students about stamps, and have them design an Otherling stamp.
- Invite students to create skits featuring a scene in which pen-pals finally meet.

Brainstormy Weather

SE-06

Grade Level: 2 through 6
Participants: Individuals or teams of two
Objectives: Exercise flexibility, originality, elaboration, creative writing, and understanding weather concepts and terminology
Time: Approximately 1 hour

Quick View

In this exercise in parody, students create outrageous weather reports by substituting unlikely words for the weather terms in real weather reports.

Example

Today's Local Tomato Forecast – In this example, the word "tomato" is substituted for "snow":

"Tomato blizzard conditions have crippled our city today, making driving difficult. Airports are closed because of low visibility and saucy landing conditions.

Schools are closed today because they are smothered in tomato paste; however, there will be a spaghetti festival in the park complete with a meatball toss this afternoon. Wear rain gear and tall boots.

Tomato conditions are expected to continue into the evening with frozen diced tomatoes later tonight. Warmer tomorrow with sun dried tomatoes. Tomato conditions will likely diminish by Thursday.

Forecast: A massive Glue Front is predicted for Friday."

Take Home

Enhanced language and meteorological skills and an outrageous weather report to share with family and friends

Materials

- Pencils
- Paper
- Sample weather reports
- Chalkboard and chalk or equivalent

Getting Ready

- Collect a few authentic weather reports from any season and region to read aloud to the class.
- Ask students to bring in two or more weather reports from the newspaper or Internet.
- Encourage students to watch a weather report on TV prior to the lesson. (optional)
- List some weather terms on the board. You can choose some from the sidebar, "Weather Vocabulary Words," and invite students to add their own ideas as well.

Jr Imagination® Creative Genius   216   **Science Explorations**

Activities and procedures

1 Read an authentic weather report aloud to the class.

2 Discuss weather terminology and some basic causes of weather conditions and systems.

3 Ask students to create their own outrageous weather reports by selecting a theme unrelated to weather, and then substituting common weather words for things (nouns) related to that theme. Also, suggest that students use theme-related adjectives and adverbs to describe the weather words in the report. TIP: Brainstorm ideas for possible themes by thinking in categories such as food, art materials, toys, hardware store items, sports equipment, etc.

4 Ask students to follow the writing style of actual weather reports and insert "creative departures" as well. Encourage students to use real weather reports, or the template below to guide them in their writing:

"Good afternoon, classmates. A low pressure system from Our Town will move across the lake on Thursday. The system will spread rain and strong winds gusting up to 50 mph. Additional showers and severe thunderstorms may develop that will extend through the valley to the river. Temperatures may drop to 40 degrees Fahrenheit. Tomorrow will be warmer as a high pressure system moves in from the west and the sun peeks through the wispy clouds."

5 After they are finished writing, students may decorate their weather reports with custom weather symbols.

6 Ask students to deliver their "weather broadcasts" to the class.

Extensions
- Have students make weather maps featuring their own creative weather symbols.
- Use this lesson as part of a science unit on weather.
- Read "Cloudy With a Chance of Meatballs" by Judi and Ron Barrett to younger students as inspiration for their reports.
- Connect this activity with a unit on careers, and invite students to research the career of a weather reporter including required education, job duties, salary, etc.
- Have students research typical weather patterns in a different country or region. Then, ask them to write a short narrative describing what would happen if the weather in that region drastically changed. For example, if temperatures dropped to below freezing for months at a time in Kenya, Africa, what would be the result?

Weather Vocabulary Words

- Air pressure
- Arctic air
- Atmosphere
- Blizzard
- Breeze
- Celsius
- Cirrus
- Climate
- Cloud
- Cloudy
- Cumulus clouds
- Cyclone
- Drizzle
- Drought
- Earthquake
- Fahrenheit
- Flash flood
- Freezing rain
- Frost
- Funnel cloud
- Glacier
- Global warming
- Hail
- Haze
- High pressure system
- High winds
- Humidity
- Hurricane
- Ice
- Jet stream
- Lightning
- Low pressure system
- Meteorologist
- Mist
- Monsoon
- National Weather Service
- Nimbus
- Overcast
- Ozone
- Precipitation
- Rain
- Rainbow
- Sandstorm fog
- Seasons
- Showers
- Severe weather
- Sleet
- Slush
- Smog
- Snow
- Snow flurries
- Snowflakes
- Sprinkles
- Storm
- Sun
- Temperature
- Thunder
- Thunderstorm
- Tidal wave
- Tornado
- Tropical storm
- Twister
- Typhoon
- Visibility
- Volcano
- Warning
- Wind chill

Reptile Relics

Grade Level: 2 through 4
Participants: Individuals
Objectives: Exercise originality, elaboration, imagination, fine motor control, researching, writing skills.
Time: Approximately 1 hour on each of 2 separate days (allow 2–3 days for clay to dry)

Quick View

This lesson plan will delight your students. They make fossils from a special nontoxic fossil-clay recipe that dries to look like real stone, and use plastic dinosaurs for imprinting. They mount and label their "finds" and write stories based on paleontology.

Examples

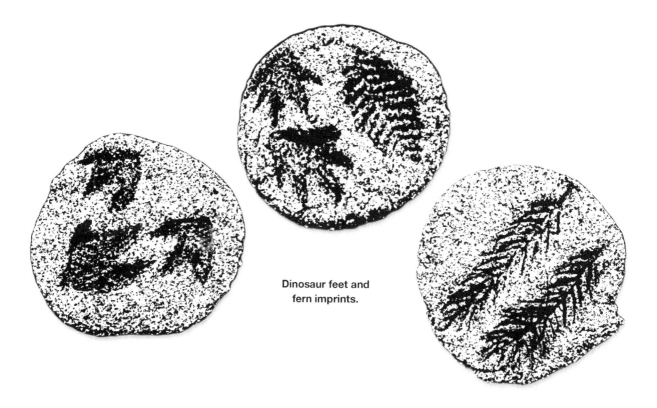

Dinosaur feet and
fern imprints.

Take Home

Authentic looking fossils, mounted and labeled, along with fact filled imaginative stories about the prehistoric creatures

Getting Ready

- Gather books and pictures of dinosaurs for inspiration.
- If time permits, read a short story about dinosaurs to the class.

Were All Dinosaurs Reptiles?

Until a few years ago, scientists believed that all the dinosaurs who inhabited the earth millions of years ago were reptiles, similar to modern lizards.

Today, scientists question whether all dinosaurs really were cold-blooded reptiles. Perhaps many were warm blooded animals, similar to modern birds or mammals.

The skeletons of baby dinosaurs suggest that their parents cared for them for long periods of time, as do birds and mammals.

Dinosaur bones often resemble the bones of birds and mammals more than they resemble the bones of reptiles.

We also know from their skeletons that many dinosaurs stood upright on two legs. This is unlike any reptile today.

The scientists who believe that not all dinosaurs were reptiles say that these giant creatures may not have fully died out. They believe, instead, that many dinosaurs were earlier forms of our modern birds and mammals.

About Fossils

What are fossils?

Fossils are the remains of living things that have been preserved in mineral form in the Earth's crust. Ten thousand to 500,000,000 years ago plants, sea life, bugs, and animals lived on Earth, many of which are now extinct. Fossils give us a history of prehistoric life on Earth by containing imprints of these earlier life forms.

How are they formed?

There are several ways fossils are formed. Here is a common way. When a living thing died, it would fall into mud or sand. Over time, its organic material would decay, and get replaced by minerals. Those minerals became part of the surrounding mud or sand, but left the imprint of the plant or animal it replaced. The mud or sand hardened into rock.

Where are they found?

Scientists have found fossils everywhere on Earth, including on mountains, under oceans, in our deserts, on beaches, buried deep underground, and inside rocks. There are places on Earth that still hold fossil secrets we have not yet discovered.

Vocabulary Words

Dinosaur: Prehistoric reptile

Carnivorous: Meat eating animal

Excavation: Digging in the ground for prehistoric bones or artifacts.

Extinct: A species that is no longer in existence.

Fossil: Impression in rock of a living thing from a prehistoric era.

Herbivorous: Plant eating animal

Omnivorous: Plant and meat eating animal.

Paleontology: The study of life forms that existed in prehistoric eras.

Prehistoric era: 270 to 65 million years ago.

Reptile Relics *continues* ➡

continued from previous page

How to Make Fossils: Fossil Clay Recipe

This clay is non-toxic and has a wonderful coffee scent

Ingredients
(makes 4 to 8 fossils)

½ cup salt

1 cup flour

½ cup cold coffee

1 cup used coffee grounds.

TIP: Large quantities of used grounds are often available at no cost from Starbucks or other coffee stores.

You Will Need
- Measuring cups
- Mixing spoon
- Large mixing bowl
- Paper plates

"We're going to make fake fossils now so we don't have to wait 200 million years."

To Make The Clay
Put dry ingredients in the bowl and blend together with a big spoon. Add cold coffee and coffee grounds. Stir and knead until the dough is smooth and thoroughly mixed.

TIP: If the clay is too stiff add a little liquid. If it is too gooey, add more flour. The clay should feel soft and resilient. The clay will dry to a lighter color and will have the texture of real stone. Store unused clay in plastic bags in the refrigerator.

Materials For Making Imprints
- Small plastic toy dinosaurs
- Twigs, seashells, chicken bones, plastic toy creatures of any kind, plastic fruits and flowers.
- Paper towels
- Soap and water for clean-up

Materials for Finishing the Fossils
- Index cards for mounting
- White glue, such as Elmer's®
- Pens or markers
- Brown paint and small brushes

Activities and Procedures

1 Explain how fossils are made: Millions of years ago plants, bugs, and animals left impressions in soft mud or liquid lava, which cooled or dried and eventually became rock. The impressions left in rock tell us about our world long before humans walked the Earth.

Making the Fossils

2 Spread paper towels or newspaper on tables or desks. Leave extra towels on the table for wiping hands.

3 Give each student a paper plate and have them write their name on the rim.

4 Break off several lumps of clay, enough for rolling into the size of golf balls. Put two or three pieces on each plate. See sidebar, "How to Make Fossils" for the clay recipe.

5 Have each student roll their clay into balls, then flatten them slightly with the heel of their hand. Do not let the piece get too thin or it will be difficult to make imprints. Approximately ¾″ depth is good.

6 Put a pile of toy dinosaurs and things for imprinting in the center of each table.

7 Push the toy dinosaur (or a part of it) into the clay and lift it out, leaving a clear impression. Don't push more than halfway down because very thin fossils may crumble as they dry.

NOTE: dinosaur feet look especially interesting. Parts of creatures work well, too.

8 The fossils need one to three days to dry thoroughly. After the fossils are dry, gently lift them off the paper plates. A spatula can be helpful.

NOTE: Sometimes fossils crack. This adds a look of authenticity to the fossils, and will not be obvious when the fossils are mounted onto cards.

Final Touches

9 Stain inside the impressions with brown paint and a small brush.

10 Prepare the cards for mounting. Students should write the name of the fossilized creature, its age, and in what part of the world it was "excavated."

11 Glue fossils to their cards.

Fossils Have Tales

12 Each student selects one of their fossils to write about. They describe a day in the life of that dinosaur.

13 State whether it was herbivorous, omnivorous, or carnivorous. In what part of the world did it live? How did it get its food? Who were its enemies? How did it care for its young? Imagine what might have happened that resulted in your dinosaur becoming a fossil—and tell the story!

Extensions
- Illustrate several different types of dinosaurs in their natural surroundings.
- Create fossils of seashells and sea creatures as a tie-in with a unit on oceans.
- Create fossils of leaves and flowers as a tie-in with a unit on plants and trees.

Notes

Social Studies

Mississippi Mud Rush

Grade level: 4 through 8
Participants: Individuals or teams of two or three
Objectives: Exercises fluency, flexibility, originality, elaboration, imagination, understanding cause and effect, understanding social behavior, critical thinking skills, writing skills.
Time: 1 to 2 hours

Quick View

Students use both critical and creative thinking skills to construct a resulting environment after the discovery of precious mud in Mississippi. Students describe their visions in short essays, which they share with the classroom.

Examples

A Mud-Worker Family

Emma and her family live near the Mississippi River.

Emma's family does not have a lot of money, but Emma has lots of friends and a happy home life. Emma's dad was a factory worker in town, but he quit his job to work for the farmer who discovered the precious mud.

Since the discovery, Emma's small town has become overcrowded. Now there are 71 students in her 5th grade classroom. She shares a desk with the new girl from New York City.

Mississippi needs to build bigger schools and wider roads. Emma used to have a ten minute ride to school. Now it takes 45 minutes because of the traffic.

Emma's mom is a fabulous cook. She makes lunches to sell to the mud-diggers. She is so busy that Emma and her brother must help before school. The extra income allows their family to save money so Emma and her brother can go to college someday.

Emma's family used to go fishing together on weekends. Now the River is closed to the public, so they go to the movies instead. Life has changed a lot since the discovery. Some changes are for the better, some changes are for the worse, and some changes are just changes.

New Hollywood, Mississippi

I am a 37 year old actress, who had a career in Hollywood, CA.

I'm the pretty "Dusty-Done" lady you've seen in TV commercials. But I'm getting older now, and there are not many roles for older women in the movies and on TV.

As soon as I heard about the age-stopping mud in Mississippi, I moved here. I wasn't the only one; dozens of my actor friends came here, too. Then movie directors, writers, and cameramen followed.

We established the town of New Hollywood outside of Biloxi. There are still some child actors in Hollywood, California, but New Hollywood, MS is taking over the industry.

Yet we miss the Pacific Ocean and the majestic mountains of the west coast. We miss friends and family back home, too. Some day I will accept getting older and move back to the land I love.

Miracle Mud

Mississippi was once a state with quiet natural beauty and historic small towns. Now every city is a congested boomtown.

Since the discovery of illness-curing mud, called Miracle Mud, there has been an overwhelming influx of new residents with serious illnesses. The state government had to set up waiting lists for newcomers to each city. Unfortunately, a long waiting time can be tragic when Mississippi Mud is one's only hope.

Medical clinics have sprung up along the borders of Mississippi. Mississippi cities are bustling with new housing development and shopping center construction. Traffic is horrendous.

Folks from every part of the world are coming here, and bringing wonderful cuisines with them. But more people means more garbage and pollution. Mississippi is struggling to keep up with her population boom.

Housing costs in Mississippi have risen dramatically, and many people cannot afford to buy or rent a place to live. Families often share small apartments and the homeless population is growing.

The President of The United States has offered a 40 million dollar reward to anyone who invents a way to preserve the mud so it can be packed and shipped to locations outside Mississippi.

Mississippi Mud Rush *continues* ➜

continued from previous page

Take Home
Enhanced critical and creative thinking and writing skills.

Materials
- Pencils
- Paper

Getting Ready
- Find and display some reference material about Mississippi.

Activities and Procedures

1 Read the following scenario to your class:

The news is out! Last month a farmer and his son discovered something astounding about the mud near their farm:

Select one:
- It has properties that stop the aging process in adults.
- It will cure any disease.
- It will raise your IQ to genius level.

Scientists around the world have confirmed that this mud is found only in Mississippi. Furthermore, a ¼ tsp must be taken fresh every day for it to continue working. It cannot be packaged and shipped anywhere or it will lose its potency.

Describe how life in Mississippi might be two years from now.

2 Instruct students to list all the changes as they can think of that might result from the discovery of the mud. See sidebar, "A Changing State."

3 Invite students to write short essays describing one or more ways life in Mississippi has changed since the discovery. The essays may be written from the point of view of
- A Mississippian
- A newcomer
- An omniscient overview of life in Mississippi since the discovery

NOTE: It may be helpful for students to learn about Mississippi so they can compare and contrast life before and after the "discovery".

4 Share the essays with the classmates.

Extensions
- Connect a study of the California Gold Rush with a fictitious story about The Mississippi Mud Rush. Compare and contrast the events.

A Changing State

The discovery of Mississippi Mud can result in great social change

1 Thousands of people want to move to Mississippi.

2 The population of Mississippi booms. What sub-effects might follow?

- Land values go up
- Industries crop up to support the increased population, such as restaurants, tourist attractions, entertainment, shopping malls, schools, churches, health care, and so forth.
- Architects and construction workers are in high demand.
- More roads need to be built.
- A chef becomes famous for writing a cookbook of recipes using the mud.
- A jewelry maker becomes famous for designing silver mud-taking teaspoons.
- A songwriter becomes famous for writing a folksong about the mud.
- A factory worker invented a tool for collecting the mud, and now makes millions of dollars on the invention.
- A taxi driver started "Mud-Ex", a popular mud-delivery business.

3 The farmer and his family become among the richest people in the world. What might be some sub-effects to his family?

4 People who want to continue getting benefits from the mud need to stay in Mississippi. Sub-effects:

- Virtual travel would become a popular new pastime.
- Many people are depressed because they can't visit family and friends.

5 The mud might be in danger of depletion. Sub-effects:

- The State government puts a tax on the mud
- The government limits the quantities per person
- It sells at a high price
- Dishonest people sell fake mud.

6 Mississippi might become the richest State in the Union.

7 Clusters of people who are strong and healthy, or who have years of wisdom and experience, or who have exceptionally high intelligence create cultural and scientific advances. Mississippi becomes the hub of a modern day Renaissance.

8 How would daily life change for families living near the muddy Mississippi River?

9 How are adjacent states affected by the changes in Mississippi?

10 List and describe additional effects the discovery might cause.

Go Ahead, Make My Holiday!

Grade Level: 3 through 8
Participants: Individuals or teams of two to four
Objectives: Exercise originality, elaboration, imagination, theme development, writing skills, speaking skills, and cultural awareness
Time: 1 to 3 hours

Quick View

In this exercise in cultural event planning, students use their powers of imagination to create original holidays. By "officially" establishing their days as national holidays and inventing unique traditions and customs, students learn about how holidays are created while simultaneously honing their own creative thinking skills.

Example

National Middle Name Day

National Middle Name Day started in the Midwest to pay tribute to those wonderful names our parents gave us that nobody ever gets to hear. On NMN Day, we reveal our middle names to each other and henceforth, respond only to our middle names.

Some of you may believe you do not have middle names, but we all have *hidden* middle names!

Find Your Hidden Middle Name

Combine the last three letters of your first name with the first three letters of your last name. For example, if your name is Anthony Martin, your hidden middle name is Onymar. If your name is Susan Nicholas, your hidden middle name is Sannic.

Baby Naming

If a baby is born on NMN Day, tradition dictates that the parents give him or her a first name that is/was the middle name of an American President. My sister, Milhous, is not so fond of NMN Day.

On NMN Day, it is customary to make middle-name tags to wear. Also, we eat only the middle fillings of ravioli, egg rolls, and creampuffs, and we dance with a middle-aged relative in the middle of a room.

NMN Day is observed on a Wednesday from midday May 15th to midday May 16th.

Take Home
Enhanced creative thinking skills and a new holiday to observe with friends and family

Materials
- Pencils
- Paper
- Chalkboard and chalk or equivalent
- 12-month calendar
- Crayons, markers, or colored pencils (optional)

Getting Ready
- Write the following words and definitions on the board:
  - *Holiday:* a day designated by law or custom in which people celebrate or commemorate a person or event
  - *Tradition:* a philosophy-based activity that is handed down from one generation to the next and has been performed for a long time
  - *Custom:* an activity that has been performed for a shorter period of time, and is done more out of habit than philosophy
- Discuss the meanings of these terms with the class.
- Invite students to brainstorm common holidays and their corresponding customs and traditions. List student responses on the board.

New, Unusual, Odd, Fun, Or Silly Holidays
(Some Are Actually Observed)

• Amelia Earhart Day	• Hopscotch Day	• National Mitten Day
• Bad Hair Day	• Hug a Middle Child Day	• National Pudding Day
• Bad Poetry Day	• It's Not My Fault Day	• Orange Day
• Ball and Jacks Day	• Johnny Appleseed Day	• Pigtail Day
• Clueless Day	• Jump Rope Day	• Save the Weeds Day
• Da Vinci Day	• Kindness Day	• Sleep All Day Day
• Fast Talker Day	• Knock-Knock Joke Day	• Slow Talker Day
• Friendship Day	• Left Hander's Day	• Susan B. Anthony's Birthday
• George Crum Day	• Lucky Penny Day	• Thomas Edison Day
• Global Forgiveness Day	• Martha Washington's Birthday	• Try a New Food Day
• Honor a Senior Day	• My Way Day	• Wiggle Your Toes Day
• Honor Corn Day	• National Goldfish Day	• Wind Day

Go Ahead, Make My Holiday! *continues* ➜

---

continued from previous page

Happy Holiday Facts

Unofficial Days

Some holidays are not recognized by Congress, but instead, are established by media and word of mouth. They often become popular and appear year after year along with a following of observers.

Chase's Calendar Of Events

This annual publication is an authority on current national and international holidays and other important dates throughout the year.

The calendar lists March 26th as the official date for "Make Up Your Own Holiday" Day.

A Wild And Happy New Year

The celebration of the New Year is the oldest of all holidays. Its first known observance occurred in ancient Babylon about 4,000 years ago. The Babylonian New Year began with the first New Moon, marking the beginning of spring.

The Babylonians first began the tradition of making New Year's resolutions. The most popular resolution is said to have been the promise to return borrowed farm equipment.

The ancient Babylonian holiday lasted for eleven days with a special festivity for each day. During these days, the King was banished from the land and the people could do as they pleased!

Upon the return of the King, in grand procession, the Babylonians went back to work and behaved properly once more, but with renewed spirit.

Activities and Procedures

1 Tell your class that today, they will invent their very own holidays.

2 Have students brainstorm ideas for new holidays and record their responses on the board. Suggest that the holidays may be serious (i.e. honoring someone for an accomplishment or celebrating something important like clean water), or they can be wacky (e.g. honoring broken crayons, pointy elbows, or plaid suspenders).

3 Provide the following tips to facilitate brainstorming:
   • Think of something that is original but important such as the first bus in your city, paving the sidewalks, or building a movie theater.
   • Think of elements in nature (i.e. honoring rain, bumblebees, snow, wildflowers, cats, owls, etc.)
   • Think of inventions and discoveries such as the wheel, fire, soap, lipstick, socks, bicycles, etc.

4 After the brainstorming session is complete, invite students to select one idea for further development.

5   Once students have selected a new holiday, have them write a description containing the following elements:
- The name of the day
- Who or what it commemorates
- When during the year it is observed
- Its origin
- Why it is important
- The customs and traditions related to the holiday such as certain foods, games, activities, songs, dances, hats, gifts, parades, colors, ceremonies, etc.

6   After the descriptions are complete, have students write mock letters to a local Congressperson in order to officially establish their new holidays. Each letter should take the form of an official proposal explaining the purpose of the holiday, why the holiday is important, and how it will be celebrated.

7   Encourage each student or team to deliver a brief presentation explaining the nature and origins of their new holiday.

8   Assign dates for student holidays and note them on your classroom calendar.

9   As a follow-up activity, allow the class to celebrate each new holiday as it arrives. Have the holiday's creator lead the class in observing one custom or tradition such as performing a special song or dance, sharing a holiday-related treat, or making and delivering greeting cards for the new holiday.

Extensions

- Research the origins of the customs and traditions of our national and popular holidays such as: New Year's Day, Christmas, Hanukkah, Thanksgiving, Halloween, Valentine's Day, Easter, April Fool's Day, Martin Luther King, Jr. Day, St. Patrick's Day, Ground Hog Day, etc.
- Create a special "Classroom Day," and plan a celebration in which classmates honor each other (and the teacher too!) by exchanging small cards with sincere compliments.
- Connect this activity with a unit on calendars.
- Integrate this activity into a social studies unit on various cultures and their holidays.

"The best way to predict the future is to invent it."
– Alan Kay

Grade Level: 2 through 6
Participants: Best for teams of two to four, but individuals can work with this, too
Objectives: Exercise flexibility, originality, and elaboration; understanding cultures
Time: Approximately 1 to 4 hours or more, depending upon depth of study

Quick View

Students apply general knowledge about cultures to imaginary cultures they develop themselves. Students collaborate to describe and display a range of characteristics for their original cultures. This activity requires research, writing, and drawing, along with focused imagination. Also it provides great opportunity to exercise elaboration.

Examples

"The Swamp People," named after their geographic locale; the "Cactus Dwellers" or "Dragon Dancers," inspired by their behavior or rituals; or a name based on an interesting sound, like "Huti-Bo-Fluti."

The Cactus Dwellers

Take Home
- Detailed description of a fictitious culture.
- Artifacts from that culture. These will vary, but may include coins made of clay, jewelry designs, maps, alphabet samples, pottery, hand-made musical instruments, and so forth.

Materials
- Pictures portraying a variety of cultures
- Information sheets about any aspect of culture
- Examples of maps, coins, artifacts, etc., from a wide variety of real cultures.
- Pencils
- Paper
- Crayons or markers
- Clay (optional)

Getting Ready
- Discuss the definition and characteristics of "culture," including:
  - *A culture is a group of people living together who have developed ways of behaving that help them survive and live together in harmony.*
  - Such people depend on each other to maintain their lifestyle.
  - The natural surroundings and climate influence the kinds of food the people eat, the way they dress and their type of shelter.
  - Additional influences come from its history, and the beliefs and artistic tastes of its people.
- Discuss a few examples of cultures around the world, from any time period. Show some examples of artifacts, give a quick summary of environments, beliefs, and behaviors.

What Makes Up a Culture?

- Name of the culture
- Arts (crafts, paintings, dance, songs, music makers, literature, etc.)
- Caring for children
- Climate
- Clothing
- Defense and protection
- Education
- Family structure
- Foods
- Games, toys, and sports
- Geography and type of environment, such as shoreline, plains, mountains, etc.
- History (where and when this culture began)
- Holidays
- Houses and buildings
- Justice system
- Language (spoken and written)
- Leadership structure
- Maps
- Medical practices
- Money systems
- Natural resources (real or fantasy) such as fruit trees, gold, purple earth, or musical flowers.
- Religion or beliefs (optional)
- Rituals
- Transportation
- Way of tracking the passage of time

My Nation Creation *continues* ➜

continued from previous page

Activities and Procedures

1 Divide the students into teams of two to four.

2 Each team creates a new country by deciding where it is and its geographic features and climate.

3 When did the country flourish—when in the past, the present, or when in the future?

4 Each team names its country. As in the Examples, the name could be influenced by geography, behavior or beliefs, or even to honor a person. There are many creative ways to name a country.

5 Draw your country's shape and place it on a real or fictitious map. Optional: Design a flag for your country.

6 Some questions to spark ideas:
   • How does your country's geography and climate affect how the people live, how they dress, how they get food, and other things they do?
   • Do the people live in two-parent families, or other groups?
   • What do they do for fun?
   • What do they use for money? Shells, gems, coins, songs, bartering things, bartering labor?
   • Do they have enemies? Do they have an army? How do they defend themselves?
   • What animal and plant life do they have?

7 Refer to the "What Makes Up a Culture" sidebar to formulate additional questions to spark ideas and activities.

8 Tell your students to offer as much detail as possible when developing their fictitious cultures. Divide the responsibility among team members. For example one member may invent the money system, another may research climate, and another may design housing. Or, some may do the writing, while others create artifacts and illustrations.

9 Teams present their cultures to the classroom, including maps, drawings of the people, their land, houses, foods, practices and customs, and their artifacts.

Extensions
Several components of this activity can be linked with other classroom studies. Likewise, parts of this activity will stand on their own for creative writing exercises or art projects. The following are excellent references to use for further study and game-play regarding cultures and civilizations, especially for older students:
   • Workbook and idea book: *Create A Culture* by Carol Nordgaarden. For grades 5 – 8. Published by Creative Teaching Press, Huntington Beach, CA, ©1995 – www.creativeteaching.com
   • Sid Meier's "Civilization" software game – www.civilization.com

"There was a time when all the animals and men were alike, and the old men say they all talked together. The animals could lay off their skins and feathers like shirts, and go about like human beings. Then came a time when men spoke different words, and did not wear skins like the bear, the wolf, and the cougar, or feathers like the eagle and the goose."

This excerpt is from the story, "He Who Made All Things First," in the book, "Indian Life and Indian Lore: Indian Days of the Long Ago" by Edward S. Curtis, World Book Company, 1914. The illustration, by F.N. Wilson, is now in the public domain.

"Without playing with fantasy, no creative work has ever yet come to birth."
– Carl Jung

Grade Level: 3 through 8
Participants: Individuals
Objectives: Exercise flexibility, originality, elaboration, understanding and identifying creativity, research, writing skills.
Time: 1 to 2 hours

Quick View

Students learn what we mean by "creativity" and why it is important. They learn that there are hundreds of creative people who have made a difference in our lives, yet whose names are not widely known. Students select a creative person and write a short biography focusing on their accomplishment. Then students identify some key characteristics of creative people shown in the behavior that led to their success.

Example

See example, "Martha J. Coston"

Take Home

An inspiring biography of a creative person.

Materials

- Pencils
- Paper
- Two lists from the section *Creativity: Mysteries Revealed*, pages 16-17: "Creative Attitudes" and "The 9 Habits of Highly Creative People."

What Does It Mean To Be Creative?

Being creative means having a lot of ideas and imagination. It also means knowing that ideas are important. Creative people write down their ideas, so they have a record of them.

Being creative means finding your own answers to questions, instead of relying on what others have told you is a right answer. It means finding new questions that need answers, too.

Some ideas you try may work well, while others may not work well. The important thing in creativity is to think of new ideas, and believe it is ok if something doesn't work well. When creative people fail, they learn what doesn't work, and they don't give up. They try solving the problem another way.

Ideas are precious because they could be the seed of something valuable. Think about the hundreds of inventions and creative accomplishments that make our lives easier, healthier, more informed, and more enjoyable: automobiles, electricity, plastic toys, medicines, movies, art, music, mobile phones, frozen foods, microscopes, telescopes, laser technologies, computers, jet planes, and so forth. They all started with an idea.

Creative people are the most important people in the world!

Martha J. Coston

Inventor of Coston flares, which produce a brilliant light without an explosion

Martha J. Coston

Martha Jane Hunt was only a teen when she married a young inventor named Benjamin Coston in the 1840's in Washington, D.C. When Benjamin died, Martha was left with four children to support.

Martha found Benjamin's sketches for signal flares. The flares, which used pyrotechnics, were intended for ships to use for communication with each other while at sea.

Martha saw important possibilities for the invention, but since she was not a scientist, she hired chemists and others to help her make the idea take form.

Then she courageously went out into the business world to sell the invention. Martha was determined to break through the prejudice against women in business that existed in her day.

She eventually convinced the U. S. Navy to purchase the signals for use on its ships during the Civil War. She also won international recognition for her maritime signals.

Throughout the years following, many accounts of rescues from shipwrecks describe the aid of Coston flares. The invention has been instrumental in saving thousands of lives.

Key characteristics of creative people are shown in Martha Coston's story:

- Benjamin Coston wrote down his ideas.
- Martha believed in possibilities.
- Martha was optimistic.
- Martha used imagination to see the importance of the invention.
- Martha, who lacked scientific knowledge, found a way to make the ideas take form.
- Martha used courage to enter a "man's" business world.
- Martha was determined, and didn't give up trying to sell the invention.

A Famous Creative Genius *continues* ➜

continued from previous page

30 Creative People

William Addis

1 William Addis – *invented mass produced toothbrushes*

2 Mary Anderson – *invented windshield wipers*

3 Georg Bauer, AKA Georg Agricola – *father of mineralogy*

4 Edwin Binney and C. Harold Smith – *invented crayons*

5 William Buckland – *discovered and identified dinosaur fossils*

6 Joseph Campbell – *originated canned condensed soup*

7 Josephine Cochran – *invented the dishwasher*

8 Martha J. Coston – *created signal flares*

9 George Crum – *invented potato chips*

10 Charles Darrow – *created the Game of Monopoly*

11 Tom Every, AKA Dr. Evermore – *scrap artisan*

Berry Gordy, Jr.

12 Abigail M. Fleck – *at 8 years old invented the Makin' Bacon® dish*

13 Charles Goodyear – *invented sneakers shoes*

14 Berry Gordy, Jr. – *founder of Motown Records*

15 Ruth Handler – *invented the Barbie Doll*

16 Grace Murray Hopper – *invented COBOL Computer Language*

17 Steve Jobs – *co-founder of Apple, Inc.*

18 Margaret Knight – *invented the paper grocery bag*

19 Hedy Lamar – *invented a secret communications system*

20 Sara Lourie – *discovered a new species of seahorses*

21 Joseph Merlin – *invented roller skates*

Antony van Leeuwenhoek

22 Pierre and Ernest Michaux – *invented the modern bicycle*

23 Edward Naire – *invented erasers*

24 James Naismith – *invented the game of basketball*

25 Spencer Silver – *invented Post-it Notes*

26 Lucy Stone – *women's rights activist*

27 E. Paul Torrance – *identified creative thinking as a cognitive skill*

28 Konstantin Tsiolkovsky – *originated systems leading to the first space rocket*

Sarah Lourie

29 Antony van Leewenhoek – *discovered micro organisms*

30 Ruth Wakefield – *invented chocolate chip cookies*

Getting Ready
- Provide copies to the class of, "Creative Attitudes," and "The 9 Habits of Highly Creative People."

Activities and Procedures

1 Read the two lists to the class and discuss the ideas on them.

2 Instruct your students to select a creative person from the list, "30 Creative People," or from their own research online and elsewhere.

   For making a selection, suggest they brainstorm inventions and things in their world whose origins they don't know, and look for individuals to write about.

   For example, you wash your face every day. Who invented soap? Perhaps it was first used in an ancient culture, but was there an individual who popularized it in modern life? Who started the first soap company? Who invented bubble bath? Who invented laundry soap?

3 Write a short story about a creative person. Describe their idea, and how they accomplished their goal. Include person's name, the era they lived, and where they lived. Explain how their invention or accomplishment improved our lives.

4 Identify and list the *Creative Attitudes* and *Creative Habits* that were shown in your story (see Example, *Martha J. Coston*).

Extensions
- Tie-in this lesson with a unit on history.
- Tie-in this lesson with a unit in language arts and writing skills.

"Be daring, be different, be impractical, be anything that will assert integrity of purpose and imaginative vision against the play-it-safers, the creatures of the commonplace, the slaves of the ordinary."
– Cecil Beaton

The Creative Hero Next Door

SS-05

Grade Level: 3 through 8
Participants: Individuals
Objectives: Exercise flexibility, originality, elaboration, understanding and identifying creativity, new perspectives, writing skills.
Time: 1 to 2 hours

Quick View

Students learn what we mean by "creativity" and why it is important. They become aware of creative people around them whose names may be unknown to the general public. Students select three creative people from school, neighborhood, or family, and write a short description of what each person does that exercises creativity.

Examples

Lizards, and Turtles, and Birds, Oh My!

My mom's friend, Carrie, is a professional photographer. But she has another side to her creativity.

Carrie and her children love animals. They will take in any pet the owners can no longer care for. They are always excited to expand their mixed-species family.

They built sanctuaries for reptiles and birds in their backyard. Feeding them, however, is expensive. So Carrie asked local grocery stores to donate the produce the stores would normally discard.

Carrie raises money for the animals' care by photographing children holding the beautiful reptiles and birds and by teaching about the wonderful creatures. Carrie's creative lifestyle brings happiness to many, both people and pets.

Do-It-Yourself Inspiration

When my grandfather was raising his family, there was not much money to spare. The growing family needed chairs, desks, shelves, and beds.

So Grandpa built them. He designed exactly the furniture that suited his family best, and built the pieces himself.

Every weekend he sawed, sanded, hammered, and shellacked wood in his workshop in the garage. When my dad was a boy he and his brothers loved watching him, and sometimes they would help.

My Grandpa met a need by being creative, and left lasting inspiration for his family, which no store-bought furniture could ever match.

Winning By Hopscotch

One summer when I stayed with my aunt, there was no place to play. She had no yard, and no playground nearby. But I made a friend who lived next door.

Elena and I found some chalk and drew a Hopscotch course on the sidewalk. We played almost every day. Then Elena and I invented more challenging Hopscotch courses, with twists and turns and difficult passages. Other kids joined our games.

By midsummer we had organized daily Hopscotch contests on our block. With a stick of chalk and a lot of creativity we turned that summer into amazing fun.

Take Home
Creative inspiration acquired from everyday people

Materials
- Pencils
- Paper
- Two lists from the section *Creativity: Mysteries Revealed*, pages 16-17: "Creative Attitudes" and "The 9 Habits of Highly Creative People."

Getting Ready
- Provide copies to the class of, "Creative Attitudes," and "The 9 Habits of Highly Creative People."

Activities and Procedures

1 Read the two lists to the class and discuss the ideas on them.

2 Ask your students to select three creative people they know or know about. Students are allowed to choose themselves.

3 Instruct students to write one or more paragraphs describing the way each of those people does something that uses creative thought.

4 Invite students share their stories with their classmates.

Extensions
- Have students conduct a formal interview with a creative person they know. Ask the interviewee about their inspirations, background, procedures, philosophy, and goals.

Where To Find Creative People

- Teachers at your school who have a special way to teach something
- Others at your school who make a difference
- Family members who do something creative at home. Do you have an aunt who makes amazing holiday decorations? Did your mom invent a great way to keep track of everyone's after school activities? Does your grandmother concoct delicious meals from leftovers? Can your uncle figure out how to fix anything? Does your cousin make up fun jumping rope games? These activities use creative thought
- People you know who are professional artists, scientists, inventors, entrepreneurs, and more
- People who donate time and efforts to charity
- People you know who have creative hobbies
- People you know who have overcome major obstacles
- Classmates and friends who write music, paint, take photos, dance, sing, act, skate, perform music, write poems and stories, bake, sew, tell jokes, build things, invent things, organize events, discover things in nature, care for unusual animals, research things, know how to get along with everyone, started a small business, organized a charity, and so on

Grade Level: 4 through 8
Participants: Individuals or teams of two or three
Objectives: Exercise flexibility, elaboration, understanding cause and effect, imagination, writing skills, United States history.
Time: 1 to 2 hours

Quick View

Students choose an event in American history they have learned about. They write a short description of the event and its impact on American life. Then they imagine how history might have taken shape had the event not happened. They write a short essay describing American life had the event never taken place.

Examples

The Transcontinental Railroad

The first Transcontinental Railroad in North America was completed in 1869. Americans considered it the greatest technological feat ever.

It connected the eastern and western parts of the United States, making it possible for goods to be transported across the country, and for people to travel to visit family and friends.

Establishing new homes in the western states became very attractive to many Americans. The "Iron Horse" as the Native Americans called the trains, had much to do with the rapid growth of the United States.

The Railroad Was Not Built

Americans who live in the western states of the United States, such as Colorado, Nebraska, and California, are lonely because they cannot visit family and friends they left behind when they traveled west from the eastern states.

These brave folks survived dangerous stagecoach trips. They are reluctant to risk their lives traveling again. They cannot travel by sea because it is expensive and requires leaving home for several months or years.

Few people want to live in the western states because life is so hard there. Western Americans have difficulty getting medical supplies, household goods, books, farm equipment, and other things that come from the eastern States.

Although the western states are beautiful and have rich farmlands, the future for these states looks bleak in 1869.

Native Americans will probably take back these lands, and the United States' western border will be re-drawn at the Great Lakes.

Take Home
Enhanced thinking skills and a deepened understanding of how events shape history

Materials
- Pencils
- Paper
- Chalkboard and chalk or equivalent

Getting Ready
- List some events on the board your students may choose from.
- Gather books and other references for the class to use.

Activities and Procedures

1 Explain to your class that they will be rewriting history as if certain events never happened or if certain battles had different outcomes. They must imagine the effects of alternate causes, and what life would then be like for Americans.

2 Invite students to select an event and write a brief description of the event and how it affected people's lives.

3 Now invite them to write an alternate history explaining life if the event hadn't happened, or if a battle had the opposite outcome.

How would eliminating that event (invention, or outcome of a battle) have affected our lives? Follow the chain of cause and effect, speculating about what would have happened instead, and how that would have affected out lives, and so forth.

4 The "un-history" essays should be three or more paragraphs, depending on grade level and number of participants per essay.

5 Share the essays with the class. These make for lively classroom discussions about history.

Extensions
- Choose events in world history.
- Choose events in ancient history.
- Choose events in natural history, such as if dinosaurs did not become extinct.
- Choose science discoveries, such as the discovery of gravity, micro-organisms, electricity, and so forth.
- Substitute events in cultural history, such as Mozart or Elvis Presley having never been born. Describe art forms if various artists in music, visual arts, architecture, literature, and drama had never been born.

Counterfactual History

Counterfactual History is a contemporary approach to studying history that attempts to answer "what if" questions. These historians explore key events in history by looking at the effects of the cause, and speculating about the impact on civilization had certain key historical events not occurred or had they resulted in different outcomes.

The purpose of counterfactual study is to become fully aware of the importance of events, incidents, people, and battles that have shaped our history. Thinking about history from an alternate point of view provides a deepened understanding of history's timelines.

Events That Shaped American History

- The Discovery of America
- The Revolutionary War
- The United States Constitution
- The Erie Canal
- The Civil War
- The Transcontinental Railroad
- Spanish American War
- Electricity
- Automobile
- World War I
- The Stock Market Crash
- World War II
- Civil Rights Movement
- Computers

Notes

Visual Arts

Create-a-Creature

VA-01

Grade Level: 2 through 5
Participants: Individuals or teams of 2 to 4
Objectives: Brainstorming techniques (especially combining), personal expression
Time: 1 to 2 hours

Quick View

Students create new creatures, never seen before, by combining parts of existing creatures and dreaming up new parts. They draw or sculpt their creatures and name the new species. They describe the creatures' lives through written stories or oral presentations to the class.

Examples

Take Home

Students who work independently may take home their creature creations. Teams may display their work in the classroom.

Materials

- Creature Cards (see "Reproducibles" pg. 326)
- Pictures of living things (optional)
- Small blank cards, 2″ x 3″ or 4″ x 5″
- Pencils
- Paper bag
- Tracing paper
- Drawing and writing paper
- Clay (optional)
- Chalk and chalkboard or large paper and marker

Getting Ready

- Gather and display pictures of all kinds of animals to spark ideas.
- Reproduce copies of the Creature Cards. The cards display "creature features" such as claws, antennae, legs, ears, hooves, eyes, snouts, tails, and so on.
- Optional: students make their own Creature Cards by drawing one feature per card. Students should make at least three cards each.

  NOTE: Realistic drawings are nice but not necessary because quirky drawings work well, too.

Activities and Procedures

1 Put all the Creature Cards in a paper bag. Each student randomly picks two or three cards.

2 Discuss creature features. For example, mention different types of grasps (pincers, hands, claws, suction cups, sticky substances) several forms of locomotion (walking, flying, leaping, rolling, floating, spinning) and so on. Make classroom lists on a board.

3 Now individuals or teams combine their cards to create new species. Students may eliminate cards or sketch additional parts, but they must combine three or more of the cards.

   Students need about 15 minutes to sketch or sculpt their creatures. The development of ideas is more important than refined artwork. Creatures can be as far out as imaginations take them.

4 Students should decide:
   - How big their creature is
   - How it defends itself
   - How it moves
   - How it obtains food
   - If it would make a good pet
   - If it's vegetarian, carnivorous, omnivorous, or eats only minerals
   - What kind of climate it needs
   - Where it lives
   - Where it sleeps
   - Who are its friends and enemies
     and so on

5 Students come up with original names for their new creature's species.

   NOTE: Coin a name by combining parts of descriptive words. For example, a scary, wiggly, slimy creature might be named "scariggly", "slimowig" or "wigglo-scarus." (See LA-06, "Name Us Famous," pg. 96, for an extensive lesson plan on creating names.)

6 Students give a written report or oral presentation about their creatures.

Extensions

- Create-an-Alien
- Create-a-Bug
- Create-a-Dinosaur
- Create-a-Sea Monster

Pass-a-Squiggle

Grade Level: 2 through 8
Participants: Small or large groups
Objectives: Exercise fluency, flexibility, originality, elaboration, and imagination
Time: Approximately 30 to 45 minutes

Quick View

Students engage in a classically inspired activity sure to unleash their inner artist. Through a collaborative effort, students create an abstract artwork by drawing a series of unique, free-form squiggles. Students quickly sketch their own squiggle and then pass it along to a team member who, offering a fresh point of view, makes their own original mark. The process continues until all artists have made their contribution. The drawing is then returned to the original artist who adds the final touches and gives the masterpiece a title.

Example

The final masterpieces will no doubt be as different as the artists themselves. Some may purposefully resemble an object or follow a theme while others may be entirely abstract. All of them, however, will be highly expressive!

Squiggle Sleigh Mobile

Take Home

Surprisingly non-traditional drawings which may become the basis for continued artistic development.

Materials
- Drawing paper
- Pencils
- Crayons or markers (optional)
- Timer
- Music of various styles and tempo (optional)

Getting Ready
- Gather all materials.
- Arrange desks so that students can pass the drawings around easily.
- Consider playing music during the activity. If you do use music, know that the pace and mood of the music will influence the sketches. You may want to vary the music during the activity to produce different effects.
- Very large groups may be divided into two or more teams for this activity.

Activities and Procedures

1 Each student writes their initials at the top right of a blank sheet of paper. Then they draw a large squiggle on the paper.

2 After a predetermined amount of time (usually a minute or two will suffice), the teacher prompts the students to pass the drawings to the right. The student receiving the drawing then turns the paper in any direction they wish and adds to the squiggle by making it into something representational, designing it with abstract shapes and lines, or adding whatever their creative visions dictate.

3 Students keep sketching and passing until every drawing has been modified by each student and the artworks have been returned to their original artists.

4 The originator adds more detail and gives the drawing a title. The title should reflect an object, idea, or feeling that the art embodies. Students have come up with creative titles such as "Silly Spaghetti on a Sea Shell," "Dancing with Triangles," "Weird Flowers On a Windy Day," and "Line-osaurus."

5 To facilitate classroom discussion, display the final artwork and ask for comments. Invite all ideas, including constructive criticism, but keep the tone positive and encouraging. Use the discussion as an opportunity to inspire students to create new pieces of art as extensions of the originals.

Extensions
For other exciting results, limit students to use the following elements in their drawings. You may instruct them to use only one or encourage them to come up with their own combinations.
- Lines – either broken, curvy, or straight
- Triangles or other shapes
- Words, letters, or numbers
- Visual symbols, such as arrows, hearts, or moons
- Colors (use markers, crayons, color pencils for colored lines)
- Use black tempera paint, large brushes, and heavy paper for a more dramatic effect.

You may also consider asking students to color in the spaces enclosed by lines in their drawings.

Grade Level: 2 through 6
Participants: Pairs or small groups
Objectives: Exercise originality, elaboration, imagination, and visual design as well as the S.C.A.M.P.E.R. brainstorming techniques
Time: ½ hour to 1 hour

Quick View

Harnessing the power of creativity and teamwork, students transform ordinary images into highly original drawings. As drawings are passed from one hand to the next, students have the opportunity to alter a classmate's artwork into something unique and special. Results will most certainly vary, but the final product will no doubt be an original and surprising adaptation of an everyday object.

Examples

Take Home

A "Stretch-a-Sketch " art piece that demonstrates the transforming effects of modification techniques on an ordinary drawing

Materials

- Paper and pencil for each student
- Timer
- Ball of clay or other pliable object
- Music or sound device (optional)
- Object Cards (see *Reproducibles,* pg. 320), or other pictures

Getting Ready

- Using a ball of clay or other visual aid, begin a class discussion of all the ways an item can change. Record student responses on the board.
- Introduce the students to the S.C.A.M.P.E.R. brainstorming techniques (see *Creativity: Mysteries Revealed,* pgs. 8–9), and encourage them to apply the strategies during the activity. Display a S.C.A.M.P.E.R. poster, or hand out copies. (See *Reproducibles,* pg. 342.)
- Have Object Cards or other pictures available to give to the students. Images may include people, animals, flowers, objects, vehicles, etc. Copies of the Object Cards work especially well because they are simple and clear.
- Distribute paper and pencils, and divide the class into pairs or small groups.
- Prepare music/sound device to indicate start and stop times (optional).

Activities and Procedures

1 Each student writes their initials on the top, right-hand side of a blank sheet of paper.

2 Students then divide the paper into nine equal sections (three across and three down) and number each section from 1 to 9.

3 The teacher randomly distributes the "Object Cards" or other available pictures. Provide extras to each pair or group so each student can have a choice.

4 Next, the student draws or pastes a picture of one recognizable item in the upper, left-hand section.

5 After a predetermined amount of time (2-3 minutes is recommended), the teacher prompts students to pass the paper to the right.

6 The student receiving the paper then draws a variation of the first item in the next section by *changing half* of the item and *keeping half* of it the same. The item can be divided in half vertically, horizontally, or in select areas depending on the student's preference.

7 As students make changes to the original drawing, the teacher should remind them of the S.C.A.M.P.E.R. techniques and encourage them to visualize changes by picturing the item as a malleable object.

8 Students continue passing the drawing until all students have made a contribution, or until time is up. The picture is then returned to the original artist.

Extensions

- To extend the activity, encourage students to:
  - Complete the entire activity individually.
  - Continue to "morph," adding nine more modifications.
  - Draw a large, detailed picture of the final product. Name their Morph item, describe what it is or what it does, and present it to the class.
  - Create an advertisement or sales flier to pitch their invention.
- For an additional full-page example of a completed Stretch-a-Sketch and a blank 9-square reproducible template, visit www.jrimagination.com/printables.

Grade Level: 1 through 6
Participants: Individuals or small teams
Objectives: Exercise fluency, flexibility, originality, and visual awareness
Time: Approximately 10 to 30 minutes

Quick View

In this exercise in artistic expression, students use their imaginations and visual awareness to transform ordinary circles into original imagery. In an effort to visualize as many round things as possible within a ten minute timeframe, students practice fluency and apply their powers of imagination as well. Use this lesson as a ten minute contest, where fluency and originality earn extra points.

Example

Circles do not have to be perfect. They can be made from a "master drawing," a circle template, or a round object like a paper cup.

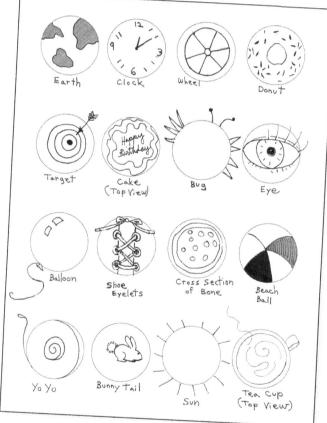

Take Home
Original sketches that demonstrate the transforming power of creativity and visualization

Materials
- Paper – three to five 8½″ x 11″ sheets per student or team.
- Printouts of "16 Circles Template" (for a free download, visit www.jrimagination.com/printables)
- Pencils
- Circle template or round object (optional)
- Chalkboard and chalk or equivalent
- Timer

Getting Ready
- Provide individuals or teams with at least three printouts each of 16 Circles Template. *Optional:* Instruct students that they will be using a pencil to draw ten to sixteen 1½″ diameter circles on a piece of paper, leaving some space around them.
- Encourage students to think of the circles as the basis for original sketches. Tell them that by adding details, the circles could become spherical things like the Earth or flat, round things like dinner plates.
- Suggest some scenarios to help spark ideas. For example, have students visualize what is in front of their houses, on their kitchen tables, or in their backpacks to mentally locate circle shapes.

- Invite students to think of objects of all sizes. For example, a poppy seed is a tiny circle whereas a lake might resemble a large circle.
- Ask students to use the following guidelines when drawing:
- If something is actually smaller than the circle, such as a coin, it is ok to sketch it in larger scale.
- Sketching tiny circles within one of the large circles (e.g. a group of small candies) is permitted.
- Sketching outside the lines of the circle lines (e.g. sketching a bug by adding legs and antennae) is allowed.
- Don't spend too much time on details; keep creating new sketches.
- Some sketches may require titles or labels for identification. For example, you may add the label "Top View" to indicate perspective.
- Only one idea per circle is acceptable; a page of ten soap bubbles, for instance, does *not* count as ten items. The end of a soap bubble wand, the lid of the soap bubble jar, and a soap bubble, however, *are* acceptable as three separate items.

Activities and Procedures

1 Tell students that they have 10 minutes to turn 30 circles into original sketches.

2 Have the first student to complete all of their circles announce, "THINGO!"

3 Write this student's name on the board and award him 10 points.

4 Ask the class to use the remaining time to complete their sketches.

5 When time is up, invite each student to present their sketches to the class.

6 As students showcase their drawings, ask others in the class to raise their hands if they sketched the same idea.

7 Award 2 points for each completed circle and 5 extra points for each unique idea (one that no one else in the class used).

8 Tally up the points and announce a winner! Present the student with an A.C.E. Award (see "Reproducibles", pg. 341), or a small (preferably round) gift.

Extensions

- Complete this activity without the contest element.
- Have students complete the activity using different shapes (e.g. Rectangle Thingo (harder), "L" Shaped Thingo (even harder), or Triangle Thingo (hardest)
- Invite students to create "shape" booklets featuring several sketches of round, rectangular, and triangular objects.

Scoring Circle Thingo

- 10 extra points for finishing first
- 2 points for each completed circle.
- 5 extra points for each idea nobody else has.
- Explain the contest to the classroom, and begin.
- Students should earn extra points for unique ideas that no one else thought of.
- Using quick pencil sketches, they go for quantity of ideas as well as unusual ideas.
- Use this fun exercise as a ten minute contest, where fluency and originality earn extra points.
- This fun activity doesn't need to have a winner.
- Consider "big circles", "small circles","big rectangles", "small rectangles", and so on.

ABC Scavenger Hunt

Grade Level: 1 through 5
Participants: Individuals or group
Objectives: Exercise fluency, flexibility, originality
Time: Approximately 15 minutes to 1 hour

Quick View

Students exercise their powers of observation and outside-the-box perceptions as they search for hidden letters in anything and everything... except for printed or written letters. Students make sketches or notes on where they find letter forms.

Examples

The letter "H" is formed by a wood window frame, the handle of a mug forms letter "D," and a wooden ruler is the letter "I". See illustration for additional examples.

Take Home

A very special ABC Book

Materials

- Pencils
- Paper
- A room or yard to search
- Magnifying glasses (optional)

Getting Ready

- Explain the activity to the classroom, showing some examples.
- Hand out the papers and pencils.

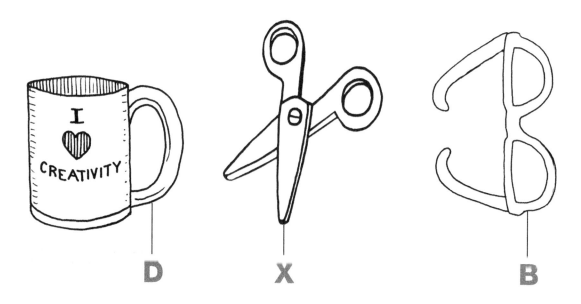

D   X   B

Activities and Procedures

1 Divide the class into teams. Large teams can each take half of the alphabet; A through M or N through Z. Smaller teams can pick fewer letters. Individuals can work on any letter group they choose.

2 Students write the letters at the top of a paper to remind them of the shapes they are searching for.

3 Teams go on a scavenger hunt in the classroom, looking for letters in shadows, furniture, a friend's shoes, school supplies. Sometimes they are upside down or sideways. Find letters anywhere but printed and written letters are not fair use.

4 Students sketch in pencil the objects in which they found their letter forms, and use color to accent the letter.

5 Add a written description, such as " Letter X in part of a scissors." Individuals or teams may compete to finish first.

6 Students combine their efforts to create a Classroom ABC Book. Use one letter per page, with a sketch and description.

Extensions

- Teams pick three-letter words, such as CAT, HOG, HAT, etc. It is important that each word has three different letters, but teams may have duplicate letters. This variation moves quickly.
- Have teams find the letters in "OBSERVE" or another word or phrase. They may like to find the letters of their names or school name. Add sketches to create an art piece.

.

*"I invent nothing.
I rediscover."*
– Auguste Rodin

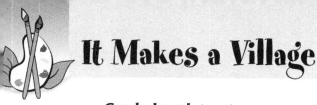

It Makes a Village

Grade Level: 1 to 6
Participants: Teams of two to 6
Objectives: Exercise flexibility, originality, elaboration, imagination, understanding communities, metaphors, concept development, architectural design, and teamwork
Time: 2 to 6 hours, depending on team size and depth of project development

Quick View

In this architecturally-inspired activity, students combine their powers of imagination with their knowledge of community building to create tangible "villages" from ordinary cardboard boxes. By working in teams to create original design themes and settings, students enhance their knowledge of architectural concepts while building on their creative thinking and social skills as well.

Examples

East Booklyn—a book village where bookworms dwell. There is a Library made from a dictionary, a School made from the Book of Knowledge, a Grocery Store, and Homes.

Booklyn Borough
Construction paper over books

Take Home
Enhanced design skills and fun village pieces for imaginative play

Materials
- Paper
- Pencils
- Empty boxes of various shapes and sizes
- Construction paper, butcher paper, or similar
- Scrap paper or newspaper
- Glue sticks
- Rulers
- Scissors
- Crayons or markers
- Pictures of building styles and villages
- Clay (optional)
- Drinking straws (optional)
- Tape (optional)

Getting Ready
- Gather pictures of village settlements and architectural styles found in books and online to display for student reference.

NOTE: There are numerous miniature village collectibles on the market today. These are ideal reference for simplified architectural styles and building types. Visit www.department56.com and other giftware websites for examples. Model railway suppliers are good sources for reference, as well.

Cereal Box Lane
Construction paper over cereal boxes

Buildings and Structures
- Amusement Park
- Bakery
- Bank
- Bowling Alley
- Candy Shoppe
- Church
- College
- Concert Hall
- Fashion Shoppe
- Grocery Store* (food necessities)
- Hardware Store
- Health Club
- Homes* (three or more dwellings)
- Ice Cream Shoppe
- Library
- Lookout Tower
- Medical Center* (health needs)
- Museum
- Playground
- Post Office* (communication)
- Restaurant
- School* (education)
- Shoe Store
- Skating Rink
- Sporting Goods Store
- Street Signs
- Theater
- Town Hall* (meetings)
- Toy Store
- Train Depot

*Buildings that are essential to village life

It Makes a Village *continues* ➜

continued from previous page

Activities and Procedures

1   Write the following word and definition on the board:

   Village: a community with a small population in which houses and buildings are clustered together for sociability and protection

2   Explain to the class that they will be constructing unique miniature villages.

3   Tell students that their villages should consist of at least eight structures including the following:
   • Town Hall
   • Private residences (3 or more)
   • Schoolhouse
   • Grocery Store
   • Medical Center
   • Post Office

4   Divide the class into Village Planning Councils (teams of 2 to 6 students each).

5   Instruct each council to elect a secretary who will take notes as the council brainstorms ideas for their village.

6   During the brainstorming session, encourage students to list ideas for the village theme, name, and setting.

   NOTE: For assistance in naming the village, suggest that students look up the word "village" in the thesaurus.

7   Provide students with the following tips designed to stimulate creative thinking:
   • Themes can be visual such as a striped city, a pink city, or a tall and narrow town.
   • Themes can be metaphors for buildings and settings. For example, if boots were buildings, would you like to live among cowboy boots in the Wild West? Your home might be a fancy cowboy boot whereas the saloon might be a scuffed-up boot. Or, would you rather live among hiking boots in the hills? Perhaps you prefer a diverse village made up of all kinds of boots.
   • Themes can be based on architectural styles such as an Alpine village, an ecologically-kind village, or an ancient Chinese village. These must display creative thought and imagination through the use of surprising surface materials, or by adding a touch of fantasy (e.g. the inhabitants are flowers that walk and talk, and so forth).

8   Once the councils have selected a theme, instruct them to decide which buildings will comprise their village.

9   Next, have the councils designate a box for each building. Ask students to consider standard scale proportions when choosing boxes (i.e. the hospital will be much bigger than a private residence).

Village Theme Suggestions

• Astro City
• Bird House Heights
• Bootville
• Cactus County
• Cake Township
• Caveman Borough
• Cereal City
• Checkerboard Junction
• Dog House Downs
• Easter Egg-Land
• Ham Hamlet
• Haunted Village
• Kitty Corners
• Musicville
• Peppermint Place
• Polka Dot Plains
• Seahorse Bay
• Turtletown

10 To construct the villages, have students follow the steps below:

Constructing the Villages
- Stuff the boxes with scrap paper to increase stability.
- Trace four sides onto paper and cut out the shapes.

  NOTE: If you are using a shape that is not rectangular such as the shape of an egg or boot, sketch the shape over the rectangle so that it fits as closely as possible within the edges of the paper.

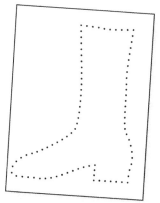

- To make roofs, cut out pieces of cardboard, fold them in half, and glue them to the tops of the boxes. Roofs can be decorated with markers or squares of paper resembling shingles.
- Sketch the doors, windows and other features onto the front, back, and side surfaces. Keep the village theme in mind and use the reference materials provided for style ideas.
- Add creative details such as signposts, billboards, greenery, authentic textures, etc.
- To assemble the village, place the buildings in a pleasant and appropriate arrangement.
- Glue the bottoms of the buildings onto a heavy flat surface such as cardboard or heavy poster board.
- Sketch and cut out streets from paper and place or glue them onto the surface.
- Create street signs by sticking drinking straws into small mounds of clay. Tape a paper street sign to the top. (optional)
- Add creative details like small figurines, artificial greenery, pebbles, and details sculpted from clay.
- Add a name plate for the front of your village.

11 Display the finished villages around the classroom and invite the students to comment on one another's work.

Extensions
- Connect this activity with a social studies unit on communities.
- Integrate this lesson into a unit on architectural design.
- Have students write a short story featuring citizens of their newly created village.

Robo-Buddies

Grade Level: 1 through 8
Participants: Individuals
Objectives: Exercise fluency, flexibility, originality, elaboration, imagination, brainstorming skills, concept development, sketching skills, perspective, and proportions
Time: 1 to 2 hours

Quick View

In this lesson, students combine science with creativity to invent and design buddy robots, or "robo-buddies," programmed to do the things they hate to do, need help doing, or simply wish they were able to do. By mixing, matching, and modifying basic shapes, students learn the "anatomy" of a robot and practice sketching simple mechanical devices as well.

Examples

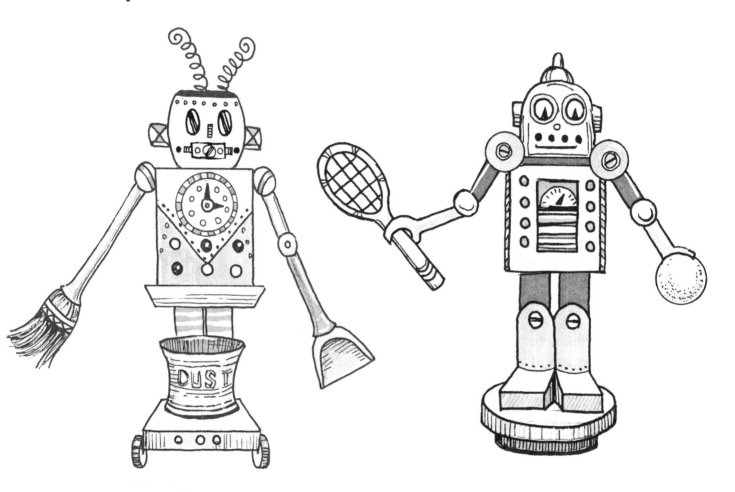

Robbles is a robot who cleans up after me   *Tennis Ro* is my partner for tennis practice

Take Home
Enhanced conceptualization skills and an imaginative design plan for a personal robot

Materials
- Plain paper
- Pencils
- Ruler
- Chalkboard and chalk or equivalent
- Pictures of retro and contemporary robots for student reference
- Crayons, markers, or colored pencils (optional)
- Graph paper (optional)

Getting Ready
- Have students brainstorm things they hate to do such as homework, clearing the table, taking out the garbage, etc.
- Ask students to brainstorm things students would like to have help with such as studying, styling their hair, or making breakfast.
- Finally, invite students to brainstorm things they wish they could do, but cannot such as running faster than anyone else, listening in on teachers' conversations, and catching the ball every time.

  NOTE: Ideas offered through classroom participation are meant to be idea-sparkers only. Students should create individual personal lists.

- Draw some basic robot shapes on the board and display pictures of retro and contemporary robots for student reference.

HEAD SHAPES

BODY SHAPES

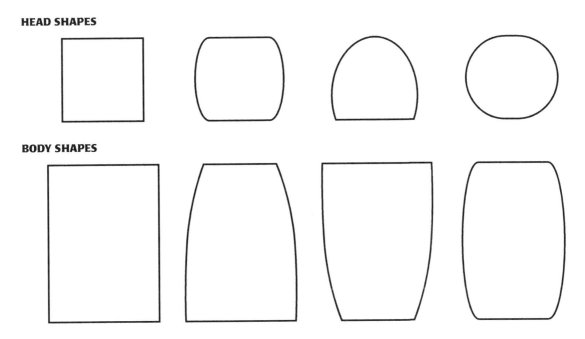

Robo-Buddies *continues* ➜

continued from previous page

Activities and Procedures

1 Explain to the class that they will each design a robot to be their helpful and loyal companion. Ask them to brainstorm and create a personal list of things they would like their robot to do.

2 Next, have students choose three of the items from their list and number them in order of priority. The list will be different for each student.

3 Suggest that students make sketches to show how the robot is designed to perform the three functions.

   NOTE: Students must adhere to the Three Laws of Robotics as they design their robots (see sidebar, "Isaac Asimov's Three Laws of Robotics").

4 To assist students in planning their robot's moving parts, encourage students to ponder which movements the robot will need to execute in order to perform the desired function. For example, will it:
   • Need storage for tools?
   • Speak?
   • Throw a ball?
   • Play music?
   • Have lights or special sensors?
   • Climb, fly, spin, or move fast?
   • Grasp things?

5 As students decide which moveable parts their robot will require, encourage them to explore a variety of options and to make sketches and notes to record their ideas.

6 After students have had sufficient time to brainstorm their robots' functions, have them begin designing the robots' appearance. Explain to students that most robots have a mechanical, engineered, boxy look. See Examples on previous page.

7 Encourage students to use graph paper to sketch in the basic shapes of their robots. If they do not have graph paper, have them draw light guidelines down and across the center of their paper using a ruler. Suggest that students adjust the shapes until they look symmetrical

8 Remind students to use light pencil line until their designs are complete.

Isaac Asimov's Three Laws of Robotics

1 A robot may not injure a human being or, through inaction, allow a human being to come to harm.

2 A robot must obey any orders given to it by human beings except where such orders would conflict with the first law.

3 A robot must protect its own existence as long as such protection does not conflict with the first or second law.

The FIRST Robotics Competition

The FIRST Robotics Competition is an international high school robotics competition organized and started by FIRST (For Inspiration and Recognition of Science and Technology) in 1992 in Manchester, New Hampshire. The founder, Dean Kamen, is an inventor whose passion is to help young people discover the excitement and rewards of science and technology.

   Every year, teams of high school students compete to build robots that can complete a particular task, which changes with each competition. Thousands of students around the world enter the competitions each year. Visit http://www.usfirst.org for more information.

9 Provide the following guidelines for students to follow as they complete their sketches:
- *Start:* Start by sketching two shapes: a head shape and a body shape.
- *Proportions:* head length to body length: 1 to 1½ or 1 to 2. The body should be wider than the head. The body should be longer than the height of the head, not counting details on top.
- *Joints:* Keep the robot's joints in mind (i.e. where appendages bend, where the head turns, antennae, etc. Illustrate the joints using rounded shapes, wedge shapes, or another logical design.
- *Feet:* There are many ways to allow your robot to ambulate such as through the use of feet walkers, wheels, a platform with wheels underneath, a platform that spins, a ball bottom, and so forth. Be creative!
- *Face Details:* Include imaginative facial features. For instance, the mouth might be a speaker. Eyes and eyebrows can give your robot a distinct personality. Noses can be knobs, dials, bulbs, etc. Robots often have lights and antennae at the tops of their heads.
- *Hands:* Depending on what your robot needs to do, consider making the hands take the form of hooks, wheels, magnets, scissors, grabbers, and so forth.
- *Other Details:* Add buttons, dials, wheels, lights, levers, springs, gears, display screens, and more to your robot.

10 Have students finalize their drawings by going back over them with a darker pencil or pen line. Encourage them to add color if they wish.

11 Invite students to name their robots and write short descriptions of their overall purposes and specific functions.

Extensions

Construct A Robot
- Have teams of students collect items from home or school to construct a robot figure. Empty paper towel rolls, tissue boxes, construction paper, empty oatmeal boxes, egg cartons, string, pipe cleaners, tin foil, bottle caps, hardware pieces, cardboard, plastic bottles, and odds and ends work well, especially when you add imagination.
- Encourage students to use glue, tape, scissors, and markers in addition to their collected items to design various robots intended for specific purposes.
- Display the finished robots in the classroom, and invite students to comment on one another's work.

Perspective
- Connect drawings of robots with an art unit on one-point and two-point perspective.

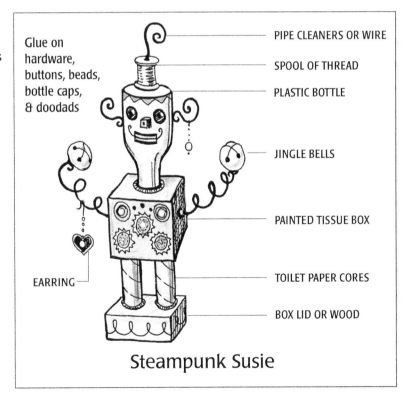

Glue on hardware, buttons, beads, bottle caps, & doodads

PIPE CLEANERS OR WIRE

SPOOL OF THREAD

PLASTIC BOTTLE

JINGLE BELLS

PAINTED TISSUE BOX

EARRING

TOILET PAPER CORES

BOX LID OR WOOD

Steampunk Susie

My Dream Bedroom

Grade Level: 3 through 8
Participants: Individuals
Objectives: Exercise flexibility, originality, elaboration, understanding scale, visual symbols, and graph making
Time: 1 to 2 hours

Quick View

In this exercise in architectural design, fantasy and reality are combined as students plan realistic, professional-looking floor plans for their dream bedrooms or suites. With permission to think big, students sketch luxurious designs while learning about architectural symbols, style, and terminology.

Example

See "My Dream Bedroom."

Take Home

A floor plan for a personal dream bedroom

Materials

- Graph paper
- Plain paper
- Pencils
- Markers, colored pencils, and crayons
- Rulers
- Examples of floor plans
- Chalkboard and chalk or equivalent

Getting Ready

- Collect and display examples of floor plans from magazines and websites for student reference.
- Gather and display pictures of doorways, window styles, balconies, staircases, floor coverings, wall coverings, and other interesting architectural features from magazines, websites, and books.
- Write the following words and definitions on the board and explain their meanings:
  - *Floor Plan* – a diagram of a room or rooms, usually drawn to scale
  - *Scale* – the ratio between the actual size of something and the representation of it
  - *Plan View* – a drawing that shows the appearance of a room when seen from above

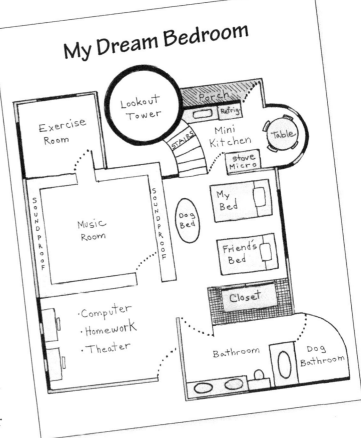

Activities and Procedures

1 Use graph paper to show students how to draw a floor plan for a room. Explain that each square represents one foot.

2 Show students example floor plans and discuss strategies for depicting door openings, windows, furniture, and other features.

3 As a class, decide on the symbols that students will use to represent typical beds, desks, chairs, doorways, windows, stairs, and more. Students may also make up symbols for atypical features such as an unusual shaped bed, an easel, or a snack dispenser.

4 Discuss the function of a bedroom and list the essentials. For example, you might suggest that every floor plan include the following:
   - Bed
   - Closet
   - Desk and chair
   - Door
   - Window
   - Hobby or activity area

5 Next, invite students to list their hobbies and interests such as:
   - Astronomy
   - Collecting sea shells
   - Listening to music
   - Painting pictures
   - Playing ping pong
   - Photography or video

   Instruct students to keep these things in mind when designing their dream bedrooms.

6 Tell students to make a list of the things they would like in their fantasy rooms. Remind them that there is no budget!

   Although the lists will vary depending on students' individual interests and preferences, some ideas are listed below:
   - Air hockey table
   - Aquarium wall
   - Bathtub with a bubbles faucet
   - Bed with a special place for your pet
   - Built-in display case for collections
   - Closet with revolving clothing racks
   - Homework room with no distractions
   - Lookout tower and telescope
   - Mini kitchen
   - Music system
   - Secret door that opens to the outside
   - Skating rink
   - Skylight
   - Sleepover room with pull-down beds
   - Special effects lighting
   - Theater
   - Trampoline bed and a very high ceiling
   - Velcro covered walls

7 Encourage students to include space and resources for all of their important activities, hobbies, collections, and dreams when designing their floor plans.

8 With these things in mind, students should create a rough sketch of their floor plans.

9 Next, ask them to use their graph paper to create a final drawing with labels for furniture and other features.

10 Invite students to use colored markers, pencils, or crayons to make their floor plans visually appealing.

11 Finally, invite students to give their plans titles and write short descriptions of their dream bedrooms.

Extensions
   - Show examples of several different architectural styles and have students learn some key features of each to include in their floor plans.
   - Encourage students to design floor plans for a home, a school, or other type of building.

Upside Downside Up

Grade Level: 3 through 6
Participants: Individuals
Objectives: Exercise flexibility, originality, elaboration, imagination, and visual awareness
Time: ½ hour to 1 hour

Quick View

Most of us have seen clever cartoon faces that transform into entirely different faces when turned upside down. This lesson shows students how to design the challenging faces, then craft them into masks or double-faced note cards.

Examples

Jake McBlister...   ...and his Charming Sister

Silly Ms. Millie...   ...and her husband Big Billy

Take Home
A novel drawing made into a mask or set of note cards.

Materials
- Plain heavy paper, approximately 8½" x 11"
- Pencils
- Crayons or markers
- Scissors
- Hole punch (optional)
- String or ribbon

Getting Ready
- Gather examples of upside-downside-up faces to show to your students. Use the examples in this book, or find more online

Upside Downside Up *continues* ➜

continued from previous page

Activities and Procedures

1   Position the paper vertically and using a pencil draw a vertical oval shape in the center. The oval should be 5″ to 7″ from top to bottom.

2   Explain to the students that the faces they draw can be silly, weird, funny, or scary. Animal, fantasy, and extraterrestrial faces work well, too.

3   Lightly draw a nose in the center of the oval. Add ears to the sides of the face.

4   Lightly sketch eyes, eyebrows, upper lip, and lower lip.

5   Optional additions: mustache, hair, beard, hat, bow, bow tie, collars, hats, forehead wrinkles, chin lines, dimples, age lines, face contour lines, and more.

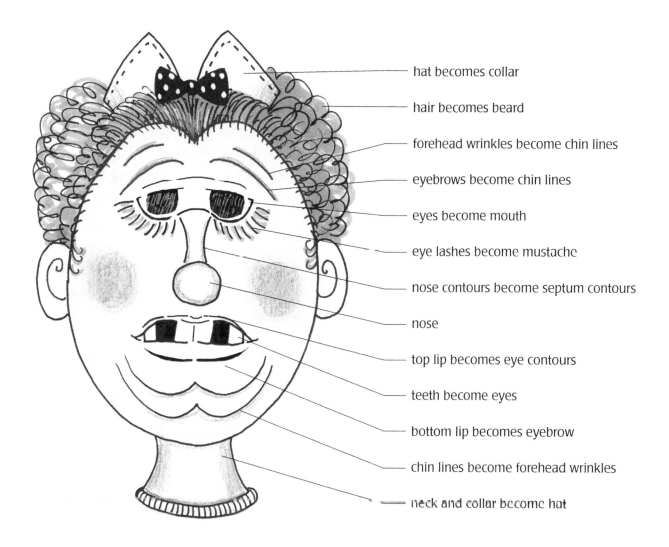

- hat becomes collar
- hair becomes beard
- forehead wrinkles become chin lines
- eyebrows become chin lines
- eyes become mouth
- eye lashes become mustache
- nose contours become septum contours
- nose
- top lip becomes eye contours
- teeth become eyes
- bottom lip becomes eyebrow
- chin lines become forehead wrinkles
- neck and collar become hat

6 Turn your paper often, to check how the opposite face is shaping up. Alter your drawing to make them the most effective for the double faces.

7 After you are satisfied with your drawing, darken the lines, and color the faces.

8 Give each face a name.

9 *Masks*
   • Cut out the faces. Cut a breathing slit or holes in the nose. Cut holes in the eyes.
   • Make holes near the ears. Knot a ribbon length through each hole and tie them together around your head. You can wear your mask two ways.

10 *Note Cards*
   • Fold a piece of heavy paper to create a note card. Position the note card so it opens on the right.
   • Photocopy the face to fit the front of the note card.
   • Now flip the card over, and position that side to open on the right. Paste a photocopy of the upside down version of the face to fit.
   • Position the cards either way for writing notes.

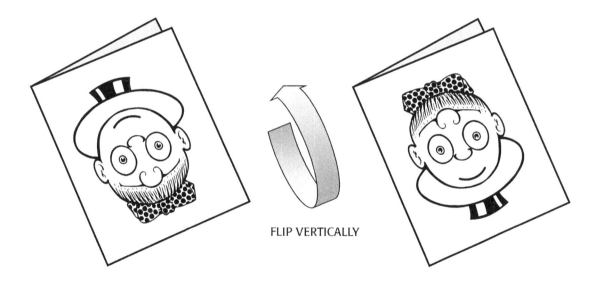

FLIP VERTICALLY

Extensions
   • Draw various face shapes.
   • Draw animal features.
   • Draw monster faces.

Grade Level: 3 to 8
Participants: Individuals
Objectives: Exercise originality, elaboration, organizing and categorizing, visualization, artistic design, jewelry-making vocabulary, and concept development
Time: 1 to 2 hours

Quick View

In this exercise in artistic accessorizing, students learn how to design and construct original charm bracelets. By brainstorming and developing themes, identifying essential jewelry parts, and following the visual planning and presentation process used by professional jewelry designers, students practice both self-expression and concept development.

Example

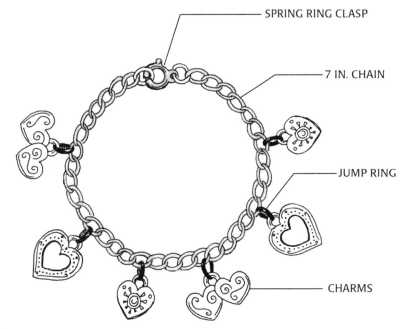

SPRING RING CLASP

7 IN. CHAIN

JUMP RING

CHARMS

Take Home

Enhanced visualization and artistic design skills as well as a ready-to-make design for an original charm bracelet

Materials

- Plain paper, 8½″ x 11″ (two sheets per student)
- Tracing paper, 8½″ x 11″ (one sheet per student)
- Plain index cards, one per student
- Pencils
- Black pens
- Glue sticks
- Scissors
- Tape
- Pictures of jewelry chains, clasps, jump rings and charms from craft catalogs or websites
- Pictures of charm bracelets
- Chalkboard and chalk or equivalent
- An example of a real charm bracelet (optional)

Getting Ready

- Gather pictures of charm styles and charms to display for reference.
- Write jewelry-related vocabulary words on the board. (See sidebar, "Jewelry Vocabulary.")
- Explain that the charms on a charm bracelet are often shaped like objects, but sometimes they depict images, words, symbols, or abstract decorations.

Activities and Procedures

1   Inform students that their assignment is to design an original charm bracelet using a procedure similar to that used by professional jewelry designers.

2   Invite students to brainstorm theme ideas for their charm bracelets. Provide the example ideas in the sidebar, "Theme Suggestions" in order to stimulate creative thinking.

Jewelry Vocabulary

Charm bracelets have been beloved accessories for thousands of years. As glamorous personal statements, they are as popular in contemporary fashion jewelry today as ever before.

Chain: a flexible length of metal formed by links

Charm: a small ornament to attach to a bracelet

Clasp: a fastener for a jewelry chain

Jewelry findings: small metal parts used within jewelry

Jewelry pliers: a tool for manipulating pieces of metal

Jump ring: small metal rings used to attach charms to a chain

Charm bracelet: a decorative wristband with miniature ornaments affixed to it

Theme Suggestions

Favorite Things: butterflies, flowers, books, animals including endangered species such as whales, etc.

Personal Memoirs: photos of friends and family, things that commemorate happy events such as birthdays, graduations, vacations, recitals, school achievements, a new puppy, a new house, etc.

Words and Phrases: uplifting messages, adages, words of inspiration, etc.

Good Luck Symbols: ladybugs, horseshoes, four leaf clovers, silver dollars, etc.

Hobbies: items related to hobbies such as a camera, an artist's palette, coins, gems, baking supplies, etc.

Fantasy and Mythology: fairies, mermaids, dragons, wizards, trolls, princesses, castles, gargoyles, etc.

Music and Dance: clef symbols, notes, tap shoes, tutus, ballerina slippers, etc.

Shoes and Fashion Items: boots, high-heel shoes, brand symbols, sundresses, prom dresses, jeans, handbags, hats, etc.

Sports: various types of sports equipment, bat and ball, soccer balls, basketballs, ice skates, team logos, etc.

Symbols: zodiac, peace, spiritual, yin yang, ankh, pyramid, keys, hearts, stars, items of personal significance, etc.

Charm School *continues* ➜

continued from previous page

3 Begin by referring to the example Charm Bracelet Specification Chart below. (For a ready-to-use blank specification chart for your students, visit www.jrimagination.com/printables.)
   - Down the left side of the chart, list:
     Chain Style – 7″ (standard bracelet length)
     Two or more clasp styles, silver or gold metal – approximately ¼″
     Jump rings, silver or gold metal, – ⅛″ to ¼″ diameter
     Three or more charms, gold, silver, or
   - enameled metal– ¼″ to ¾″ (not to exceed ¾″ in any direction)
   - Fill in information across the chart.
   - Sketch or paste photos under "illustrations."
   - Give each chain, clasp, ring, and charm a Style No.

Charm Bracelet Specification Chart

ITEM	STYLE NO.	MATERIAL: SILVER OR GOLD	QTY	ILLUSTRATIONS	SIZE
CHAIN	A-01	GOLD	1		7 inches
RING CLASP	A-02	GOLD	1		¼ inch - large
JUMP RINGS	A-03	GOLD	5		¼ inch - large
HEART CHARM	A-04	GOLD	2		¼ inch - small
DOUBLE HEART CHARM	A-05	GOLD	2		¼ inch - small
OPEN HEART CHARM	A-06	GOLD	2		½ inch - small

4 Instruct students to adhere to the following guidelines for designing the charms:
   - Brainstorm as many as items as you can that fit into the category of the selected theme.
   - Select five or more things to develop as charms, and sketch them. Charms should be between ¼″ and ¾″, no part to exceed ¾″ in any direction.
   - To create a sizing stencil, cut out a square template from an index card. With light pencil line, trace the "not to exceed" limits. Sketch the charms within those borders.
   - If the charms are miniature sculptures of things, add a loop at the top for attaching to the chain with a jump ring.
   - If the charms are flat shapes, plan a tiny hole near the top for attaching to the chain with a jump ring.
   - Refine pencil sketches with black pen line.

5 Invite students to follow the steps below to create the final bracelet design:
   - Write a descriptive title at the top of a sheet of plain paper. For example, "**Hearts and Keys Charm Bracelet**"

- Add a sub-title. For example, "**Gold hearts and silver keys commemorate special friends**"
- Sketch or glue on a 7″ bracelet chain, chosen from the chart.
- Sketch the clasp, chosen from the chart, on the right end.
- Cut out the charms. Arrange them under the bracelet chain. Make sure you leave room between the chain and the charms for the jump ring attachments.
- Glue the charms in place and sketch in the jump rings.
- Add color to make the design more visually appealing (optional).

6 Have students label the bracelet design by taping a sheet of tracing paper to the top of the final bracelet design drawing. It should be the same size as the drawing beneath it. Then, instruct them to label the different bracelet parts and draw lines leading to the parts.

Extensions

- Have students extend their research on jewelry chain and clasp styles to include six or more of each. Invite them to make a chart of photos or sketches with their style names such as snake chain, cable chain, box chain, lobster claw clasp, toggle clasp, and hook and eye clasp.
- Integrate this activity with an art history unit by creating charms inspired by a specific style in art history such as pop art (soup cans and ordinary objects), Matisse-inspired shapes, Fauvist-inspired colors, ancient Greek pottery, ancient Egyptian motifs, architectural wonders, and Picasso-inspired imagery.
- Connect this lesson with a math unit on millimeter and centimeter conversions.
- Use the activity with a social studies unit and have students make charms to commemorate landmarks, events, or important people.
- Incorporate this activity into a science unit by encouraging students to create charms that signify endangered species, sea creatures, prehistoric creatures, butterflies of the world, etc.

Make A Play Charm Bracelet

1 Cut 14″ lengths of ribbon. Braid the ribbon and knot the ends.
2 Draw five or more ¾″ charms on index card stock. Color them, and paint a coat of acrylic gloss medium on them.
3 Cut out the charm shapes and push a small safety pin through a spot near the center top, about ⅛″ to ³/₁₆″ from the top edge.
4 Attach small safety pins at intervals along the length of braided ribbon 4″ in from each end.
5 Attach the charm's safety pin to a safety pin on the braid.
6 Use silver or gold thread with large needles to form thread attachments (optional).
7 Tie the bracelet onto your wrist.

Make A Play Charm Necklace

Use approximately 36″ lengths of ribbon, and follow the procedure above.

Make Sculpted Charms

1 Sculpt charms from self-hardening clay.
2 Insert a small paper clip or safety pin (opening end in, small loop out) in the clay at the top of the charm for attaching to braided ribbon with another safety pin or heavy thread.
3 Let the charms dry, color with paint or markers, and coat with acrylic gloss medium.
4 Sculpt charms from clay that hardens by oven baking such as Sculpey.
5 Make a hole ³/₁₆″ or more from the edge and large enough to pull a large blunt needle and heavy thread through.
6 Bake according to directions on package.
7 Let cool and color charms with paint or markers. Coat with acrylic gloss medium.
8 Attach charms to braided ribbon with cord or heavy thread.

Grade Level: 2 through 6
Participants: Individuals
Objectives: Exercise originality, elaboration, theme development, writing skills, and sketching skills
Time: 2 to 3 hours

Quick View

In this whimsical activity, students pay tribute to the nostalgic Jack in the Box toy by creating an original character to replace Jack and developing a theme, jingle, and setting around their new character. By creating a new twist on a traditional concept, students express their creativity while practicing their concept development skills as well.

Examples

Lion Jingle

(to the tune of *Pop! Goes The Weasel*)

The lion is the king of beasts,

His roar is loud and scary,

Through the jungle he roams free,

Animals be wary.

Take Home

An original replica of a Jack-In-The-Box toy

Materials

- Photocopies of the box template, one per student. (For a free, printable download, visit www.jrimagination.com/printables)
- Five squares of heavy paper 2½″ x 2½″ for each student
- Heavy paper, 5″ x 2½″ per student. When folded in half, the paper should be a square the same size as the other five squares
- Small pieces of heavy paper, one per student
- Pencils
- Tape
- Glue sticks
- Scissors
- Crayons, markers, or colored pencils

Getting Ready

- Provide photocopies of the box template, one per student.
- Cut out and tape together boxes for your students. (optional)
- Cut five squares of heavy paper to fit onto the box sides and top.
- Gather pictures of Jack-in-the-Box toys and an actual toy, if possible.
- Write the following words and definitions on the board and discuss their meanings with the class:
  - Analogs: words related to a theme
  - Motifs: a repeated design or pattern related to a theme

Activities and Procedures

1 Using a picture or an authentic toy as a model, explain to the class what a Jack-in-the-Box toy is and how it works.

2 Inform students that they will be designing their own original Jack-in-the- Box, substituting their own character for Jack.

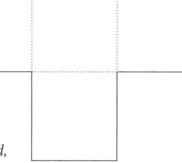

Box Template

3 Have students brainstorm character ideas such as *a dinosaur, monkey, kitten, bug, rock star, fashion model, butterfly, mermaid, basketball star, queen of hearts, shark, elephant, Abe Lincoln,* or *Vincent Van Gogh.*

4 Ask students to select a character from their brainstorming list and make a sketch of it.

5 To begin developing a design theme, invite students to list what they know about their character including its environment, the food it eats, what it does, its physical characteristics, popular myths about it, its colors, and anything else related to the character.

6 Have students make a list of analogs related to their chosen character. For example, if a lion were selected, students may list words associated with a lion including *jungle, safari, paw prints, African sunsets, king, crown, yellow and orange, jungle animals,* and *African tribal designs.*

   NOTE: Analog lists are important reference for developing a design theme. Professional designers use these processes when developing their creations.

7 Encourage students to select some motifs from their analog lists. For example, some lion-related motifs are *paw prints, a jungle leaf,* and *a king's crown.*

8 Invite students to sketch three or more motifs.

Jack-Not-in-the-Box *continues* ➜

continued from previous page

9 Instruct students to use at least two motifs to sketch borders associated with their character. For example, one might combine African tribal motifs with yellow and orange crowns to create a border design.

10 Next, have students sketch at least one environment for their characters such as an African sunset with trees.

11 Then, ask students to think of names for their characters. The names can be as simple as "Lion" or unique as "Lionell, A Likeable Lion." Sketch a few ways of drawing the letters.

12 Encourage your students to make up jingles about their characters to the tune of Pop! Goes The Weasel. A simple poem for one stanza with four lines will do. Remind older students to follow the meter of the tune.

Lion Jingle (to the tune of *Pop! Goes The Weasel*)

The lion is the king of beasts,

His roar is loud and scary,

Through the jungle he roams free,

Animals be wary.

13 Have students use the
   box templates provided to
   construct the boxes. Tell
   them to press down firmly
   on the folds and tape the
   edges together.

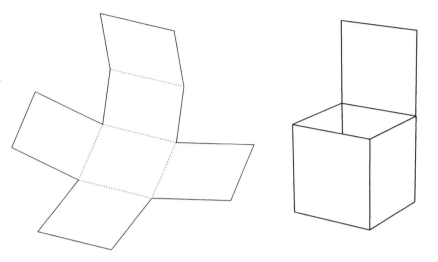

14 To construct the
   pop-up lid, instruct
   students to fold and
   cut heavy paper as
   shown.

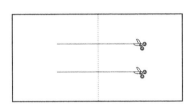
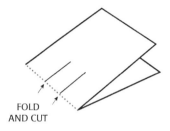

FOLD
AND CUT

15 Tell students to use a glue stick to adhere the top part
   of the pop-up lid to the inside of the box lid as shown.
   Have students tape the bottom of the pop-up piece to
   form a top surface for the box as shown.

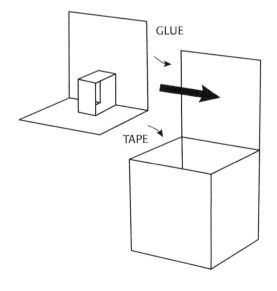

GLUE

TAPE

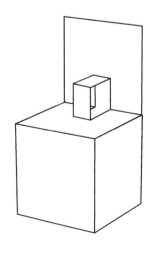

Jack-Not-in-the-Box *continues* ➜

continued from previous page

16 Suggest that students refer to their analog lists and prior sketches as they follow the instructions below to decorate the panels of their boxes:

- *Front Panel:* Draw decorative letters for your title. Color them in, and add designs to the rest of the square. Glue it to the front panel of your box.
- *Right Side Panel:* Draw a handle similar to the one shown on the template. Color it, and add a border design. Glue the square to your right side panel of the box.
- *Left Side Panel:* Using a straight edge, draw guidelines on a paper square. Write lyrics and add a border. Glue the square to your left side panel of the box.
- *Back panel:* On the bottom of the square write: "Designed by (your name)." Add the date, and draw and color a setting. Glue the square to the back panel of your box.
- *Top Lid:* Decorate the top lid any way you wish, but be sure to add a border.

17 Have students draw their characters onto small pieces of heavy paper. The character should be approximately half the height of the square lid, but no taller.

18 Invite students to add color to their characters, making the outlines around it heavier than the inside lines.

19 Instruct students to cut out their character sketches and glue them inside the lid on the vertical plane of the pop-up fold so that when the lid is closed, the character will fold down under the lid and when the lid is opened, the character will pop up.

TIP: It's ok for the top and sides to stick out, but the bottom should not exceed the fold.

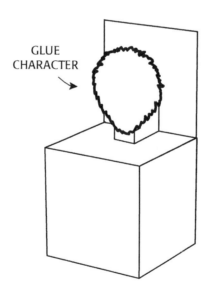

GLUE CHARACTER

NOTE: As optional enhancements, students may also wish to decorate the inside panels or punch a hole at the center front of the lid and tie string through it to create a pull for lifting the box lid.

20 Display the "Jack-Not-In-The-Boxes" for all to see, and invite students to comment on each other's work.

Who Is Jack?

The Jack-in-the-Box is a classic children's wind-up toy that consists of a box with a crank. As the crank is turned, it plays a melody, usually "Pop! Goes the Weasel." At the end of the tune, the lid pops open, and a clown figure pops out of the box.

Where Did Jack Come From?

Early in the 16th century, a German clockmaker named Claus made a toy for a local prince's fifth birthday. It was a wooden box with a handle that, when turned, produced a simple tune. At the end of the tune, out popped a paper mache "Jack", a comical figure on a spring which was believed to stave off bad luck.

As other nobles saw the toy, the idea spread. Contemporary adaptations include a variety of characters and tunes as well as the timeless Jack and the familiar tune.

Traditional American Jack-In-The-Box Jingle—Pop! Goes The Weasel

> A penny for a spool of thread,
>
> A penny for a needle,
>
> That's the way the money goes,
>
> Pop! Goes the weasel.

There are additional verses to this song, and several more versions of the lyrics. The earliest written record of the song goes back to 1855, in England. Scholars debate the meaning of the lyrics.

Extensions:

- Integrate this activity into a social studies unit by having students select historical characters such as Benjamin Franklin or Abe Lincoln for their "Jack-Not-In-The-Box" characters. Encourage them to write short biographies in place of song lyrics and use photos for the pop-up characters.
- Connect this lesson with special themes such as:
  - Endangered Species
  - Holidays
  - Greek Mythology
  - Inventions
  - Plants and Flowers
  - Poets
  - Sea Creatures

Grade Level: 4 through 8
Participants: Individuals or teams of two to four
Objectives: Exercise flexibility, originality, elaboration, categorizing ideas, understanding strategy and cause and effect, concept development, writing skills, design skills, construction skills
Time: Approximately 4 to 6 hours

Quick View

Creating a board game is easier than it might seem—especially for youngsters who get immersed in play on a daily basis. Kids are accustomed to making up new games and altering the rules of established games. Harness this natural creativity as students learn how to generate a game concept, plan it, design it, evaluate it, make a prototype, and have fun playing with classmates.

Examples

Professional designers often rethink an existing game to create an original game. For example, the TV game, Wheel of Fortune, is an elaboration of the humble "Hangman." Below are four directions students can follow to create their games.

Elaborate on a Simple Game
- *The Game of Tic Tac Total* – Tic Tac Toe made into a more challenging strategy game: 25 squares to fill in instead of nine. There's an element of luck with dice.

Simplify an Established Game
- *The Game of Triplettes* – Scrabble structure, but uses no more and no less than three letters per move. Change the ratio of letters available, and use fewer commands on the spaces.

Alter an Established Game
- *Schoolopoly* – Beginners can copy the structure of a familiar game like Monopoly®, making it their own by giving it a new theme.
  - **Object:** To earn the highest grade point average.
  - **Play:** Students pass a number of Subjects (Properties) around the board by landing on them. They may buy them with Study Cards (Monopoly Money) thereby earning "B's". When they own three of a subject they earn "A's." This precludes others from earning "A's" in that subject. Winner has highest grade average at the end of the game.
  - **Details:** Adapt details such as Go To The Principal's Office (Go To Jail), School Events (Community Chest), and Homework (Chance).
  - **Board Design:** The Schoolopoly board design is structured as the Monopoly board, but words and colors are new.
  - **Parts and Pieces:** Use dice and tokens from discarded games or make your own. Cards can be made from index cards.

Create a New Game
- *The Battle for China* –
  - The Great Wall of China is sculpted onto a board.
  - The Ancient Mongolian Army and the Ancient Chinese Army battle for control of the Great Wall. They roll dice, which determines how many men can move a space at a time, into each other's territory. Ten men is a controlling number.

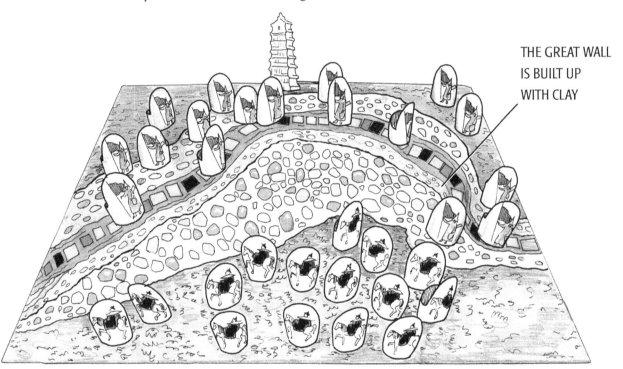

THE GREAT WALL
IS BUILT UP
WITH CLAY

The Battle for China

Take Home
A compelling new board game to play with friends and family. Perhaps it is destined to become a classic game in the marketplace someday!

Materials
- Plain paper
- Grid paper (optional)
- Ruler
- Pencil
- Glue sticks
- Tape
- Large sheets of heavy paper or smaller sheets taped together.

- Markers
- Large sheets of cardboard or discarded game boards. Heavy paper is a reasonable substitute
- Game pieces, or materials for making them, such as paper, buttons, pebbles, and self-hardening clay
- Plastic sandwich bags

Let the Board Games Begin *continues* ➜

continued from previous page

Getting Ready

- Gather a few familiar board games, such as Scrabble®, Monopoly®, Candyland®, Clue®, and Sorry® as examples.
- **Homework Assignment:** Invite students to watch a TV game show or play a board game and write a review identifying the theme and strategy of the game. Determine whether the game depends on luck or strategy, or what percentage of each.

Activities and Procedures

1 **Discuss board games and their playing pieces:** dice, spinners, timers, cards, tokens, and board designs. Show samples. Explain the difference between strategy and luck. A blend of both makes games fun.

2 **Brainstorm ideas for games:** Watch TV game shows and play board games and card games. Becoming familiar with a variety of games can be a springboard for new ideas. Other ideas may be sparked by things around you. Brainstorming with others can help spark ideas, too. Jot down all your ideas before settling on one to develop.
   - Think about strategies for your game. What is the challenge? What is the cause and effect of a player's moves?
   - Strategy games usually have randomizers to bring in the element of luck. These are often chance landings on spaces or cards you pick that offer good and bad luck. Think of ways to add randomizers to your game.

3 **Choose a theme:** Board games have themes that accompany their strategies. The theme for Monopoly is acquiring property. The theme for The Game of Life is family life. The theme for Scrabble is words. If you have a game strategy in mind, think of a theme that fits it. If you have a theme in mind, think of a strategy that fits it.

4 **Describe your new game:**
   - Name of the game (refer to lesson plan, "Name Us Famous," pg. 96)
   - Appropriate age range
   - How many players
   - Objective of the game: What the players do toward winning
   - How to win
   - How the game proceeds
   - How long it takes to play the game

Making Fun

Games depending on strategy to win are called destiny driven. With these games, players' decisions and skills help them win.

Games depending only on luck to win appeal most to players age 7 and younger.

A blend of both luck and strategy make games more fun for all ages. The elements creating luck in a destiny driven game are called randomizers.

Board Game Categories

Abstract strategy: chess, checkers, etc.

Educational games: Shakespeare, Cleopatra, etc.

Eurogames: The Settlers of Catan, Carson City, etc.

Race games: Parchesi, Backgammon

Roll-and-move games: Monopoly, The Game of Life, etc.

Trivia games: Trivial Pursuit, etc.

Social games: Pictionary, Dictionary, etc.

Wargames: Risk, Attack, etc.

Word games: Scrabble, Boggle, etc.

...and more, yet to be invented.

5 **Write clear rules for your game, including**:
  - How to set-up before beginning to play
  - Explain the object of your game
  - Who goes first
  - A list in logical sequence of what to do to play
  - Explain details and how to deal with special situations in your game
  - How players earn points; how to score the game
  - How to win

6 **Design the board and game pieces:** Game boards are usually 19″ square but they can be any size or shape.
  - *Concept sketches:* Start with simple sketches of ideas for what your board might look like. How do players move along or through the board? Will there be a path the players must follow? Make the design compatible with what choices you want your players to have.
  - *Prototype model:* Make an actual size drawing of your game board. If necessary, tape sheets of paper together. Use pencil and ruler to sketch the surface design. Graph paper may help.
  - *Use a discarded game board:* Tape your paper to it to use as a support for your game board. Thrift stores often sell used games that have boards. Cardboard will work, too.
  - *Post-its:* These are flexible aids for figuring out spaces, and index cards make handy prototype cards.
  - *Color the playing surface:* Use markers and glue down pieces of colored paper as needed.
  - *Add features:* Self hardening clay is useful for forming mountains, bumps, ridges, bridges, and more.
  - *Parts and pieces:* Decide which pieces your game needs, such as timers, dice, tokens, decks of cards, spinners, and so forth. Gather these parts from other games or improvise to make them. TIP: Keep small pieces in plastic sandwich bags.

Tokens: Tokens can be painted pebbles, or small clay sculpts, and more. Paper tokens can be made from paper strips glued or taped to form cylinders with a images on the front.

CREATE ARTWORK FOR FRONT WHILE GAME PIECE IS FLAT

THEN, GLUE OR TAPE ENDS TOGETHER

Spinners: Make spinners from cardboard and brads.

7 **Focus Groups:** Classmates test out each other's games, and anonymously rate them (1-5) for fun. Ask classmates to add suggestions that might help the inventor improve their game.

Extensions
  - Connect this activity to a language arts unit on writing instructions.
  - Connect this activity to a social studies or history unit.
  - Have students write advertisements for their games.

Twenty Textures

Grade Level: 2 through 8
Participants: Individuals
Objectives: Exercise fluency, flexibility, originality, visual and tactile awareness
Time: 1 to 2 hours

Quick View

This activity broadens a student's visual repertoire of textures, and opens minds to new possibilities in painting. Students find objects with distinct textures that can be used as stamps or rubbed over to create rich textures. They mount and identify the sources of their textures. The lesson culminates by painting a picture that incorporates wonderful textures.

Examples

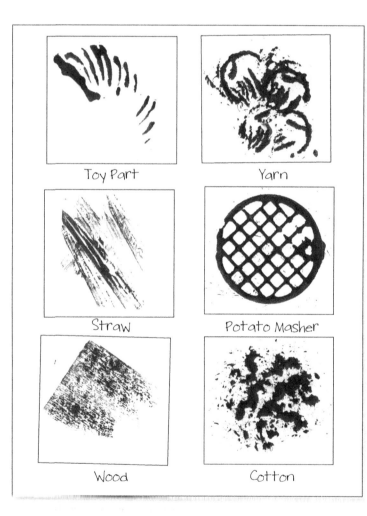

Toy Part

Yarn

Straw

Potato Masher

Wood

Cotton

Golden Ebony (detail). From a painting by the author.

Take Home

Textures for reference and a wonderful painting

Materials
- Heavy paper
- Tempera paint or similar
- Brushes
- Crayons
- A variety of objects that can be used for stamping, or rubbing over
- Glue stick
- Pencils

Getting Ready
- Gather a variety of objects that can be used for this lesson
- Gather some examples of paintings that use texture. Websites showing contemporary art are a good source of examples.

Activities and Procedures

1 Explain the word texture to your class. There are two kinds of textures: (a.) those that you can feel, and (b.) those that look like surfaces you can feel, but are really flat marks on a surface.

2 Find objects with distinct textures that can be dipped in paint and used as stamps. Flat shapes work well, but bulky surfaces can be rolled onto paper, too. Surfaces can be rubbed over, using thin paper and the side a crayon.

3 Look for leaves, wildflowers, bark, bricks, scraps of cloth, spiral notebook edges, stucco walls, crumpled paper, discarded items. Be imaginative; help students find the unexpected and see new possibilities in familiar items.

4 Students search to identify many textures. Next they stamp or rub samples of textures onto paper, cut them into squares, and mount and label them. They should have at least 6 textures.

5 Now students select from these textures to use within a painting. For example, applying the bark texture to a tree trunk will achieve an authentic looking tree.

6 For creative paintings, apply textures in *new, unexpected ways*. For example, apply bark texture in pale colors for a cloudy sky.

7 Encourage students to think about the look of the textures regardless of their source. For example, a texture resulting from rubbing a crayon on paper over a rough stone may look like soft fur.

8 Textures may be used in abstract paintings, as well, focusing on their aesthetic appeal.

9 Textures may be applied collage style, or stamped or rubbed directly onto the final paintings.

Extensions
- Make a collage using textures only to match their source. For example, the texture created on paper by rubbing over wood grain can be cut and used to represent a wood surface in the painting.
- Make a collage using textures only in ways that represent anything *but* the surfaces that were their source. For example, the texture made by stamping with a flower can be used to represent shingles on a roof.

Grade Level: 3 through 8
Participants: Individuals
Objectives: Exercise flexibility, originality, visual concept development, and art skills such as drawing, composition, painting, and color harmony
Time: 1 to 2 hours

Quick View

In this lesson, student artists take their places among painters from the Renaissance to modern day by creating their very own art movements, or "isms." By defining their unique style of expression and then applying it to a still-life, students enhance their creativity while paying homage to the great artists of the past.

Examples

Original still life shapes

Dab-ism

Square-ism

Take Home

Enhanced visualization and artistic skills and an original painting with the potential of sparking a new art movement

Materials

- Plain paper
- Pencils
- Heavy paper or board for painting or drawing, 9″ x 12″ or larger, one sheet per student
- Water based paints such as tempera, watercolor, or acrylics
- Brushes, mixing palette, water container, and paper towels
- Oil pastels, chalk pastels, or crayons in many colors (optional)

Setting Up a Still Life

- Start with one main item of a large, simple shape.
- Add two or three smaller items, nothing complex.
- Put a solid neutral background behind the items. A large sheet of paper, cardboard, or cloth works well.
- Set up the still life in a place where the lighting is good and all can see it well.

Getting Ready

- Set up a still life using objects on hand, or ask students to bring in some props from home.
- Gather examples of a few "isms" from the art world such as Pointillism, cubism, expressionism, surrealism, etc., and put these on display for student reference.
- Cover the tables or work surfaces with plastic cloth or equivalent.
- Place art materials within the reach of all students.

Activities and Procedures

1 Explain the meaning of "ism" in art: an art movement in which a group of artists, working in the same time period, explore creative expression using a certain system.

2 Show some examples of paintings from an "ism" movement.

3 Show the class the still life set-up and ask them to decide on a special process (an "ism") for portraying the still life in a new way.

4 Provide students with the following "ism" suggestions. Students may select from the list or invent their very own "isms."

   - Cross-hatch-ism
   - Dab-ism
   - Diagonal-ism
   - Drip-ism
   - Thumbprint-ism
   - Orange-ism
   - Rain-ism
   - Round-ism
   - Splotch-ism
   - Square-ism
   - Stretch-ism
   - Stripe-ism
   - Swirl-ism
   - Wiggle-ism
   - Zigzag-ism

   NOTE: Do not allow more than 2 or 3 artists to use the same "ism." It's most exciting to generate a variety of artistic perspectives in the classroom.

5 Have artists put the name of their "ism" in the upper right corner of their painting surface.

6 Next, ask students to sketch the main shapes of the still life, handling the proportions as their chosen "ism" inspires.

7 Invite artists to apply paint according to their "ism" vision. They should fill the whole surface of their paintings including the background.

   NOTE: It may take some trial-and-error for artists to find their way. Encourage this exploration as it is an important part of the learning process.

8 Encourage students to present their finished art pieces to the class by explaining their "ism" and the process they used to create their new "art movement."

Extensions

- Randomly assign the "isms" and have students interpret them according to their personal perspectives.
- Ask students to do a second painting of the same still life using another "ism."
- Invite students to create a painting of the still life using an established "ism" such as impressionism.

Suggestions for Main Items

- Backpack
- Beach toy
- Cake
- Cowboy boots or hat
- Musical instrument
- Plush animal
- Pumpkin
- Sports equipment
- Stack of books
- Teapot
- Terra cotta flower pot
- Toy sailboat
- Umbrella
- Watering can

Grade Level: 1 through 4
Participants: Individuals
Objectives: Exercise flexibility, originality, elaboration, imagination, visual awareness, and drawing skills
Time: ½ hour to 1 hour

Quick View

In this exercise in personal perspective, students learn that true art is in the eye of the beholder as they discover unique images within their classmates' simple drawings. Using their powers of visualization and creativity, students transform ordinary sketches into original masterpieces.

Example

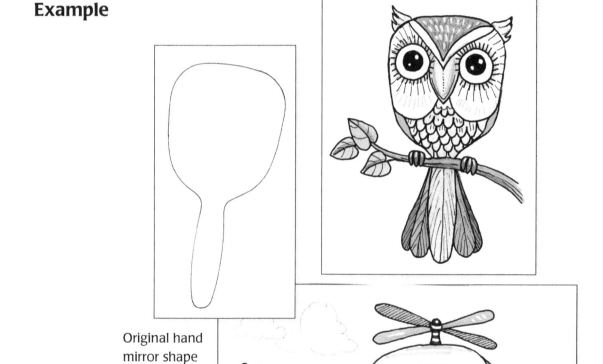

Original hand mirror shape

Take Home
Enhanced visualization and artistic skills as well as an original masterpiece to share with family and friends

Materials
- Heavy paper, 8½″ x 11″ or larger
- Pencils
- An assortment of everyday objects
- Crayons or markers

Getting Ready
- Gather the objects and place them in a box or in the center of a table.
- Distribute paper to the students.

Activities and Procedures

1 Invite students to select three objects and use pencil to trace the outlines of the objects onto their drawing papers. Instruct them to trace the outline shape only, not the interior lines or details.

2 Provide the following suggestions to guide students as they trace their chosen objects:
   - Look for interesting outside "contours."
   - Allow the objects to overlap if you wish.
   - It's ok if parts of the objects do not fit onto the paper.

3 Instruct students to write the name of the object(s) they traced on the backside of their papers.

4 Collect the drawings, shuffle them, and redistribute them.

5 Invite students to look for new images in their classmates' outline drawings. Suggest that they position the outline drawings in several directions to gain new perspectives.

6 Instruct students to add lines within, between, and/or around the shapes to create new objects or images. Tell students not to erase any of the original outlines, however.

7 Explain that the shapes must become something *other* than the original traced object. For example, the stapler can become a dinosaur head, a rock formation, or part of a design, but *not* a stapler.

8 When the new drawings are complete, encourage students to use crayon or markers to add color and create visual effects.

9 Finally, invite students to give their pictures creative titles.

10 Display the final drawings and ask classmates to guess which objects first inspired the final works of art.

Extensions
- Have students continue passing the drawings to transform them into collective masterpieces designed by the entire class.
- For a personalized effect, invite students to use the letters of their names as the original objects for their drawings.

What to Trace?
- Crayons
- Banana
- Book
- Crumpled paper towel
- Eyeglasses
- Hairbrush
- Hand
- Magnifying glass
- Mug
- Necklace
- Pencil box
- Scissors
- Shoe
- Stapler on its side
- Tape dispenser on its side
- Water bottle
- Yo-yo and string

Switch-a-Pic

Grade Level: 3 through 8
Participants: Three or more individuals
Objectives: Exercise flexibility, originality, elaboration, imagination, concept and composition development, and visual awareness
Time: ½ hour to 1 hour

Quick View

In this exercise in artistic perspective, students create simple sketches and pass them to their classmates who add unique details and elaborations. As the drawings are passed from student to student, they are transformed into complex and sometimes abstract masterpieces. By witnessing and participating in this transformation, students gain an appreciation of both artistic diversity and teamwork.

Example

Take Home

An original artwork demonstrating the powerful and diverse influence of the creative mind

Materials

- Heavy paper, 8½″ x 11″ or larger, one per student
- Pencils
- Crayons, markers, or colored pencils

Getting Ready

- Arrange desks so that students can pass drawings around easily.
- Explain to the class that during this activity, they will create simple drawings and then swap their sketches back and forth with their classmates to get the benefit of fresh points of view until the drawing is returned to them for completion.

Activities and Procedures

1 Invite students to select the subject matter for the original drawing. Encourage them to choose any object they wish, whether abstract or realistic.

2 Give students five minutes to sketch their original drawing. Tell them that they may use color at any stage of the process.

3 When time is up, instruct each student to pass their drawing to the classmate on their right.

4 The student who receives the drawing then has five minutes to add details to the original sketch. Instruct students to add any details they wish including straight lines, curves, squiggles, symbols, or realistic objects.

5 When the five minutes have passed, instruct the student to return the drawing to the initial artist who then has five minutes to elaborate on the changes made to the original work.

6 When time is up, instruct the artist to pass the drawing again, this time to the student on their left who will add their unique artistic touch to the work in progress.

7 Continue this process for a few rounds or until time is up.

8 At the end of the final round, ask students to return the drawings to the original artist for completion.

9 As students complete their drawings, encourage them to think of ways to visually unify all of the elements.

10 Invite students to share the finished works of art with the class. Encourage students to comment on the art as a whole as well as their individual contributions.

Switch-a-Pic Procedure

Each student begins a drawing, then switches at teacher's command with another student, who adds to it, then switches back to the original artist, in this order:

- Original artist – 5 minutes
- Student on the right – 5 minutes
- Original artist – 5 minutes
- Student on the left – 5 minutes
- Original artist – 5 minutes

Extensions

- Have students respond to oral cues as they draw. For instance, call out various objects intermittently as the students work such as *tree, tower, dragon, sunrays, rain, sailboat*, etc., and encourage artists to incorporate the items into their drawings. Compare the drawings to demonstrate how similar subject matter can be depicted by a medley of artists.
- Encourage students to use only abstract images in their drawings. Call out shapes such as triangle, rectangle, circle, oval, square, free form, half circle, etc., and ask students to incorporate these shapes into their sketches.

A-Maze Yourself

Grade Level: 3 through 8
Participants: Individuals
Objectives: Exercises flexibility, originality, elaboration, visualization, concept development, and mathematical skills
Time: Approximately 1 hour

Quick View

In this "a-maze-ing" activity, students design and publish original maze puzzles to share with their classmates. As students learn about and reproduce intricate aspects of mazes such as junctions, spirals, and blind alleys, they enhance their visualization and conceptualization skills while applying geometrical concepts as well.

Example

Hey, stop! Come back with my homework!

START

FINISH

Take Home

Enhanced visualization and conceptualization skills and an original maze to share with family and friends

Materials
- Paper
- Pencils
- Erasers
- Rulers
- Pens
- Examples of mazes from workbooks or websites
- Graph paper (optional)
- "Dot Grid" sheets. (For a printable download visit www.jrimagination.com/printables.)

Getting Ready
- Write the following word and definition on the board:
  maze- (n.) a puzzle of interconnecting lines that require the solver to find their way from start to finish by following the correct pathway and avoiding misleading pathways
- Show some examples of mazes and discuss their similarities and differences.
- Have each student work a sample maze and discuss strategies for successfully completing maze puzzles.

A-maze-ing Facts
- A **maze** has false pathways that mislead solvers as they try to find their way from start to finish.
- A **simply-connected maze** is formed from a continuous wall so that it can be solved by keeping one hand in contact with the wall.
- **Multiply-connected mazes** are intensely challenging mazes that include both dead ends and blind alleys.
- A **labyrinth** has a single path that leads the solver from the start (entrance) to the finish (exit).
- The first known labyrinths were the **Cretan Labyrinth at Knossis**, built about 4000 years ago, and **The Egyptian Labyrinth**, built in the 5th century, B. C. There are intriguing theories about the purpose of these mysterious structures.
- **English castle garden mazes** date back to the late 1600s. Their walls were made by hedges, and the mazes were often used as secret meeting places. Garden mazes have a "key," or strategy to find one's way out. There are over a hundred garden mazes to visit in England.
- Since the early 20th century, scientists have used **mazes to test the behavior of rats**.
- In 2008, **Dole Plantation Giant Pineapple Garden Maze** in Hawaii was declared the world's largest maze. The fastest finishers win a prize.
- A **corn maze** is a maze cut from a cornfield. They are popular attractions in the U.S., usually at farms where pumpkins are sold.
- **Adrian Fisher** of England designed the world's first corn maze. He designed over 500 mazes in 30 countries and holds several world records for his designs.
- Hand-drawn **maze puzzles** have been enjoyed around the globe since the fifteenth century.
- An electronic, **interactive Maze Pix** was developed in the 1990's in Japan.

A-Maze Yourself *continues* →

continued from previous page

Practice Makes Perfect Mazes

Draw pathway walls by keeping lines parallel, whether they are straight or curved

Students who love a challenge can experiment with placing spirals, kernels, and other configurations

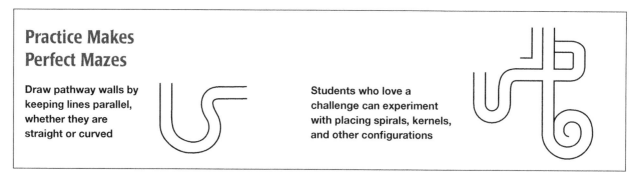

Making the Maze

Dot Grid sheets have dots that are spaced ¼ inch apart.

Lightly sketch a pathway through the grid from the S point to the F point.

Have students add junctions, blind alleys, or dead ends leading off the S to F pathway.

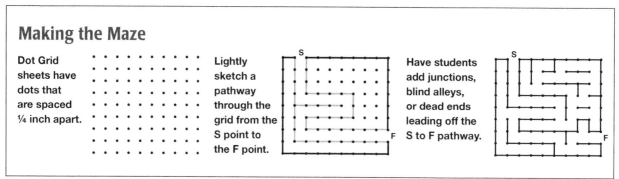

Activities and Procedures

Practice

1 Inform students that they will be designing their very own mazes for others to complete.

2 Have students begin by sketching lightly with a pencil. Encourage them to let their ideas flow freely as they generate at least three concepts for further development.

3 Suggest that students practice drawing pathway walls by keeping the lines parallel and of a consistent width, whether they are straight or curved. (See "Practice Makes Perfect Mazes.")

4 Invite students who love a challenge to experiment with placing spirals, kernels, and other configurations into their maze sketches. (See "Practice Makes Perfect Mazes.")

Drawing the Maze

5 Using the "Dot Grid" sheets, instruct students to use a ruler to draw a large rectangle or square on plain paper or graph paper. These lines will be the "outer walls" of the maze.

NOTE: If you are unable to download and print the "Dot Grid" sheets, have students use graph paper or a ruler and pencil to draw a dot every ¼ inch, both across and down. (See "Making the Maze.")

6 Direct students to choose a start point and finish point on the outer walls of the maze, and mark them with the letters **S** and **F**. Tell students to lightly sketch a pathway through the grid from the **S** point to the **F** point. (See "Making the Maze.")

7 Suggest that students make several corner turns so that the maze will be fun to solve.

8 Instruct students to fill in the areas within the outer walls with pathways.

9 Next, have students add junctions, blind alleys, or dead ends leading off the **S** to **F** pathway. (See "Making the Maze.")

TIP: To create a junction, make an opening in the wall of an established pathway, and draw a new pathway leading from it.

TIP: Make sure the new pathway does not end too quickly. It should fool the eye of the solver.

10 Direct students to erase the lines that cross the new pathways.

11 Instruct students to reinforce the outer walls and pathway lines with pen.

12 Tell students to erase any remaining pencil lines.

13 Finally, encourage students to give their maze a title, make photocopies, and trade mazes with their classmates.

Extensions

- Invite students to make 3-D miniature garden mazes from cardboard or clay. Have them paint and decorate the mazes, and create a figure to move through the maze as well.
- Encourage students to design mazes with circular or irregular outer walls, or those which use only curved line pathways.
- Have students embed their initials, names, words, or phrases into their mazes.
- Allow students to create holiday-themed mazes, adding illustrations and decorative elements.
- Suggest that students work together to create a classroom book of mazes.
- Connect this lesson with a social studies unit on ancient labyrinths and mazes.
- Integrate this lesson with a geometry unit which explores concepts such as right angles, triangles, curves, and symmetry.

Mazes' Phrases

❶ Blind Alley – once entered, leads back to the original pathway

❷ Curves – curving pathways

❸ Corners – right-angle turns along a pathway

❹ Dead End – a pathway that ends

❺ Junctions – a point where three or more pathways meet, forcing the solver to make a decision

❻ Kernels – a spiral type design with pathways around it; can take the form of shapes such as a flower, a ship, or an initial

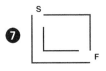

❼ Outer Walls – the outside limits of a maze

❽ Pathway – a passage in a maze in which the solver stays between the walls and does not cross any lines

❾ Spirals – optical illusions that are visually confusing, adding extra challenge

❿ Start and Finish – the entrance and exit points in a maze

Doorway to a Dream

Grade Level: 4 through 8
Participants: Individuals
Objectives: Exercise flexibility, originality, elaboration, imagination, concept development, intuitive design, and surrealist techniques
Time: 1 to 3 hours

Quick View

In this eye-opening adventure in creative expression, students combine drawings with collages to develop Surrealist concepts. By creating "doors" that reveal unique and unexpected imagery, students express their artistic intelligence and inspire their audience to view ordinary images in new and surprising ways.

Example

"I Wandered Lonely as a Cloud"

This example shows dislocation (an easy chair on the ocean), juxtaposition (an elephant in the scene), symbolic imagery (peace sign, words), and more.

Take Home

Enhanced visualization and artistic skills and an original Surrealistic artwork for friends and family to interpret

Surrealist Techniques

JUXTAPOSITION: a technique in which seemingly unrelated or incongruent objects are placed alongside one another.

Examples

Juxtaposing time periods:

- *Shakespeare singing with Elvis*

Unexpected objects put together:

- *String of pearls on a basket of fish*

The famous Surreal artist Rene Magritte painted umbrellas with glasses of wine on top.

DISLOCATION: a technique in which objects are placed in unusual places.

Examples

Environmental dislocation:

- *A chocolate sundae inside the hood of a car*

Geographical dislocation:

- *The Sphinx floating on an iceberg*

TRANSFORMATION: a technique in which a familiar object is turned into something unusual, disturbing, or puzzling.

Example

- *A building that has roaring lions emerging from the windows or a backpack that has slime oozing out*

FALSE PROPORTIONS: a technique in which objects are depicted in unrealistic scales or proportions.

Example

- *A cowboy riding a horse across a cherry pie*

DISTORTIONS: a technique in which objects are shown in an abnormal physical state by being stretched, melted, made transparent, broken, etc.

Example

- *A mountain cracked wide open down its center*

The famous Surreal artist Salvador Dali painted melted clocks.

SYMBOLIC IMAGERY: a technique using visual depictions of things that do not have physical properties.

Example

- *Words, thoughts, or sounds shown as tangible objects, such as words pouring out of a faucet, or a peace symbol flying away*

ABSURDITY AND HUMOR: a technique which uses ridiculous, exaggerated, and nonsensical images.

Example

- *A thought balloon of Mona Lisa talking about a laundry detergent*
- *A lady walking a pigeon on a leash*
- *A pirate on a pogo stick*

DREAM IMAGERY: a technique which employs symbolic images and writings that come from the artist's subconscious mind.

Example

- *Wings, clocks, eyes, animals, suitcases, fruit, mirrors, and more*

Doorway to a Dream *continues* ➔

continued from previous page

Materials
- Magazines, old calendars, newspapers, and/or print-outs from the Internet
- Plain paper, 8½″ x 11″, two per student
- Cardstock or heavy paper, 8½″ x 11″, two per student
- Pencils
- Markers or colored pencils
- Scissors
- Glue sticks

Getting ready
- Gather pictures of Surrealistic artworks from books or online. (Artists Salvador Dali and Rene Magritte are highly regarded Surrealists.)
- Display and distribute the materials.

Activities and Procedures

1   Explain the concept of *Surrealism*: an art movement that began in the 1920's in Europe and America. Surrealistic works feature the element of surprise by positioning objects alongside one another that don't usually belong together. Surrealists create subject matter that the viewer must interpret. The Surrealists were the first to use *collage* in their artworks.

2   Explain the term *collage*: an artistic work made by adhering various materials such as pieces of paper, fabric or photos to a surface.

3   Explain to the students that they will be making Surrealist artworks by combining photos and drawings in a collage.

4   Provide the following guidelines for the project:
   - Compositions must include two or more surrealist techniques such as juxtaposition, dislocation, transformation, dream imagery, etc. See sidebar, "Surrealist Techniques."
   - Works must include "doors" that open to reveal unexpected imagery such as written messages, humorous juxtapositions, unusual visions, symbols, etc.
   - There must be two layers of imagery:
     The Bottom Layer, which the top layer opens to reveal, is a collage of photos, writings, and drawings. Heavy paper works best.
     The Top Layer will have large "doors" or images with openings. Each opening is a flap that opens and closes.

5   Invite students to follow the steps below to design the top layer:
   - Draw a light pencil line border one to two inches wide around the edges of the paper. See Diagram 1A.
   - Decide on an image that has an opening such as a castle door or a pelican's mouth. See sidebar, "Some Things That Have Openings."
     Draw the shape of the opening in pencil line inside the border. Make the shape large enough to be cut open. Use dotted lines for the edges that get folded. See Diagram 1B.

Some Things That Have Openings

- Animal mouths: hippo, alligator, whale, etc.
- Backpack
- Barn
- Book
- Boxes
- Cave
- Closet
- Coat, robe, shirt, kimono
- Cupboard

- Eyes
- Gate
- Hollow tree trunk
- House – haunted, dollhouse, mansion, castle, storybook, shack, dog house, White House, etc.
- Landmark structures – Taj Mahal, Stonehenge, Pyramid, Eiffel Tower, Empire State Building

- Locket
- Lunch box
- Mailbox
- Paint box
- Pendulum clock door
- Refrigerator, stove, other appliances
- Robot panels
- School
- Sea shells

- Stores – bakery, candy, shoe, toy, sporting goods, grocery
- Treasure chest
- Tunnel
- Vehicles – car, bus, train, airplane, boat, rocket ship, flying saucer, submarine
- Windows

DIAGRAM 1

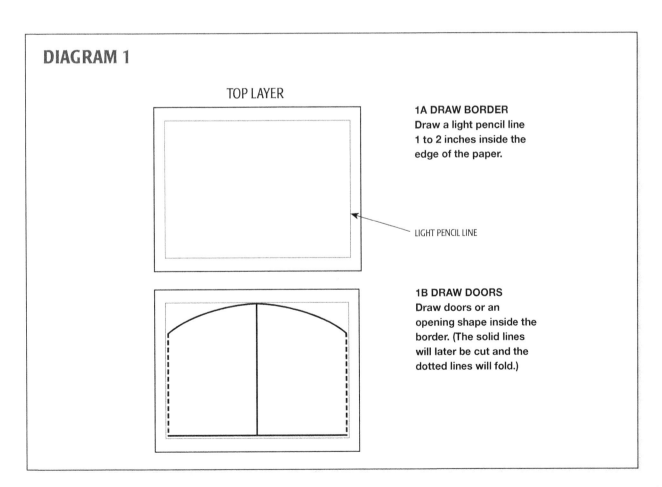

TOP LAYER

1A DRAW BORDER
Draw a light pencil line 1 to 2 inches inside the edge of the paper.

LIGHT PENCIL LINE

1B DRAW DOORS
Draw doors or an opening shape inside the border. (The solid lines will later be cut and the dotted lines will fold.)

Doorway to a Dream *continues* ➜

continued from previous page

DIAGRAM 2

TOP LAYER

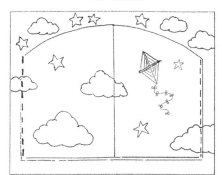

2A DRAW SKY IMAGERY
Draw clouds shooting stars, moons, planets, galaxies, constellations, and more. Go beyond the edges of what will become the doors.

2B CUT DOORS
Cut the doors open and fold them back. More sky imagery and words can be added to the inside flaps.

BOTTOM LAYER

2C TRACE SHAPE
Place the top layer over the bottom layer. Trace the shape created by the opening of the doors onto the bottom layer.

2D CREATE ARTWORK
Working within the traced shape, draw images, paste collage pictures, and add words. Unleash your imagination!

FINISH

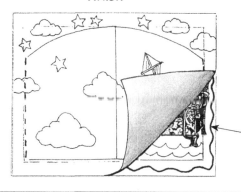

2E GLUE TOP TO BOTTOM
Finish by adding glue to the bottom layer around the edges only. Place the top layer flush over it, being careful not to glue the doors shut.

APPLY GLUE ALONG EDGES
OF BOTTOM LAYER

- Draw and color sky around and on the "doors." Sky imagery contributes to a dreamlike mood. Examples include clouds, shooting stars, moons, planets, galaxies, constellations, starry nights, rainbows, sunsets, stormy skies, balloons, kites, flying saucers, fairies, angels, planes, rockets, birds, bugs, and things that float or fly in the sky. See Diagram 2A.
- Cut the doors open and fold the flap back. Younger students may need assistance. Add sky and words (optional) to the inside flaps. See Diagram 2B.

6 Instruct students to follow these guidelines:
- Use the top layer's opening as a stencil. Place it flush over the bottom layer paper. Open the doors and lightly trace the inside shape. See Diagram 2C.
- Peruse the pictures provided to brainstorm ideas for the bottom layer's imagery. Try putting two unrelated photos together; ordinary objects in unlikely places take on new meanings. Let subconscious intuition and imagination direct you as you glue down and draw images within the area traced. Add writings if you wish. Let the pictures overlap the shape's outline. See Diagram 2D.

   NOTE: For writings, use printed or hand written words such as a fragment of a poem, an absurdity, a newsprint story, humor, or whatever moves you. Adding words that relate to your images will enhance their importance.

- Add glue to the bottom layer around the edges only. Place the top layer flush over it, opening the doors to prevent gluing them shut. Firmly press around the edges and let dry. See Diagram 2E.

7 Invite students to give their Surrealist artworks intriguing titles. Provide the examples below to spark students' imaginations:
- Painting titles by Salvador Dali:
   "Melting Clock At Moment Of First Explosion"
   "Woman With A Head Of Roses"
- Painting titles by Rene Magritte:
   "The False Mirror"
   "The Empire Of Light"

8 Allow students to share their masterpieces with the class, and invite classmates to comment on and interpret each other's work.

Extensions
- Integrate this activity into an art history unit on Surrealism.
- Use this lesson as part of a unit on psychology (i.e. dreams and the subconscious).
- Connect this activity to an art unit on shading and light source.
- Align this lesson with a literature unit on "stream of consciousness" writing.
- Advanced students may wish to add a third layer under their bottom layer. Cut door openings into the bottom (now second) layer and fold flaps back to reveal imagery that you've added to the third layer. Glue edges of third layer to the layer above it.

Grade Level: 3 through 8
Participants: Individuals or teams of two
Objectives: Exercise flexibility, originality, elaboration, learning about patents, concept development, and drawing skills
Time: Approximately 1 to 2 hours

Quick View

In this inventive inquiry, students are challenged to design vehicles from randomly-assigned objects, combining the parts of each to invent a new form of transportation. By making sketches with notations and naming their Odd-mobiles, students practice their creative thinking skills while exploring the actual invention process.

Example

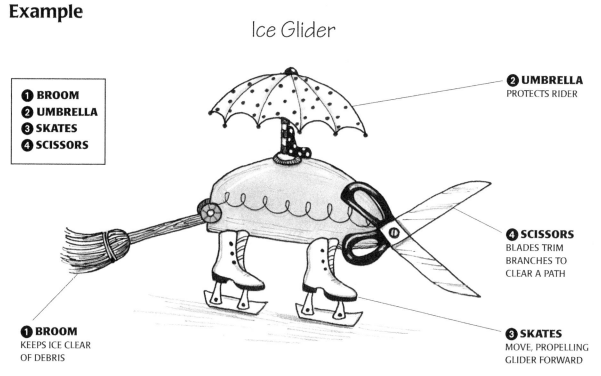

Ice Glider

❶ BROOM
❷ UMBRELLA
❸ SKATES
❹ SCISSORS

❷ **UMBRELLA**
PROTECTS RIDER

❹ **SCISSORS**
BLADES TRIM
BRANCHES TO
CLEAR A PATH

❶ **BROOM**
KEEPS ICE CLEAR
OF DEBRIS

❸ **SKATES**
MOVE, PROPELLING
GLIDER FORWARD

Take Home

Enhanced conceptualization skills and an imaginative new invention with a trademark name, design, and award

Materials
- Pencils
- Paper
- Object Cards (see *Reproducibles,* pg. 320)
- Award
- Paper bag
- Magazines for cutting, with pictures of anything *except* vehicles (optional)
- Crayons or markers (optional)

Getting Ready

- Find samples of trademarks in magazines (e.g. Coca Cola, Apple, Inc., Kodak, 3M, etc.), and cut them out.
- Make copies of Object Cards, at least 6 per participant.
- Trim and gather the Object Cards, shuffle them, and put them in a bag. You may need to make duplicates, or supplement them with pictures cut from magazines depending on the size of your class.
- Write the following word and definition on the board: *vehicle*: (n.) any means by which a person is carried in travel

Activities and Procedures

1 Begin a classroom discussion by asking students to brainstorm:
- Types of vehicles-train, plane, automobile, sled, spaceship, bicycle, scooter, glider, etc. Students may invent brand new vehicles or create hybrids.
- Methods for creating movement: wheels, runners, feet, wings, floating, rolling, air currents, etc.
- Sources of power: horses, electricity, mechanics, steam, water pressure, wind, etc.

2 Have individual students pick six cards from the bag at random. Teams of two students should pick three items each, and combine their objects.

3 Inform students that their challenge is to design a vehicle using the items on their cards.

4 As they brainstorm, encourage students to imagine the various parts of the objects. Tell them that they may add additional pieces to connect parts.

5 Suggest that students not worry about technical realities, but come up with an explanation, however fantastic, of how their vehicle is powered and how it moves.

6 Invite students to ponder the following questions as they work:
- Who would use my vehicle?
- What special features will it have?
- How is my vehicle better than others?
- Of what materials will it be made?
- How will it move?
- How will it be powered?

Steps for Inventing

1 Brainstorm many ideas.
2 Select the best idea.
3 Design it on paper. Include notes that describe its function, how it is made, and how it works.
4 Make a model or prototype of it.
- A model is handmade and looks like the final invention.
- A prototype is handmade and looks and works like the final invention.
5 Name it.
6 Patent it by filling out a Patent Application.
7 Trademark it by designing a mark and filling out a Trademark Application.
8 Sell it. Think of venues in which you might sell your invention. You could sell it to another company or sell directly to the public online, in stores, or at special events and other locations.

Odd-mobiles *continues* ➜

continued from previous page

Intellectual Property

Patents, trademarks, and copyrights are often called "intellectual property." Intellectual property is produced by creative thought. It has value just as physical property such as a bicycle or a computer.

- A **Copyright** is an exclusive right of ownership granted to the author or creator of an original work. Creations such as written works, art works, music, and photographs are protected by copyright laws. In general, nobody else is allowed to copy it for sales or to make new works derived from the original work without the author's permission. A copyright notice should be placed on every original work. It is indicated with ©, the year of completion, and the name of the author/creator. For example, ©2012 Marjorie Sarnat. For strongest legal protection register a copyright with the United States Copyright Office at www.copyright.gov. For an overview about copyright especially as it pertains to the visual arts, including Fair Use, Public Domain, and Creative Commons, see "Understanding Copyright and Licenses" at Smashing Magazine, http://bit.ly/jPGz4Q.

- A **Trademark** is any name, design, logo, initials, numbers, words, slogan, image, symbol, or sound that distinguishes your company or product from those of others. A trademark makes it easy to identify a company, product, or service. The trademark usually appears on the product, its packaging, or in advertisements. In general, the owner of the trademark has exclusive rights to use it in its product category. The trademark may be indicated by a ™ after the trademark name to establish its use. For stronger protection of a trademark register it with the United States Patent and Trademark Office. Trademarks that are registered with the U.S.P.T.O. carry the ® mark, such as Coca-Cola®.

- A **Patent** is a grant by the United States Government to the inventor of something that is new, useful, and non-obvious. The patent allows the inventor to "exclude others from making, using, offering for sale, or selling" their invention. Such a patent is granted for a period of time, usually 20 years. Others who wish to manufacture or sell the invention must obtain a license and likely pay the inventor.

Patent laws are recognized in many other countries besides the U.S. as well. New inventions are important because they inspire new technologies, create jobs, and improve the quality of our lives. The first U S. patent was granted in 1790 to Samuel Hopkins of Philadelphia, PA for a formula used in soap making.

Links:
Trademarks and Patents: For official application forms and more information visit www.uspto.gov

Teacher and student resources about intellectual property: Visit www.uspto.gov/kids/.

Copyright: For more information or to register a work visit www.copyright.gov

In the classroom, use the Award of Creative Excellence (see *Reproducibles,* pg. 341) to provide your students a "certificate" to "protect" their Copyright, Trademark, or Patent creations.

Disclaimer: I am not an attorney. This overview is for educational purposes only and is not meant to provide legal advice.

7 Instruct students to make sketches of their vehicles with notations, and name their Odd-mobiles. (See lesson plan, "Name Us Famous: Tips for Creative Naming," pg. 96.)

8 Discuss the concept of trademarks with the class, and ask students to design unique trademarks for their inventions.

9 Hold an "Odd-mobile show" showcasing the students' new inventions.

10 Award students for their work by giving special recognition to the distinct features of each Odd-mobile. You may use the ideas listed here or come up with your own:

- Best air travel
- Best all-terrain
- Best designed
- Best developed
- Best family
- Best hybrid
- Best land travel
- Best sand travel
- Best use of animal inspiration
- Best use of mechanics
- Best vertical travel
- Best water travel
- Fastest
- Funniest
- Most attractive
- Most colorful
- Most comfortable
- Most creative
- Most fantastic
- Most imaginative
- Most innovative
- Most luxurious
- Most outrageous
- Most practical
- Most technologically advanced
- The "Oddest"

Extensions

- Have students make models of their odd-mobiles from clay, wood, cardboard, or other materials. Consider using a toy vehicle and altering it with clay, cardboard, glue, and paint.
- Encourage students to make larger sized odd-mobiles from corrugated boxes and paint them.
- Connect this lesson with a unit on physical science and energy.
- Integrate this lesson with a social studies unit and have students write reports on the history of patents.

"The essential part of creativity is not being afraid to fail."
– Edwin H. Land

Grade Level: 1 through 6
Participants: Individuals
Objectives: Exercise flexibility, originality, elaboration, brainstorming, visualization, imagination, and sketching skills
Time: Approximately ½ hour

Quick View

In this exercise in artistic expression, students transform simple squiggle drawings into unique masterpieces. By experimenting with different perspectives and sketching techniques, students practice visualization skills while getting in touch with their inner artists.

Examples

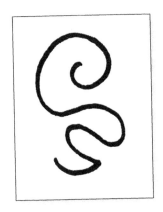

Foundation Squiggle

Swirly Design

Snake in the Grass

Take Home

Enhanced visualization skills and an original work of art to share with family and friends

Materials

- Pencils
- Photocopies of a squiggle, at least two per student
- Chalkboard and chalk or equivalent
- Timer or equivalent

Getting Ready

- Create a squiggle drawing in bold, black line for making photocopies.
- Make at least 2 photocopies per student.
- Draw a similar squiggle on the board for demonstration.

Activities and procedures

1 Distribute two squiggle copies to each student.

2 Tell students that they will be creating original artwork using the squiggle drawing as a starting point.

3 Instruct students to use pencil lines to transform squiggles into representational objects or abstract designs.

4 Demonstrate the process using the squiggle on the board.

5 Encourage students to view their squiggles from all sides when planning their drawings.

6 Inform students that they will have two minutes to plan their drawings and ten minutes to complete them.

7 When time is up, invite students to give their drawings short titles.

8 Repeat steps 6 and 7 using a new squiggle template to create a new drawing, different from the first.

9 Display the finished drawings in the classroom, and invite students to share positive comments and responses. Discuss how the different pieces illustrate a variety of interpretations.

Extensions

Have students complete the "Squiggle Sketch-its" activity as follows:

- Distribute large sheets of paper (11″ x 14″ or larger) and have students divide each sheet into four or six sections.
- Instruct students to draw one squiggle in each section.
- Encourage students to develop a theme among their squiggles by adding lines, shapes, patterns, and/or color schemes, or by transforming the squiggles into representational objects such as flowers or silly creatures.

Foundation Squiggles

Squiggle Wiggles

Squiggle Scenics

- For a related activity, see lesson plan "Pass-a-Squiggle" on pg. 248

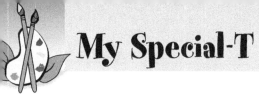

My Special-T

Grade Level: 2 through 6
Participants: Individuals
Objectives: Exercise fluency, originality, elaboration, and sketching skills
Time: ½ hour to 1 hour

Quick View

In this "tee-riffic" activity, students practice fluency and creativity as they challenge themselves to see how many original T-shirt designs they can generate within a specific timeframe. After participating in this activity, students will never view an ordinary T-shirt the same way again!

Examples

Take Home

An extensive selection of original designs for T-shirts, some of which may be created at home

Materials

- Page of six T-shirt outlines (Download a free template at www.jrimagination.com/printables)
- Photocopies of T-shirt outlines page, at least 2 per student
- Pencils
- Pictures of real T-shirts collected from catalogs and websites
- Crayons, markers, or colored pencils (optional)
- Actual examples of decorated T-shirts (optional)

Getting Ready
- Make photocopies of T-shirt outlines, six T-shirts per page. You will need at least two copies per student.
- Display pictures or real T-shirts for student reference.

Activities and Procedures

1 Show your class examples of T-shirt designs and ask the class to brainstorm different types of designs. Some examples include:
- Abstract designs
- All-over designs, such as animal skin look, flowers, checks, etc.
- Add-ons like beads, fringe, collars, or pockets
- Animal paw-prints
- Color effects
- Images tossed all over
- Looks like tuxedo or another garment
- One large picture
- Original logos
- Symbols
- Tie-dye
- Words, phrases, and/or letters

Tell your class that any school-acceptable decoration is acceptable.

2 Give each student two pages of T-shirt outlines.

3 Give students a predetermined amount of time (usually 10-15 minutes will suffice) to sketch as many different T-shirt designs as they can. Encourage them to use their imaginations to create unique and imaginative patterns and decorations.

4 Invite students to add color to their designs if they wish. Crayons, markers or colored pencils work well.

5 Allow students to share their designs with the class, and invite classmates to comment on each other's work.

Extensions
- Consider implementing variations of this activity by having students design:
  - Backpacks
  - Butterflies
  - Cars
  - Cats
  - Christmas stockings
  - Cows
  - Cowboy boots
  - Flying saucers
  - Guitars
  - High-heel shoes
  - Horses
  - Monster faces
  - Sailboats
  - Sprinkling cans
  - Vase of flowers
- Have students choose one design to recreate on an actual T-shirt with acrylic paints or paints made for painting cloth (available from craft stores). Allow students to wear the shirts on the following school day to debut their creative new fashion statements.

Grade Level: 2 through 8
Participants: Individuals
Objectives: Exercise flexibility, originality, puns, homophones, and homonyms, humor, writing skills, drawing skills, planning and design skills, construction skills.
Time: 1 to 2 hours

Quick View

Students use a beloved theme, knock knock jokes, to create booklet-ornaments shaped like miniature houses with opening doors. Behind the doors are silly knock knock jokes to make you smile (or groan.) Students draw wood grain and brick textures, plan and design booklets, and learn strategies for making up original knock knock jokes. This activity is great fun and yields delightful, highly creative products.

Example

Knock Knock
Who's there?
Ha Hotch
Ha Hotch who?
Geshundheit!

Take Home

An amusing novelty booklet that makes a cute ornament or special gift for any occasion

The History of Knock Knock Jokes

Knock Knock
Who's there?
Wyza
Wyza who?
Wyza door on your cave?

Within minutes of the invention of the door came the invention of the knock knock joke. We're not sure exactly where knock knock jokes started, but we know they have been told in English speaking countries for hundreds of years.

In Shakespeare's Macbeth, Hamlet utters a version of a knock knock joke. Here's another knock knock joke from Shakespeare's era, overheard one evening at a castle entrance:

> *Knocke Knocke*
> Who goeth there?
> *A goode knight*
> A goode knight who?
> *And a goode night to you, too*

Knock knock jokes are old standbys still used by contemporary comedians such as Kathy Griffin

and Jerry Seinfeld, who are said to sometimes include them in their comedy routines.

Knock knock jokes are fun because they engage the jokester and the audience in a dialogue.

> *Knock Knock*
> Who's there?
> *Boo*
> Boo Who?
> *I tried to make you laugh, not cry*

Materials
- Plain paper, 8½″ x 11″, (one per student)
- Scrap paper for joke writing practice
- Crayons or colored pencils (do not use markers)
- Stapler
- Construction paper (any colors)
- Brads (one per ornament)
- Scissors
- Glue sticks
- Ribbon or string (6″ per student)
- Examples of wood grain and brick from the internet or elsewhere.
- Chalkboard and chalk or equivalent
- Hole punch (optional)

Knock Knock
Who's there?
Dorky
Dorky who?
Dorky doesn't work, so I had to knock

Getting Ready
- Gather a dozen or more knock knock jokes for student reference. These are readily available online and in books. Ask students to contribute some favorites, as well.
- Draw examples of wood grain and bricks on the board.

The Knack of Knock Knocks *continues* ➔

continued from previous page

How To Write A Knock Knock Joke

Formula

All *knock knock* jokes follow a formula. They have five lines. The first two lines are always the same:

1 **The Jokester:** Knock Knock
2 **The Recipient:** Who's There?
3 **The Jokester:** gives a response—usually a name
4 **The Recipient:** repeats the response and adds "who?"
5 **The Jokester:** The punchline, or final payoff, is usually a pun or funny words that sound similar to the response words. "Sam and Janet who? Punchline: "Sam and Janet Evening" (Some Enchanted Evening)
   Sometimes the punchline is a funny response to the words in line 4. "Hoo Who?" Punch line: "What are you, an owl?"

Sample joke:

Line 1, **Jokester:**   Knock Knock

Line 2, **Audience:**   Who's there?

Line 3, **Jokester:**   Doris

Line 4, **Audience:**   Doris who?

Line 5, **Jokester:**   Doris locked. Let me in!

Punchline

Write knock knock jokes using a name for line 3 and using it again to form a punchline for line 5.

Write fill-in-the-blanks knock knock jokes using names, such as:

1 Knock Knock
2 Who's there?
3 Daryl
4 Daryl who?
5 Daryl_____
   (Pun for "there will." Answers will differ)

Hoo

Words that end in oo sound can be formed from the word, "who," at the end of a phrase. When said fast, the "h" sound in "who" is silent. For example, cash + who= cashew.

The word "who" is phonetically, "hoo." This sound, doubled with another word, as in 'Who's there?' "Yoo." "Yoo who?" creates a new meaning: Yoo Hoo. Many puns can be made with the "who" sound at the end. For example, "chooch" combined with "who" sounds like "choo choo." "Tatt" combined with "who" sounds like "tattoo, and so forth."

"Who" (hoo) sound endings: choo choo, yahoo, yoo-hoo, cashew, ha-choo, hoo-hoo, kazoo, shampoo, tattoo, kangaroo, Kalamazoo, and more can be used as puns.

Sample joke:

Line 1, **Jokester:** "Knock Knock"

Line 2, **Audience:** "Who's there?"

Line 3, **Jokester:** "Chooch"

Line 4, **Audience:** "Chooch who?"

Line 5, **Jokester:** "What time does the next train leave?"

Creating The Booklet

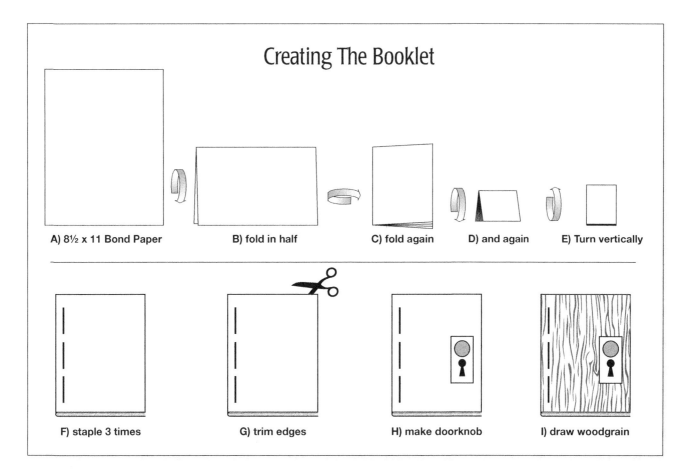

A) 8½ x 11 Bond Paper   B) fold in half   C) fold again   D) and again   E) Turn vertically

F) staple 3 times   G) trim edges   H) make doorknob   I) draw woodgrain

Activities and Procedures

Refer to diagram, "Creating the Booklet," for steps 1 – 3 below.

1 Assembling the booklets
   • Fold a sheet of plain 8½″ x 11″ bond paper in half, held vertically, top to bottom, then in half again, in half again, and one final time horizontally for a total of four folds.
   • Staple the folded paper in place, like hinges on a door, on the long side that has no open edges.
   • Cut open all folded edges on the remaining three sides, to create a booklet. You will have 32 pages, including the front and back covers.

     NOTE: Younger students will need assistance to assemble their blank books.

   • Apply tape over the staples on the back outside cover to smooth sharp edges.
   • If necessary, have students number the pages, starting with the front cover as page 1.

2 Creating the "door"
   • Draw a doorknob on the right side of the outside front cover of the booklet.
   • Insert a brad for the doorknob.

3 Wood grain texture
   • Color the outside front cover of your booklet a light color. Draw darker wood grain lines over it. Grain lines run vertically, but are irregular, and sometimes form "V" shapes. Occasionally a knot appears between grain lines, as well.

The Knack of Knock Knocks *continues* ➜

continued from previous page

What's In A Name? Puns

Example puns on first names, to be said in lines 3, 4, 5:

- Annie… Annie who? (Annie body home?)
- Anita… Anita who? (Anita borrow a dollar)
- Candice… Candice who? (Candice be love?)
- Carrie… Carrie who? (Carrie me back home)
- Bella… Bella who? (Bella no work, so I knock)
- Daryl… Daryl who? (Daryl be a party here tonight)
- Donna… Donna who? (Donna why I knocked on your door)
- Doris… Doris who? (Doris locked. Let me in)
- Eileen… Eileen who? (Eileen on the bell, but it didn't ring)
- Dorky… Dorky who? (Dorky doesn't work so I had to knock)
- Gwen… Gwen who? (Gwen are you coming out to play?)
- Harvey… Harvey who? (Harvey too late for the party?)
- Isaac… Isaac who? (Isaac and tired of knocking on the door)
- Justin… Justin who? (Justin time for dinner)
- Ken… Ken who? (Ken you open the door?)
- Maida… Maida who? (Maida cake for your birthday)
- Maya… Maya who? (Maya hand hurts from knocking)
- Misty… Misty who? (Misty bus. May I wait inside?)
- Morris… Morris who? (Morris on the way to your house)
- Sherwood… Sherwood who? (Sherwood like to come in)
- Stella… Stella who? (Stella your #1 fan)
- Theodore… Theodore who? (Theodore was closed, so I knocked)
- Wanda … Wanda who? (Wanda why I knocked on your door)
- Willoughby… Willoughby who? (Willoughby staying here for a few days)

Comedy Vocabulary Words

1. Audience
2. Comedian
3. Comedy routine
4. Dialogue
5. Humor
6. Humorist
7. Joke
8. Joke format
9. Joke formula
10. Joke structure
11. Jokester
12. Monologue
13. Payoff
14. Pun
15. Punchline
16. Punster
17. Set-up

4　Booklet requirements
- Students have room for five knock knock jokes starting with the words, "Knock Knock" on the front cover.
- One or more jokes should be original. Have students begin on scrap paper by numbering 1–5 down the left side of the paper. Line 1: Knock Knock. Line 2: Who's there? (See sidebar, "How To Write A Knock Knock Joke," for lines 3, 4, 5.)
- Add other favorite knock knock jokes as needed for five jokes.
- The inside back cover should have the student's name and date.

See sidebar, "Page Designations," for order sequence for all the pages in the book.

5 Designing the pages
- Fill in the pages in the order shown in the sidebar, "Page Designations."
- Color and decorate the pages, making sure your lettering shows clearly.

6 Assembling the ornaments
- Cut two shapes from 2 colors construction paper: Rectangle- 3¾" x 3" and Triangle- 3" wide at base, 2" high at peak. These shapes will become a house front and roof.
- Glue the triangle 3" edge to the house front 3" edge. Overlap approximately ½". Reinforce the back seam with tape (optional).
- Glue the outside back cover of the booklet to the house front, lining up the bottoms of each.
  Brick texture Draw brick texture onto the house front by drawing horizontal lines, and alternating vertical lines between the horizontals.
  Details Add flowers, decorative trims, or roof details.
  Loop for hanging Poke a hole at the top center of the roof. Tie a ribbon though it to form a loop for hanging the ornament.

Extensions
- *Organize a Contest*: Have a *Classroom Knock-Knock-Off* for the best (or worst) knock knock jokes. Read submissions anonymously, and have the class vote. Award special certificates, "Door Knockers," to the winners.

Knock Knock
Who's there?
Bella
Bella who?
Bella no work, so I knock

Page Designations
For 32-page Knock Knock Book

1 Outside front cover – Knock Knock (and drawing of a door)
2 Left side – Who's There?
3 Right side – a name
4 Left side – repeat name (and) Who?
5 Right side – punchline
6 Left side – solid color, no words
7 Right side – Knock Knock (and drawing of a door)
8 Left side – Who's There?
9 Right side – a name
10 Left side – repeat name (and) Who?
11 Right side – punchline
12 Left side – solid color, no words
13 Right side – Knock Knock (and drawing of a door)
14 Left side – Who's There?
15 Right side – a name
16 Left side – repeat name (and) Who?
17 Right side – punchline
18 Left side – solid color, no words
19 Right side – Knock Knock (and drawing of a door)
20 Left side – Who's There?
21 Right side – a name
22 Left side – repeat name (and) Who?
23 Right side – punchline
24 Left side – solid color, no words
25 Right side – Knock Knock (and drawing of a door)
26 Left side – Who's There?
27 Right side – a name
28 Left side – repeat name (and) Who?
29 Right side – punchline
30 Left side – solid color, no words
31 Date and "By" (name of author)
32 Outside back cover – leave plain. This surface gets glued to the construction paper ornament

Notes

Reproducibles

The Picture Prompt Cards consist of three sets of 50 cards each:

- *Object Cards* – things
- *Creature Cards* – creature "parts"
- *Personality Cards* – people

Throughout the book, there are many lesson plans in which these are used. In addition, you can use the cards on their own to spark creative activities as described here. Photocopy the cards on bond paper or card stock, which will be more durable, and trim on the dotted line.

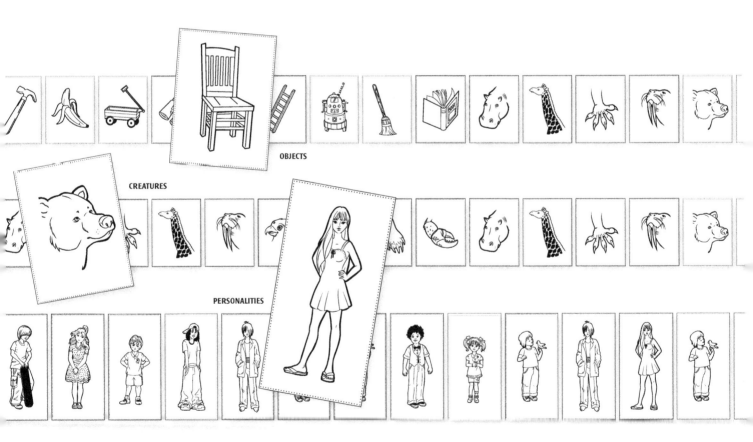

OBJECTS

CREATURES

PERSONALITIES

Object Cards

Object Cards challenge innovative minds to make new connections and find relationships between unlikely things and ideas. Use the cards to provide new concepts for inventions, elements in story plots, and for exercising creative thinking skills.

Inventive Idea Prompts
- Find relationships between two or more randomly chosen objects
- Invent something new using two or more randomly chosen objects
- Write a story that includes two or more randomly chosen objects
- Combine a randomly chosen object with a vehicle
- Randomly combine an object card with a personality card and explain the relationship between the two
- Tell a story through a randomly chosen object's point of view
- Find five or more new uses for a randomly chosen object
- Sketch five or more variations of a randomly chosen object
- Apply the S.C.A.M.P.E.R. techniques to an object

Creature Cards

Creature Cards inspire creative minds by showing features from nature's life forms. Use the cards to conjure up fantasy critters, suggest new inventions and machines, and envision imaginary worlds.

Imagination Prompts
- Combine two or more cards to create a visual portrayal of a fantasy beast
- Combine creature parts to create a mythological beast and write its story
- Attach an animal part to another animal in an unexpected way. Explain why the animal has this anatomy
- Create new inventions by interpreting animal features as mechanical parts
- Design an article of clothing inspired by a creature card
- Invent an organism by combining a creature part with a plant
- Give an animal feature to a human for developing a character with special abilities. Write a story about your character

Personality Cards

Personality Cards spark imaginations through a focus on characters and human interactions. Use the cards to create unexpected scenarios and to develop insight into human behavior.

Writing and Drama Prompts
- Name your character and explain why you chose that name
- Describe your character's personality, motivations, and background
- Create a relationship between two characters
- Create dialog between two randomly chosen characters
- Insert characters into story lines to alter an established story
- Write a story using three or more random characters
- Tell about an incident from your character's point of view and in their style of expression

Object Cards

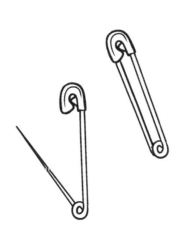

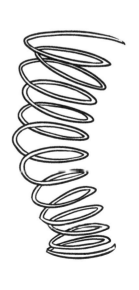

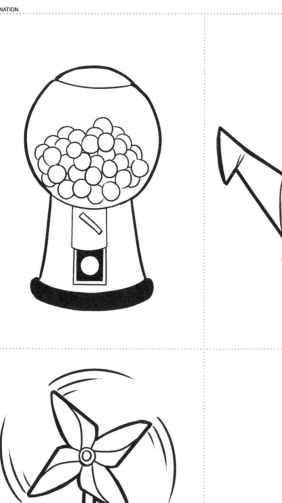

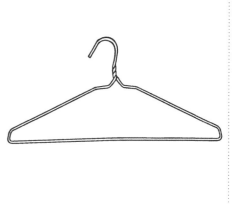

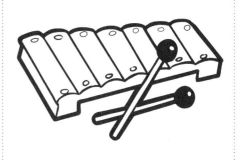

Creature Cards

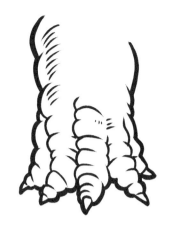
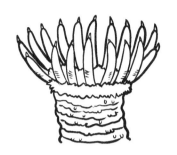

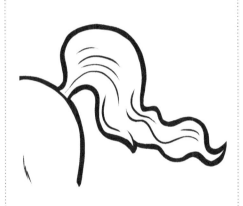

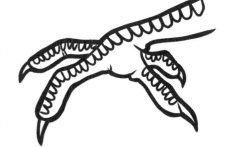

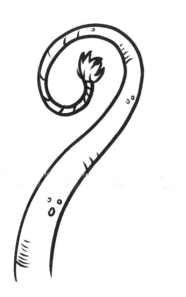

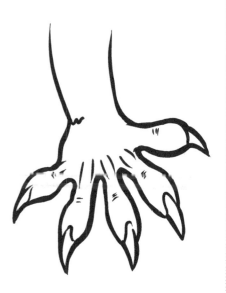

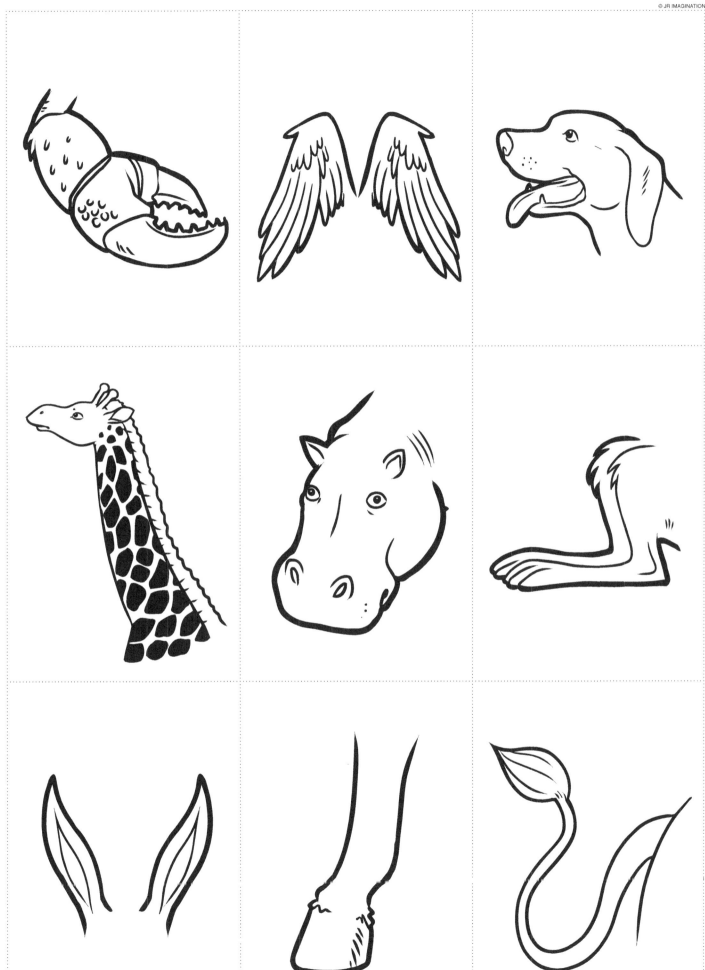

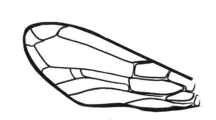

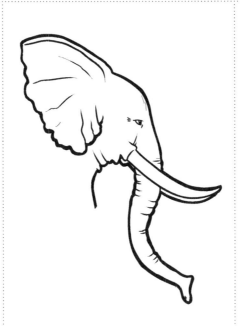

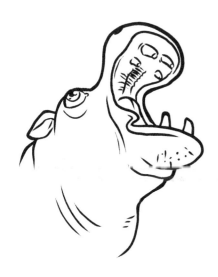

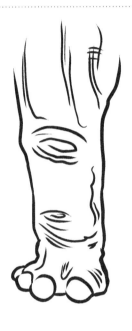

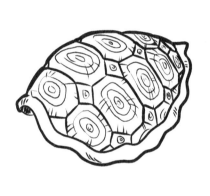

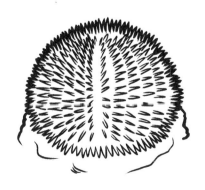

Personality Cards

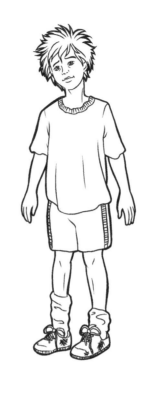

A·C·E

Award of Creative Excellence

presented to

_____

Name

for

_____

Achievement

This certificate is awarded for demonstrating exceptional accomplishment in

Creative Thinking

_____

Date

_____

Awarded By

CREATIVE GENIUS · JrImagination®

©2012 Jr Imagination www.jrimagination.com

S.C.A.M.P.E.R.

Brainstorming Idea Generators

S

Substitute a part for something else

C

Combine things or add something new

A

Adapt by changing the materials or procedure

M

Modify by enlarging or reducing

P

Put to a new use

E

Eliminate something or simplify

R

Reverse or rearrange

Appendix

BOOKS FOR KIDS

Hopscotch: Around the World
by Mary D. Lankford
A Beech Tree Paperback Book, © 1992
Fascinating *Hopscotch* shows and describes multicultural hopscotch games. Besides familiarizing kids with cultures and locations elsewhere on the globe, the book could inspire kids to design their own hopscotch courses, as well. Wonderful illustrations. All grades.

How To Be An Inventor: Create Amazing Innovations
by Murray Suid
Hawker Brownlow Education, © 2003
Packed with intriguing stories and the pragmatic information every young inventor needs to know. All grades.

How To Build Your Own Prize-Winning Robot
by Ed Sobey
Enslow Publishers, © 2002
Learn the fundamentals of robotics, resources for supplies, competitions, clubs, and more. Best for grades 5 and up.

Inventing Stuff
by Ed Sobey
Dale Seymour Publications, © 1996
How to invent toys, games, and solutions to everyday problems. This is a great resource for science fairs and invention contests. Best for grades 5 and up.

Inventing Toys
by Ed Sobey
Zephyr Press, © 2002
Encourages students to work in teams to design and make working toys while learning the fundamentals of science, design, tool usage, and the creative process. The science concepts behind many suggested projects are explained for teachers. Best for grades 4 and up.

Kids Make Music
by Avery Hart & Paul Mantell
Williamson Publishing, © 1993
Lively musical fun for kids of all ages, especially early elementary. Hand-clapping, foot-stomping singing and dancing in several styles of music. Includes instructions for creating simple sound-makers.

Nature Got There First: Inventions Inspired by Nature
by Phil Gates
Kingfisher Publishers, London and New York, 2010
Discover what in our world's natural environment inspired our most useful inventions, and how the inventors made creative connections. Ages 9 to 12.

Rubber-Band Banjos And A Java Jive Bass
by Alex Sabbeth
John Wiley& Sons, Inc. © 1997
Information about musical instruments and how to create home-made versions of them. Best for grades 5 and up.

Sing My Song: A Kids Guide to Songwriting
by Steve Seskin and a chorus of creative kids
Tricycle Press, © 2008
Shows young readers the steps for writing songs and setting them to music. It's encouraging, fun, and informative for beginning songwriters. Grades 1 to 5.

Snack Art: Eat What You Create
by Elizabeth Meahl
Teacher Created Resources, © 2004
Foods are used as craft materials. All ages will have fun eating their creativity.

BOOKS FOR EVERYONE: TEACHERS, PARENTS, AND KIDS

Composition For Young Musicians
by Jennifer Wilson
Alfred Publishing Co., Inc. © 2005
An award-winning book that teaches the basics of composition and encourages musical creativity. Includes a CD.

Funny You Should Ask
by Marvin Terban
Clarion Books, © 1992
This book clearly shows how to make up jokes, riddles, and more with wordplay.

The Imagineering Workout
by The Disney Imagineers
Disney Editions, © 2005
Exercises and inspiration to stimulate imaginations and generate creative ideas along with advice from an array of Disney artists. Effective and fun for adults and children.

The Inventive Mind in Science: Creative Thinking Activities
by Christine Ebert & Edward S. Ebert
Teacher Ideas Press, © 1998
A discussion of creative thinking as it applies to science, along with wonderful activities to integrate into a science curriculum.

Kids & Inventing! A Handbook for Young Inventors
by Susan Casey
John Wiley & Sons, © 2005
Inspiring stories and guidance in all the stages of inventing. Young and not-so-young will find this book a valuable help.

Kids Who Laugh: How To Develop Your Child's Sense of Humor
by Louis R. Franzini, PhD
Squareone Publishers, © 2002
Humor is an important coping skill, and a characteristic of creative people. This book shows how to nurture a healthy sense of humor in your child, and how teachers can use humor in the classroom to get positive results.

Learning About Creativity From The Life Of Steven Spielberg
by Erin M. Hovanec
PowerKids Press, © 1999
A short biography of the filmmaker and the powerful creative drive behind his movies. The inspiring insights are motivating to youngsters and adults.

101 Drama Games For Children
by Paul Rooyackers
Hunter House Books, © 1998
This is a handy and versatile book of fun games for stirring imaginations in all age groups.

101 Improv Games for Children and Adults
by Bob Bedore
Hunter House Books, © 2003
This is a handy and versatile fun book for stirring imaginations in all age groups.

Paid To Play: The Business of Game Design
by Keith A. Meyers
iUniverse, Inc., © 2008
Simple steps to turning your game concept into earnings in today's growing game market. This is an easy to follow guide for inventing games by a successful and experienced game designer.

Twyla Tharp: The Creative Habit
by Twyla Tharp
Simon & Shuster, © 2003
An uplifting book by a famous chore-ographer, Tharp shows how and why artists must actively seek and nurture inspiration. The advice applies to turning any work of art, invention, or creative endeavor into a viable product. Creative students who wish to follow their dreams would benefit from reading this book.

BOOKS FOR PARENTS AND TEACHERS

Applied Imagination
by A. F. Osborn
Scribner's, © 1963
A classic overview of creative problem solving that has been the foundation of several later books on creative thinking techniques, particularly the inspiration for Robert Eberle's S.C.A.M.P.E.R. techniques.

Caffeine For The Creative Mind: 250 Exercises to Wake Up Your Brain
by Stefan Mumaw and Wendy Lee Oldfield
FW Publications, © 2006
Daily exercises to get imaginations in top shape.

Cambridge Handbook of Creativity
James C. Kaufman, Editor
Robert J. Sternberg, Editor
Cambridge University Press, © 2010
Provides a comprehensive, definitive, authoritative review of the study of creativity. This is a compilation of engrossing writings by distinguished leaders in the field. The book offers a solid education on the topic.

Cracking Creativity: The Secrets of Creative Genius
by Michael Michalko
Ten Speed Press, © 2001
The author has researched history's greatest creative thinkers to show readers how they think and how to put their secrets to use. This book has a series of idea-inspiring resources, techniques, and exercises to bring out your awesome creative mind.

Creativity 101
by James C. Kaufman
Springer Publishing Company, LLC, © 2009
Engaging introduction to cutting-edge studies in the field of creativity by an international leader in the field. Discusses how creativity influences personality, motivation, intelligence, and talent.

Creativity: Flow and the Psychology of Discovery and Invention
by Mihaly Csikszentmihalyi
Harper Collins, © 1996
Investigations of "optimal experience" that reveal what makes a creative experience so satisfying. During a conscious state called "flow" people typically experience deep enjoyment, creativity, and full involvement with life. Learn how to achieve flow.

Creativity in the Classroom: Schools of Curious Delight
by Alane Jordan Starko
Lawrence Erlbaum Associates, © 2001
Helps teachers link creativity research and theory to the everyday activities of classroom teaching. Highly informative, easy to read, and packed with wonderful case examples, lesson ideas, strategies for supporting students' creativity, and more.

The Creative Journal For Children: A Guide For Parents, Teachers, and Counselors
by Lucia Capacchione
Shambhala Publications, Inc., © 1982
Imaginative writing and sketching ideas that help children understand their feelings and form positive self-images.

Growing Up Creative
by Teresa M. Amabile
C.E.F. Press, © 1989
Explains how a home environment can either spark or crush a child's natural urge to be creative. Gives examples of creativity in the daily lives of children and adults.

Guiding Creative Talent
by E. Paul Torrance
Prentice Hall, © 1962
The author is known as the "father of creativity." When first published, this was a ground-breaking book identifying creativity as a cognitive skill. Torrance offers an eye-opening view of the creative child in a traditional school environment.

Language Is Served
by Cheryl Miller Thurston
Prufrock Press, © 2008
Wonderful food-word games and activities for teaching language arts with creative thinking as a main ingredient. All grade levels.

Lateral Thinking: Creativity Step by Step
by Edward de Bono
Harper & Row, © 1970
Introduces a creative way of reasoning and decision-making. De Bono coined the term, "lateral thinking," a type of divergent thinking. He makes the concept easy to understand.

From Ordinary to Extraordinary: Art & Design Problem Solving
by Ken Vieth
Sterling Publishers, © 2000
Addresses creative thinking in art education, as well as the fundamentals of design and techniques. Students are encouraged to find highly individual solutions to visual problems. For art teachers of all grade levels.

The Ultimate Guide For Student Product Development & Evaluation
by Frances A. Karnes & Kristen R. Stephens
Prufrock Press, Inc., © 2009
Ideas for integrating creative products into an existing curriculum, and steps for planning, evaluating, and developing new product ideas, including ways to get the creations noticed. Adapts to all age levels.

A Whack On The Side Of The Head: How You Can Be More Creative
by Roger Von Oech
Business Plus, © 2008
The author has been helping people break through mental blocks and unlock their creativity for many years. This edition offers anecdotes, exercises, metaphors, cartoons, and more designed to systematically produce creative thinking.

A Whole New Mind: Why Right Brainers Will Rule The Future
by Daniel H. Pink
Riverhead Books, © 2006
Pink's premise is that we are in transition to a right-brain dominated society where the keys to our success are in cultivating designers, inventors, teachers, storytellers, and other right-brain thinkers.

GAMES FOR EVERYONE

MindTrap
Ages 12 & up
Outset Media
Puzzles, trick questions, and more that challenge everyone's creative thinking skills

Cranium Cadoo
Ages 7 and up
Hasbro
A variety of thinking, creating, and humorous activities

Scrabble
Ages 8 and up
Hasbro
The foremost of all word games. Players use flexible thinking to see word possibilities and form a variety of combinations from the letters on their racks. For ages 5 and up, consider "Scrabble Junior."

Dictionary
Ages 6 and up
All versions
This classic game idea has seen many commercial incarnations over the years. Writing bogus but convincing definitions takes originality, elaboration, and plenty of imagination.

Mad Libs
Ages 6 and up
Price, Stern, and Sloan
There are dozens of Mad Libs˚ games, which use random substitution words to elicit laughter. Mad Libs is a modern counterpart to its hysterical predecessor, "The Comical Game of Dr. Quack," first published in the 1930s. See page 138 for our adaptation, "Forever Funny, Dr. Quack."

Gin Rummy, Canasta, and Variations
Ages 6 and up
All versions
Card games such as these have been reinvented in a number of card games for kids, but their basic concept calls upon flexible thinking to combine cards in ways that optimize your score.

Monopoly®
Ages 8 and up
Hasbro
This longtime favorite depends mostly on luck until later in the game when players must apply creative thinking skills to stay in the game.

Rory's Story Cubes
Ages 8 and up
Gamewright
Creative story generator with a number of ways to play

Acting Out!
Ages 7 and up
Swingset Press
Creative improvising as players act out random combinations on the spot

WEBSITES

Buffalo State College – International Center for Studies in Creativity
www.buffalostate.edu/creativity/
This appealing website is a clearinghouse for information on creativity, creative problem solving, creative leadership, and creativity education. Buffalo State offers credentials in creativity, as well, through their Center for Studies in Creativity. View their Creativity 101 video series on the website; The short videos are easy to follow and highly enlightening.

By Kids For Kids
www.BKFK.com/home
Encourages kid-driven innovation. Find fabulous articles and ideas for parents and teachers. *Kid Friendly*

Childspace
childspace.wordpress.com
A blog that features issues impacting the lives of children and adolescents with an attempt to understand them, and with a lot of creativity and humor thrown in.

Courageously Creative
www.courageouslycreative.com
Thoughtful articles about how creativity permeates our lives.

Crayola
www.crayola.com
This lively website offers creative crayon techniques, inspiring examples of crayon art, tips for teachers, classroom ideas, info about children's art development, and more. Children will enjoy their Kids' Playzone. *Kid Friendly*

Creativity Portal
www.creativity-portal.com
Fascinating articles and more written by creative people from a variety of backgrounds. Packed with information and all kinds of ideas for exploring and expressing one's creativity.

The Creativity Post
www.creativitypost.com
A non-profit web platform committed to sharing the best content on creativity from scientific discovery to philosophical debate, from entrepreneurial ventures to educational ventures to educational reform, from artistic expression to technological innovation. Good articles on education.

Creative Slush
www.chrisdunmire.com
Bubbly website jam packed with downloadable fun, ebooks, humor, ideas, and creative activities for teachers, parents, kids, and everyone else to use. *Kid Friendly*

Creativiteach
www.creativiteach.me
Dr. Alane Starko's website makes concepts about the psychology of creativity easy to understand and apply. She's a former elementary school teacher and is now a Professor in the Dept. of Education at Eastern Michigan University, and author of "Creativity in the Classroom: Schools of Curious Delight." Check out her blog, too. This beautiful site is filled with insightful tips for parents and educators who wish to foster creativity in their kids.

Destination Imagination
www.idodi.org
A non-profit organization that provides programs for students to learn and experience creativity, teamwork, and problem solving. They offer a core program in which student teams solve open-ended challenges and present their solutions at tournaments across the U. S. and in 30 countries. Check out their exciting challenges.

Education Week Free Content
www.edweek.org/ew/section/free-content/
For those who happen not to be subscribers to *Education Week*, there's a quite a wealth of free content available on this area of their website, including two dozen blogs.

Edutopia
www.edutopia.org
The George Lucas Educational foundation has a vision for a new world of learning. This website is a hub for educators providing and showcasing ways to help students to become lifelong learners and thrive in their careers and adult lives.

4 2 eXplore
www.42explore.com
Activities, definitions, explanations, resources, and more for a multitude of school topics, presented in an upbeat, engaging way. For each topic you'll find "4 good starting points." *Kid Friendly*

Imagination Soup
www.imaginationsoup.net
Playful literacy and learning ideas. A bright and exciting website that's dedicated to making education exciting and creative.

Imagineering Disney
www.imagineeringdisney.com
The happiest place(s) on earth began in the imagination of Walt Disney and the talented people within the company. This all volunteer, non-official site has gorgeous concept art, vintage photos, maps, diagrams, and history.

Kahn Academy
www.khanacademy.org
Offering free education to anyone, this non-profit has over 3,300 videos on everything from arithmetic to physics, finance, and history. It also has tools for teachers, coaches and parents and nearly unlimited practice material.

Minds in Bloom
www.minds-in-bloom.com
Rachel Lynette's lively website for teachers of grades 1 – 8 offers a wealth of strategies and activities to promote creative and critical thinking. You'll find unique lesson plans there, too.

National Center on Education and the Economy
www.ncee.org
Created in 1988, it focuses on how the international economy affects American education and seeks to support policy change and develop resources to accomplish their goals. It designs education systems to improve student performance.

OPDAG – Original Paper Doll Artists Guild
www.opdag.com
Tips, news, showcasing opportunities, and history of the art and fashion of paper dolls.

Partnership for 21st Century Skills
www.p21.org
A national organization that advocates for 21st century readiness for every student. Their mission is to fuse the 3R's with the 4R's (critical thinking, communication, collaboration, and creativity) in U.S. education systems.

Planet Fassa
www.planetfassa.com
Mainly geared toward kids, this exuberant website helps expand your child's curiosity, imagination, creativity, and love of reading. *Kid Friendly*

Psychology Today – Creativity
www.psychologytoday.com/topics/creativity
This "topic" section of the magazine's online site has a wide range of contributors.

Psychology Today – Creative Thinkering Blog
www.psychologytoday.com/blog/creative-thinkering
This is the blog of author and speaker Michael Michalko. He gets "under the hood" of the subject of creative thinking with in-depth articles, profiles, techniques and more.

Quirky
www.quirky.com
A one-of-a-kind website where visitors present and evaluate each others' new product ideas.

Science News for Kids
www.sciencenewsforkids.com
A non-profit organization that advances the popular understanding of science through publications and educational competitions and programs. They inform, educate, and truly inspire.

United States Copyright Office
www.copyright.gov
Their mission is "to promote creativity by administering and sustaining an effective national copyright system." They serve the copyright community of creators and users, as well as the general public by offering news, publications, and information for and about those who design and write things.

United States Patent and Trademark Office
www.uspto.gov/kids
Information about the USA Science and Engineering Festival, and "trading cards" which are actually short narratives about inventors, written for kids and accompanied by caricature portraits. For teachers, follow the i-CREATM link for valuable resources to use in your classroom or homeschool. *Kid Friendly*

Wiley Walnut
www.wilywalnut.com
Articles on creative thinking, creativity in the news, book reviews, readers' comments, and more. *Kid Friendly*

Another Personal Story With a Happier Ending

In college I took a course called "Psychology of Personality." I had read all but two chapters among the required books. As poor luck would have it, the final exam (90% of our grade) consisted of one essay question: Apply the principles of analysis to Mr. X, where "X" is a specified character in a chapter I had not read!

Realizing I could flunk the class, I tried to salvage what I could. At the top of my paper I wrote a note to the professor, admitting the truth and asking if I could get credit for the bit of knowledge I could demonstrate. And I expressed hope that he'd enjoy my writings regardless.

Since I knew the principles of analysis I applied them to someone familiar: Benjamin Franklin. With little to lose and an hour to kill, I wrote a humorous essay using Ben Franklin's proverbs to prove my points. While my classmates struggled and sweated, I giggled my way through the final. "A penny saved is a penny earned" shows an anal retentive personality and "Fish and visitors stink after three days" describes an OCD personality with a possible fish phobia. I explained how it all works.

A few days later I was astounded to see an A+ on my exam, along with a note from the professor: "The highest goal of psychology studies is to help people cope with life. You earned an A+ ."

Creative thinking works wonders.

Marjorie Sarnat

Marjorie Sarnat

Having had a lifelong interest in creative thinking, Marjorie Sarnat cofounded *Jr Imagination* to fulfill a goal of growing the creative potential in all children.

She is a successful author, painter, inventor, and designer. Marjorie has teamed with major manufacturers to create hundreds of products based on her artwork in the gift, fashion, and craft industries. People worldwide enjoy her award-winning books and products.

With a unique understanding of creativity both academically and artistically, as well as with her extensive background in product development, Marjorie is able to generate extraordinary content for teachers, parents, and kids.

Marjorie is a featured author at creativity-portal.com. She received her Certificate of Training for "Putting Ideas into Action" from the International Center for Studies in Creativity from Buffalo State University, N.Y. Marjorie has taught art to children and teens, and is past editor of *Arts & Activities* magazine. She is an alumna of the School of the Art Institute of Chicago, and is a graduate of Eastern Michigan University.

Also by Marjorie Sarnat:

151 Uncommon and Amazing Art Studio Secrets: To Boost Your Creative Output
Jr Imagination © 2011
Winner of two 2011 Global eBook Awards, this book offers a treasure trove of wisdom and techniques for making art, presented in short, easy to grasp passages. Includes dozens of kid friendly art ideas. The companion site for the book can be found at www.sarnatart.com where expanded and additional tips and techniques are available.

151 Effective and Extraordinary Art Studio Secrets: To Ignite Your Personal Expression
Jr Imagination © 2012
This second book in the series, to be published in Fall 2012, offers another 151 gems for making art, presented in simple, clear passages. Includes dozens more of kid friendly art ideas.

Creativity is as important to a student's future as any other educational goal

About Jr Imagination
The company started with one goal in the mind—to grow the creative potential in all children. Its guiding principle is that creative genius can blossom in any child, anywhere and that creativity is as important to a student's future as any other educational goal.

www.jrimagination.com
Visit the companion site to this book and you'll find activities, resources and more ways for kids, parents, families, and teachers to kickstart creative thinking in their lives. For supplemental materials to this book go to http://www.jrimagination.com/printables.

Raising a Creative Genius Blog
Marjorie's *Raising a Creative Genius* blog is a place to share knowledge and discuss advancing the creative thinking skills of children. Go to www.jrimagination.com/blog

Creative Genius On-the-Go!
Ages 5 and up
Jr Imagination
This app for iOS has 150 diversions, challenges, and scenarios to spark imaginations, exercise creative thinking skills, and provides amazing fun for everyone. Available in the App Store and qualifies for an educational discount.

Made in the USA
Columbia, SC
07 September 2021

45047121R00200